Microprocessors:
Design and
Applications

Microprocessors: Design and Applications

Andrew Veronis

Reston Publishing Company, Inc.
A Prentice-Hall Company
Reston, Virginia

Library of Congress Cataloging in Publication Data

Veronis, Andy.
  Microprocessors.

  Includes index.
  1. Microprocessors. I. Title.
QA76.5.V47   621.3819'58   78-2958
ISBN 0-87909-493-1

©1978 by Reston Publishing Company, Inc.
A Prentice-Hall Company
Reston, Virginia 22090

10 9 8 7 6 5 4 3 2 1

Printed in the United States of America

*This book is dedicated
to my dearest son, Michael,
and to my dearest wife, Liz.*

Contents

Preface

We live in an ever-expanding electronic age. The birth and rapid development of the microprocessor is proof of this. Microprocessors have grown in popularity because digital systems designed around them require relatively few integrated circuits.

The microprocessor, a fairly new component for logic designers, is a major breakthrough in system design. It is changing the way products are designed and is making new products economically practical. Competing with TTL and, in some cases, with custom LSI, it has brought computer architecture into such applications as cash registers, process control systems, gasoline pumps, data-collection terminals, and traffic lights.

The word *microprocessor* is applied to LSI chips that are combined in a computer-like central processor to complete arithmetic and logic operation under program control. The purpose of this text is to describe a microprocessor system today, how it is programmed, how one learns to use it, and the advantages of its use.

The importance of the microprocessor is evident. Because of its low cost, the device brings data processing to many new classes of products. Competition with TTL and minicomputers is relatively insignificant. Far more important to the world are all the new products generated by microprocessors.

Faster design time is one of the major benefits of the microprocessor circuit approach. Designers' productivity is probably increased by a factor of five when they switch to programming logic.

Product cost is reduced, also. Flexibility, both in design and in making changes to meet individual requirements, is another major benefit.

Extensive research effort has gone into the preparation of this book, and it is the sincere hope of the author that the material covered will provide the reader with an adequate description of the subject for his or her purposes. Yet there is always more material that could be covered, and this is especially true when one realizes the almost limitless applications of microprocessors in the future.

The author wishes to extend his gratitude to the following for their valuable assistance in the preparation of this book: Motorola, Intel, Texas Instruments, National Semiconductors, Rockwell International, RCA, and Mostek.

Andrew M. Veronis

Part One
Theory and Applications

1

Basic Concepts

1.1 INTRODUCTION

Extensive activity has been recently noticed around microprocessors, and yet this type of device has just entered its "electronic adolescence." For the digital designer unfamiliar with computers, all this has come as a great shock. Safely able to ignore the vagaries of software in the past, many engineers have begun to learn that some of their hard-won skills are becoming obsolete overnight. For years, for example, the objective was logic minimization; later, engineers successfully retrained themselves into minimizing systems cost (usually synonymous with minimum package count). Now, after all that, the package count for incredibly complex systems is on the order of 10 off-the-shelf chips, and all the important logic is in software.

Once the prospective user acclimates to the unique suite of microprocessor characteristics such as word, size, and speed, one of the hard tasks begins. How, in such a new and burgeoning field, with new major announcements actually crowding each other out of space in the trade press, does the system architect select the one best processor for the job? For that matter, how does an old hand at micros know when there are significant new advances worthy of attention? Or, for that matter, how does an engineer or technician broaden his experience? The answer to these questions lies in this text and several other good books recently published that discuss the subject of microprocessors.

But, what is a microprocessor?

Several fallacies still exist in the interpretation of the term. Some call a microprocessor an entire system that incorporates the particular device; others call a microcomputer the device that is included in a system.

A *microprocessor* is usually considered to be the "heart" of an entire microcomputer system—in other words, the *central processing unit*. A *microcomputer* is the system that contains the device and its auxiliary circuits.

1.2 COMPUTER BASICS

The term *computer* is applied to a rather wide field of functions. It defines a machine or system, which, once assigned a particular problem, performs a computation automatically and without human intervention. Two main factors that closely associate computers and electronics are: (1) no known principle other than electronics allows a machine to attain the speeds now commonplace in both large- and small-scale computers, and (2) no other principle permits comparable design experience.

In particular, digital computers use numbers that are represented by the presence of a voltage level or pulse on a given signal line. A single pulse defines one *bit* (abbreviation for *bi*nary digi*t*, a base 2 number). A group of pulses considered as a unit is called a *word*, where a word may represent a computational quantity or a machine directive. A byte consists of 8 bits.

An electronic computer, for solving simple mathematical expressions, may be compared to a human being. Figure 1-1 is a block diagram of a basic digital computer.

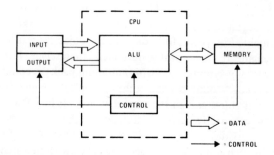

Fig. 1-1. Basic Elements of a Computer

The system consists of an input/output (I/O) device, a memory, a control section, and an arithmetic and logic unit (ALU), which is the computational element. The arithmetic/logic unit and the control section are the system's central processing unit. A person and a conventional calculator basically comprise the same system. The person's fingers represent the input, the human eyes coupled with the calculator's output represent the system output, the calculator electronics function as the ALU, and the human brain serves as the memory and control sections. The sequence of events that occur when our person–calculator solves, say, the problem 5 + 8 = ? are as follows:

1. Brain accesses first number to be added, a "5."

2. Brain orders hand to depress "5" key.

3. Brain identifies addition operation.

4. Brain orders hand to depress "+" key.

5. Brain accesses second number to be added, an "8."

6. Brain determines that all necessary information has been provided, and signals the ALU to complete computation by ordering hand to depress "=" key.

7. ALU (calculator) performs computation.

8. ALU displays result on readout.

9. Eyes signal brain; brain recognizes this number as being the result of the particular calculation.

10. Brain stores "13" in a location that it appropriately identifies to itself to facilitate later recall.

Let us now expand this basic system and add some memory and other stages that will increase the capabilities of the computer. Figure 1-2 illustrates a memory composed of storage space for a large number of words.

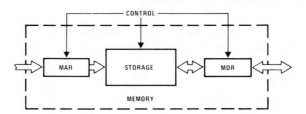

Fig. 1-2. Elements of Memory

The program memory serves basically as a place to store instructions, the coded pieces of data that direct the activities of the central processing unit (CPU). A group of logically related instructions stored in memory is referred to as a *program*. The CPU "reads" each instruction from memory in a logically determinate sequence and uses it to initiate processing actions. If the program structure is coherent and logical, processing procedures produce intelligible and useful results.

The data memory is used to store the data to be manipulated. The CPU can access any data stored in memory, but often the memory is not large enough to store the entire bank required for a particular application. The program can be resolved by providing the computer with one or more inputs. The CPU can address these ports and input the data contained there. The addition of input enables the computer to receive information from external equipment (such as a paper tape reader) at high rates of speed and in large volumes.

Almost any computer requires one or more output ports that permit the CPU to communicate the results of its processing to the outside world. The output may go into a display, for use by a human operator, to a peripheral device that produces *hard copy,* such as a line printer, to a peripheral storage device such as a magnetic tape, or the output may constitute process control signals that direct the operation of another system, such as an automated assembly line. Like input ports, output ports are addressable. The input and output ports together permit the processor to interact with the outside world. The CPU unifies the system. It controls the functions performed by the other components. The CPU must be able to fetch instructions from memory, decode their binary contents, and execute them. It must also be able to reference memory and I/O ports necessary in the execution of instructions. In addition, the CPU should be able to recognize and respond to certain external control signals, such as interrupt and stop requests. The functional units within a CPU that enable it to perform these functions are described below.

1.3 ARCHITECTURE OF A CPU

A typical central processor unit is illustrated in Figure 1-3 and consists of the following interconnected functional units:

1. Registers.

2. Arithmetic and logic unit.

3. Control circuitry.

Registers are temporary storage units within the CPU. Some registers, such as the program counter and instruction register, have dedicated uses. Other registers, such as the accumulator, are for more general-purpose use.

The accumulator usually stores one of the operands to be manipulated by the ALU. A typical instruction will perhaps direct the ALU to add the contents of some other register to the contents of the accumulator and store

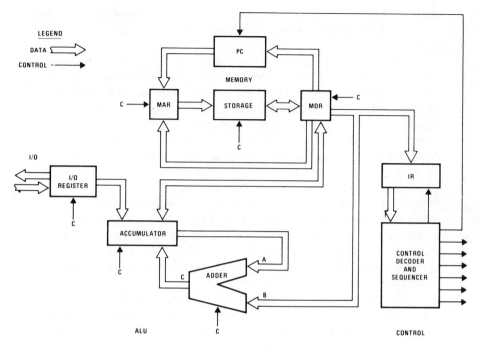

Fig. 1-3. CPU and memory

the result in the accumulator itself. In general, the accumulator is both a source (operand) and a destination (result) register. Often a CPU will include a number of additional general-purpose registers that can be used to store operands or intermediate "scratch-pad" data.

The instructions that make up a program are stored in the system's memory. The central processor examines the contents of the memory in order to determine what action is appropriate. This means that the processor must know which location contains the next instruction.

Each of the locations in memory is numbered to distinguish it from all other locations in memory. The number that identifies a memory location is called its *address*.

The processor maintains a counter that contains the address of the next program instruction. This register is called the *program counter*. The processor updates the program counter by adding "1" to the counter each time it fetches an instruction so that the program counter is always current. Programmers therefore store their instructions in numerically adjacent addresses so that the lower addresses contain the first instructions to be executed and the higher addresses contain later instructions. The only time the programmer may violate this sequential rule is when the last instruction in one block of memory is a jump instruction. The next instruction may be stored in any memory location as long as the programmed jump specifies the correct address.

During the execution of a jump instruction, the processor replaces the contents of its program counter with the address embodied in the jump. Thus, the logical continuity of the program is maintained. A special kind of program jump occurs when the stored program accesses or "branches" to a subroutine. In this type of jump, the processor is logically required to "remember" the contents of the program counter at the time that the jump occurs. This enables the processor to resume execution of the main program when it is finished with the last instruction of the subroutine. Refer to Chapter 3 for a formal definition of the term "jump."

A subroutine is a program within the program. Usually, it is a general-purpose set of instructions that must be executed repeatedly in the course of a main program. Routines that calculate the square, the sine, or the logarithm of a program variable are good examples of the functions often written as subroutines. Other examples might be programs designed for inputting or outputting data to or from a particular peripheral device.

The processor has a special way of handling subroutines in order to ensure an orderly return to the main program. When the processor receives a jump to subroutine instruction it increments the program counter and stores the counter's contents in a register memory area, known as the *stack*. The stack thus saves the address of the instruction to be executed after the subroutine is completed. Then the processor stores the address specified in the subroutine jump in its program counter. The next instruction fetched, therefore, will be the first step of the subroutine. The last instruction in any subroutine is a branch back. Such an instruction need specify no address. When the processor fetches a branch-back instruction it simply replaces the current contents of the program counter with the address on the top of the stack. This causes the processor to resume execution of the program at the point immediately following the original branch.

Subroutines are often nested; that is, one subroutine will sometimes call a second subroutine. The second may call a third, and so on. This is perfectly acceptable as long as the processor has enough capacity to store the necessary return addresses and the logical provision for doing so. In other words, the maximum depth of nesting is determined by the depth of the stack itself. If the stack has space for storing three return addresses, then three levels of subroutines may be accommodated.

Processors have different ways of maintaining stacks. Most have facilities for the storage of return addresses built into the processor itself. The integral stack is usually more efficient, since fewer steps are involved in the execution of a call or a return.

1.4 INSTRUCTION REGISTER AND DECODER

Every computer has a word length that is characteristic of that machine. A computer's word length is usually determined by the size of its internal storage elements and interconnecting paths (referred to as *buses*); for example, a computer whose registers and buses can store and transfer 4 bits of information has a characteristic word length of 4 bits and is referred to as a *4-bit parallel processor.* The characteristic 8-bit field is sometimes referred to as a *byte;* a 4-bit field can be referred to as a *nibble.*

Each operation that the processor can perform is identified by a unique binary number known as an *instruction code.* An 8-bit word used as an instruction code can distinguish among 256 alternative actions, more than adequate for most processors.

The processor fetches an instruction in two distinct operations. In the first, it transmits the address in its program counter to the memory; in the second, the memory returns the addressed byte to the processor. The CPU stores this instruction byte in a register known as the *instruction register* and uses it to direct activities during the remainder of the instruction execution.

The mechanism by which the processor translates an instruction code into specific processing actions requires more elaboration than we can afford here. The concept, however, will be intuitively clear to any experienced logic designer. The 8 bits stored in the instruction register can be decoded and used to selectively activate one of a number of output lines, in this case up to 256 lines. Each line represents a set of activities associated with the execution of a particular instruction code.

The enabled line can be combined coincidentally with selected timing pulses to develop electrical signals that can then be used to initiate specific actions. This translation of code into action is performed by the instruction decoder and by the associated control circuitry.

An 8-bit field is more than sufficient, in most cases, to specify a particular processing action. There are times, however, when execution of the instruction code requires more information than 8 bits can convey. One example of this is when the instruction references a memory location. The basic instruction code identifies the operation to be performed but cannot specify the address as well. In a case like this, a two-word instruction must be used. Successive instruction bytes are stored in sequentially adjacent memory locations and the processor performs two fetches in succession to obtain the full instruction. The first byte retrieved from memory is placed in the processor's instruction register, and the second byte is placed in temporary storage, as appropriate. When the entire instruction is fetched, the processor can proceed to the execution phase.

1.5 ADDRESS REGISTERS

A CPU may use a register or register pair to temporarily store the address of a memory location that is to be accessed for data. If the *address register* is programmable (i.e., if there are instructions that allow the programmer to alter the contents of the register), the program can "build" an address in the address register prior to executing a memory reference instruction (i.e., an instruction that reads data from memory, writes data into memory, or operates on data stored in memory).

1.6 ARITHMETIC/LOGIC UNIT

A block diagram of an arithmetic/logic unit is shown in Figure 1-4. All processors contain an ALU, which by way of analogy, may be thought of as a super adding machine with its keys commanded automatically by the control signals developed in the instruction decoder and the control circuitry. This is essentially how the first stored-program digital computer was conceived. The ALU naturally bears little resemblance to a desktop adder. The major difference is that the ALU calculates by creating an electrical analogy, rather than by mechanical analogy. Another important difference is that the ALU uses binary techniques rather than decimal methods for representing and manipulating numbers. In principle, however, it is convenient to think of the ALU as an electronically controlled calculator.

The ALU must contain an adder which is capable of combining the contents of two registers in accordance with the logic of binary arithmetic. This provision permits the processor to perform arithmetic manipulations on the data it obtains from memory and from its other inputs.

Using only the basic adder, a capable programmer can write routines that will subtract, multiply, and divide, giving the machine complete arithmetic capabilities. In practice, however, most ALUs provide other built-in functions, including hardware subtraction, Boolean logic operations, and shift capabilities.

The ALU contains flag bits which register certain conditions that arise in the course of arithmetic manipulations. Flags typically include carry and

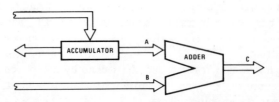

Fig. 1-4. Arithmetic and Logic Unit

zero. It is possible to program jumps which are conditionally dependent on the status of one or more flags. For example, the program may be designed to jump to a special routine if the carry bit is set following an addition instruction. The presence of a carry generally indicates an overflow in the accumulator and sometimes calls for special processing actions.

1.7 CONTROL CIRCUITRY

The *control circuitry* is the primary functional unit within a CPU. Using clock inputs, the control circuitry maintains the proper sequence of events required for any processing task. After an instruction is fetched and decoded, the control circuitry issues the appropriate signals (to units both internal and external to CPU) for initiating the proper processing action. Often the control circuitry will be capable of responding to external signals such as an interrupt request. An interrupt request will cause the control circuitry to temporarily interrupt main program execution, jump to a special routine to service the interrupting device, then automatically return to the main program. Interrupts may or may not be important, depending upon two factors: (1) Does the application require real-time quick response to external events? (2) Does the software design strategy encourage the use of interrupts? Many applications will not require interrupts—even real-time applications. Instead of allowing mainline processing programs to be interrupted, software organization may assure the testing of some external status signal frequently enough to guarantee service. There are some software design philosophies that consider interrupts as nuisances to be avoided, except for nearly catastrophic fault conditions; the software designer should make a choice before the processor is selected. The discussion above should give you a rough idea of what a microprocessor and its peripheral devices consist of and what they do.

1.8 PROCESSOR SELECTION

Selection of a microprocessor is not a job that can be accomplished easily; the requirement of the application must always be kept clearly in view. In general, almost any processor can satisfy almost any application's requirement so long as speed is not a major factor. However, most applications have real-time constraints, so processor selection is an important activity in successful system design.

Some processors are naturally easier to use for certain applications than others. Some of the available processors, like the Intel MCS-4, Fairchild F-8, and Electronic Arrays' device, make the handling of small arrays very easy. Others have features that allow simple input/output interfaces. Each processor tends to have some strong points and some weak when viewed in the light of typical applications of microprocessors. However, a processor's particular strong point may prove worthless in some specific applications; and a weakness may disappear in other uses.

Viewed from the vantage point of the system as a whole, the experienced designer can see three major areas for investigation:

- Software design, which covers those features of the microprocessor as seen by the programmer.

- Hardware design, including the requirements of the environment in which the processor must operate.

- System design, which affects the interface conventions between hardware and software design.

1.9 SYSTEM DESIGN CONSIDERATIONS

In the design phase of microprocessor-based applications, the choice of a processor, ideally, should be an open question. In those cases where the selection of some arbitrary processor is not overridden by prior organizational commitment to a particular technology, the first decision point comes during design. In order to select from the myriad of processors, some well-placed questions can probably eliminate several contenders. In general, if various processors can be dropped from further consideration, the designer's job is simplified because a smaller number of processors need to be examined in detail.

Some major features of microprocessors are:

Interrupt structure.

One-chip CPU packaging.

Microprogrammability.

DMA ability.

Arithmetic modes.

These factors, although not the only important features of microprocessors, are important enough to be considered among the first items to examine. If, for instance, the application demands the ability to accept or emit large blocks of data quickly, then processors without a DMA ability can probably be rejected from further consideration.

Interrupts have been discussed previously.

One-chip CPU packaging has a substantial effect on assembly and repair costs as well as an effect on the size of the finished product. Even among one-chip CPUs, there are tremendous varieties in the number of integrated circuits (ICs) that must be added before achieving a working computer. A

CPU that multiplexes addresses through the same pins as data requires several external packages to catch and hold a memory address. Most of the larger packages avoid this multiplexing. Other areas that frequently require substantial amounts of supporting logic are state decoding and I/O control. The signals required to enable interrupts, enable and address I/O ports, write into storage, and interrupt or reset the system may be available at CPU pins, or they may require as many as 10 or 20 packages of decoding, storage, and timing logic. While the parts cost of these extra chips is relatively small, it can double or triple the manufacturing costs of a computer.

Microprogrammability allows the fine structure of the microprocessor to be changed while the gross structure remains. In particular, the number of registers the programmer sees and the suite of instructions can be modified within limited realms, but gross changes are not possible. Microprograms are usually stored in read-only memories (ROMs), either on the computer's control chip or externally in standard ROMs connected to the control logic. Some of these ROMs are mask-programmed (during their manufacturing process), while others can be field-programmed or replaced with read/write storage to ease the development of customized instruction sets. Microprogramming is important when a microcomputer is being designed that will emulate some other (more popular) computer, or when some specialized applications—oriented instructions—need to be implemented to augment an existing instruction set. Common, but time-consuming, software routines (such as multiply) can be implemented as microprogrammed instructions to speed up application execution. Virtually, any program can be reduced to a microprogram. Relatively complicated processing tasks (like fast Fourier transforms) will execute much faster if implemented as a microprogram.

DMA (direct memory access) has been a popular option on minicomputers for a long time. DMA lets high-speed peripheral devices gain direct access to main storage without bothering the CPU; the alternative requires the software to read/write each and every word between main storage and the peripheral equipment. For DMA to work, the CPU must be prevented from interfering with main storage while the data transfer is going on. Some microprocessors have special controls that suspend the CPU cycles (and, in fact, remove the device from the data/address bus by disabling three-state output drivers) whenever DMA is in progress. Processors that do not have an inherent ability *can* be used in DMA applications, but the additional hardware is often complicated.

Arithmetic is almost always performed in two's-complement form on microprocessors. In addition, some processors have special instructions designed for handling binary-coded decimal (BCD) numbers. Whether these instructions are important or not depends upon whether the I/O data must be in BCD form. If BCD data are presented to the computer, or required from it, the BCD arithmetic instructions may be required. Remember that if BCD quantities are converted to binary for arithmetic operations and then reconverted to BCD for output, there may be some slight inaccuracies; the quantity 0.1, for example, cannot be represented in binary, so 0.1 + 0.1 will not yield exactly 0.2.

1.10 HARDWARE DESIGN CONSIDERATIONS

Microprocessors require other ancillary parts to make entire application systems work. As an absolute minimum, a microprocessor needs a program store (although the Burroughs Mini-D has it on the CPU chip). Some microprocessors are easy to interface to storage, and others are hard. To the extent that the vendor has put all the necessary interfacing circuitry on the CPU, memory, and I/O ports, a family exists.

Completeness

Completeness of the parts family is an important selection parameter. Some vendors seem to feel that, if the processor can be connected to a RAM, regardless of the number of additional chips involved, then their RAM is a member of the parts family. Other semiconductor manufacturers have taken special pains to be sure that storage and processing and I/O ports can all fit together without intervening logic; the latter systems are considered to complete parts sets.

Master Clocks

Clocks are required for most microprocessors, although some of the newer processors only require a frequency-controlling two-terminal device (crystal or *RC* net). Some of the vendors offer clock or clock-driver chips. In many designs DIP-socket-sized crystal oscillators, such as those from Motorola Vectron, are used. In others, crystal-controlled stability is not important. Clock frequency has little to do with relative data-manipulation speed and should not be used as a selection criterion. The number of phases, however, is important; four phases are harder to generate than one or two. In clock schemes with multiple phases (particularly common in MOS processors), the requirements for overlapped or closely controlled relative rise and fall periods should be investigated. Sometimes four phases are easier to make than overlapped, synchronized two-phase clock signals.

Power

Voltages and power dissipation are considerations in many systems. Many of the MOS processors require two supplies (usually +5 and -9, or -10) to be TTL-compatible; if that compatibility is unnecessary, these can be operated from a single supply. Power dissipation is most often a function of the intended operating speed range.

Compatibility

Electrical compatibility with other logic circuitry is required in most applications. Most of the microprocessors offer some degree of TTL (transistor-transistor logic) compatibility, but read the fine print carefully. Numerous variations in I/O logic levels are common, even in one-chip systems. MOS-to-TTL conversion is "delicate" at best, and the manufacturer's recommendations should be followed religiously. TTL's compatibility high-input-current requirements frequently demand that buffers be added between MOS and TTL portions of mixed-logic systems. The speed of MOS circuitry frequently degrades as more loads are paralleled, requiring the addition of buffers even within portions of MOS-only systems.

1.11 SOFTWARE DESIGN CONSIDERATIONS

After the system is designed and the hardware has taken shape, someone has to program the microprocessor. What the programmer sees is largely determined by the architecture of the computer and the environment in which that native architecture operates.

Word Size

Word size is nearly always the first parameter specified during microprocessor selection, even though it should be the last. Word size affects the microscopic efficiency of some common kinds of software operations, but it seldom affects the overall design. In many applications, 4-bit processors outperform similar designs on 8-bit processors, although the opposite is also true.

In general, ease of programming is inversely proportional to:

1. Word size, because smaller word sizes require multiword operations on practical data quantities.

2. The number of different register sizes in a computer because simple register-to-register data transfers are limited.

Computers with small word sizes (4-bit; and, to a lesser extent, 8-bit) always require a different register size for storing some addresses. For example, the program location counter is often made an integer number of native words in size. When the word size is small, the manipulation of storage addresses and program addresses is complicated. Remember, word size affects the ease of programming, not the overall application efficiency.

Throughout the history of the development of computers there have been no 4-bit word computers, and only a few 8-bit words, until the advent of the microprocessor. Until the limitations of restricted semiconductor real estate were imposed, there was little economic incentive to develop small-word computers. Difficulty of programming may, in the future, make the smaller word sizes appropriate only for special high-volume and extremely cost-sensitive applications.

Addressing Capacity

How large a program can be written without resorting to special external hardware and internal software techniques is defined by the program *addressing range.* The ideal processor for an application has neither too small nor too large a capacity. A too-small range means that extra hardware will be required to extend the addressing. On the other hand, excessive capacity means that extraneous address bits will be carried in every instruction that refers to storage; those bits cost money.

Addition Time

Register-to-register *addition time* is a popular estimate of the computing speed of a computer. This instruction is chosen as a selection factor, because nearly every computer has an add instruction. Microprocessors with more than one programmer-accessible register for data manipulation on the CPU chip can usually perform a fast register addition in a minimum instruction execution time. Some processors, however, are organized as one-accumulator computers so that register-to-register additions are not provided; in this case, the addition of the contents of an arbitrary storage location to the accumulator is often scored as the minimum addition time. The incrementing of a register by one is not considered a good test of addition time.

Addition time should not be the only criterion used in timing estimation. Computer makers have been known to treat that one instruction uniquely, so that the machine appears to the casual observer to be faster than it really is.

Register Complement

The number of registers in the microprocessor is probably the most important feature of its architecture. Different registers in a computer have different uses; the ways that they may be used are embodied in the instruction set.

The most precious resource that the programmer can allocate in software is the set of CPU registers. The more registers there are, the less likelihood there is of main storage references. Generally, references to main storage are more expensive in time than the references to on-chip registers.

ALU registers are those on which ALU functions can be performed; the register can be a source or destination of operands for the operation.

Registers that can supply but not receive operands for the ALU are not considered arithmetic registers.

An *index register* is a programmer-accessible register that is implicitly included in certain references to main storage. Unless the contents of the register can be added to another value (from, say, the instruction itself) during the storage addressing cycle, it is not an index register.

All other programmer-accessible data registers in a microprocessor (excluding the ALU and index registers) are called *general-purpose* or *scratch-pad registers.* (In some large-scale computers, a general-purpose register can be used in any of these three modes; that practice is not popular in microprocessors.)

Return Stack

Return addresses are usually handled through the medium of a pushdown stack in microprocessors. Except for the Intersil 6100, which emulates the DEC PDP-8, microprocessors put subroutine return addresses into a pushdown stack in a read-write memory; that memory may be on the CPU chip or in external main storage. Return addresses are not saved within the program storage area as in many microprocessors, because most programs for microprocessors are stored in read-only memories.

When the return addresses are stored in an on-the-chip pushdown stack, there is some natural limit to the number of dynamic subroutine calls. If there are eight stack positions, then generally only seven subroutine calls may be active at one time; if interrupts are anticipated, the real used stack size must be kept to allow some stack depth for the interrupt service routine.

When return addresses are stored in RAM, an on-the-chip stack pointer is maintained in the CPU. When a subroutine is called, the return address is pushed into the RAM stack, and the pointer is updated.

The on-chip stack allows faster subroutine calls because RAM does not have to be accessed. Stacks in RAM are of potentially huge depth which allows certain kinds of algorithms to be easily programmed. If the on-chip stack is accessible to the programmer, the depth of that stack can be extended by software. Most on-chip stacks are not accessible, and this imposes a rigid limit on the allowed depth of subroutine calling.

Addressing Modes

The addressing of data and program segments in storage is an area that presents enormous variations from computer to computer. The problem is to allow references to be made to any arbitrary word in the addressing space, yet eliminate the need for a full set of address bits in each and every instruction. If the full address is required in each instruction, program sizes tend to grow. Most microprocessors take advantage of the fact that most data program references are local in scope; that is, references are most often close to the address of the current instruction being executed or close to the last datum references to main storage.

Each microprocessor vendor seems to adopt a unique vocabulary for describing machines. Sometimes, the intent is obviously to allude to the features by names that do not really exist. In other cases, the reason is ignorance. In the descriptions of addressing modes that follow, most of the popular techniques will be covered using industry-standard terminologies. In comparing computers, compare the addressing modes by what they do, not by what the documentation calls them.

Direct addresses are the most common kind and are represented by instructions that contain a storage address wide enough to refer to any point in main storage.

Abbreviated addresses are similar to direct addresses, but only *part* of the address is carried in the instruction. The rest of the bits of the address are contained in a register that is usually part of the CPU. Most commonly, the address part that is supplied from the instruction represents the least significant bits of the intended address.

Immediate addressing means that the instruction does not have an address part at all; the program location counter is issued to storage as the datum address. The datum fetched, then, is part of the instruction itself. Certain instructions, like jump and call, nearly always have immediate operands. Many microprocessors have other data-processing instructions that admit immediate operands.

Relative addressing shortens the address part of the instruction by permitting references within some narrow range relative to a CPU register. Most often that register is the program location counter. The address field of the instruction is added to the program location counter's value (in some cases with sign extension) to arrive at a datum address. In larger computers, the base-displacement form of addressing is used; this relative form uses a special (base) register plus the displacement carried as an abbreviated address in the instruction to compute a storage address.

Indexed addressing is similar to relative addressing, but a special register is used. To compute a datum address, the address part of the instruction is added to the contents of the index register by the CPU.

Indirect addresses allow a named location to contain, instead of data, the address of data. Therefore, the instruction refers to a word that, in turn, refers to the datum. This is particularly important in generalized software. In some computers, one of the bits of the address that has been fetched indirectly may further specify indirection. This multilevel indirect addressing is intellectually stimulating but seldom useful.

Register addressing is used when the CPU has several possible registers that can be referred to. Since the number of registers is relatively small, only a few bits are necessary to select a register.

Register-indirect addressing combines the last two addressing schemes. The instruction specifies a register address and indirection. The selected register contents are used to address main storage; this keeps the number of address bits in each instruction very small.

The register-indirect form of data addressing is so common in microprocessors that it deserves special mention. Many of the 4- and 8-bit processors offer only this addressing mode; therefore, all the data addresses must be in CPU registers. This frequently makes programming difficult, particularly when making references to isolated words in storage. When accessing contiguous elements of an array, the register-indirect form is sufficient. Unfortunately, most actual programs do not spend much time cycling through array elements.

As this last example has illustrated, it is possible to combine two or more of these addressing schemes into more elaborate combinations. It is quite common, for example, for microprocessors to provide for abbreviated but indexed addresses.

EXERCISES

1-1.   Give, in block diagram form, the basic functions of a computer.

1-2.   Which are the main functional units of a central processing unit?

1-3.   Describe briefly the function of each unit in Exercise 2.

1-4.   Describe the control circuitry of a central processing unit.

1-5.   What are some of the system features in the selection of a microprocessor system?

1-6.   Describe briefly the hardware design considerations of a microprocessor system.

1-7.   Describe the software design considerations of a system.

1-8.   Describe addressing modes.

1-9.   In your opinion, what are the advantages of microcomputers compared to computers that have been on the market for many years? What are their disadvantages, if any?

1-10.   What are the two main factors that closely associate computers with electronics?

2

Types of Microprocessors

2.1 GENERAL

This chapter is perhaps one of the most valuable in the entire book because it provides summarized, yet substantial information on the various types of microprocessors on the market today. However, since microprocessors are still rather expensive, it must first be decided if the use of a microprocessor justifies the additional expense. For instance, if your system calls for 30 TTL integrated circuits, or for programming capabilities or for complex arithmetic or logic, the use of a microprocessor is well justified. On the other hand, microprocessors have their limitations as well. They are certainly not the total solution to speed, nor do they offer large word lengths. Last but not least, microprocessors are not suitable if the memory size is extremely large, usually in excess of 64 kilobytes.

Let us now see what the manufacturers offer in the microprocessor line.

2.2 AMERICAN MICRO-SYSTEMS

7200

The American Micro-Systems 7200 microprocessor was the most sophisticated and comprehensive design until recently. The schematic of the system is shown in Figure 2-1. By the way, this system never got off

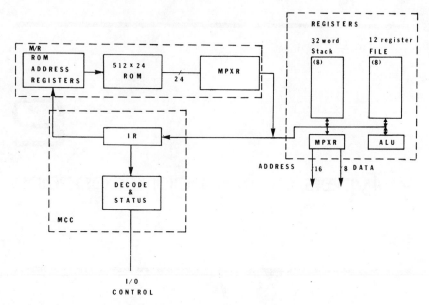

Fig. 2-1. AMI 7200 (Courtesy of AMI)

the ground. AMI apparently could not build it. As an object lesson in architectural ambition, however, it serves as a good model. It also serves as a warning to those who design around "paper tigers."

The 7200 was designed to be implemented on three chips with a microprogrammable 8- or 16-bit data word structure. Microinstructions were to be held in a 512-word, 24-bit ROM, with most control logic on a separate chip. An 8-bit register and ALU (RALU) chip was to be cascaded into a 16-bit version. The RALU's 12-word register file was to have held two accumulators, four index registers, two program counters, and four temporary registers. Because pairs of important registers were designed in, interrupt servicing would have been simplified.

The control logic called for time slots of 90 nanoseconds (ns), and a 540-ns microinstruction execution time. This was the weak point of the design because it stretched the capabilities of PMOS technology.

The MIR (microinstruction ROM) was to have held the microprogram for the particular 8- or 16-bit instruction/data configuration. The instruction register was designed to be part of the microcontrol chip (MCC), and 9 bits were to be used as an address into the 24-bit microcode ROM. In addition to the instruction register, the MCC held all master control functions and instruction decoding that was dependent upon external status conditions, and an interval timer.

The register and ALU was designed with a 32-word, 8-bit pushdown stack for data and subroutine return addresses, and a file of 12 registers.

The register file was probably designed as a 15-word 8-bit array, with several of the register pairs treated as single 16-bit registers by the programmer. ALU operations were on 8-bit quantities, and addresses were designed to be 16 bits wide.

7300

The AMI 7300 appeared at first glance to be similar in architecture to other "slice" architectures. Such was not the case. The 7300 (also recently withdrawn) was composed of a control chip, a register chip, and had a 22-bit-wide microinstruction. There, however, the similarity with other architecture ended. One chip held the microinstruction ROM and basic controls, while the other contained the registers and ALU. The data bus was arranged for 8 bits, and the interchip bus was 11 bits wide (Figure 2-2). (The microinstruction was passed to the ALU in two phases.)

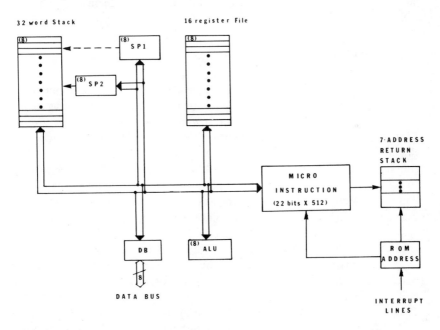

Fig. 2-2. AMI 7300 (Courtesy of AMI)

to other "slice" architectures. Such is not the case. The 7300 was (was, because, like its predecessor the 7200, the 7300 has been withdrawn) composed of a control chip, a register chip, and it had a 22-bit-wide microinstruction. There, however, the similarity with other architecture ends. One chip held the microinstruction ROM and basic controls, while the other contained the registers and ALU. The data bus was arranged for 8 bits, and the interchip bus was 11 bits wide (Figure 2-2). (The microinstruction was passed to the ALU in two phases.)

The design of the RALU chip included a 32-byte array that, with two pointers, could be used as one or two pushdown stacks. There were 16 general-purpose, 8-bit-wide registers, and the ALU was to operate on 8-bit quantities from registers, the stack, or the data bus to the rest of the system (including main storage and peripherals). The MIR was designed to be a 512-word, 22-bit mask-programmable ROM. The ROM address was held in a 9-bit register and attached to a seven-level pushdown stack so that microsubroutines could be easily created. External control and interrupt lines fed a starting-address register for interrupt recognition and I/O control lines came from the MIR.

In the 7300 design, each microinstruction required 4 microseconds (μs) for execution, and execution of one microinstruction was to be overlapped with the fetch of the next. There were no intrinsic features for peripheral device or main storage control.

2.3 BURROUGHS MINI-D

The Burroughs Mini-D is a unique departure from contemporary design. It was obviously conceived quite some time ago and was designed to minimize on-chip real estate. All data flow in and out of the chip goes over a 1-bit bus; internally, however, the Mini-D is organized as an 8-bit processor (Figure 2-3). All instructions are contained on a ROM located on the CPU chip itself; the ROM may contain 256 12-bit instructions. Reference to data storage is, like access to peripherals, through the sole 1-bit-wide data bus. While the Mini-D is microprogrammable, most applications are probably programmed directly into the ROM. Since the ROM is part of the processor chip and must be custom-mask-programmed, it is practical only for very large volumes, such as those found in consumer-credit terminal applications.

The internal organization of the processor provides four general-purpose 8-bit registers and a serial arithmetic logic unit. The program location counter need be only 8 bits long to address the entire program ROM. The instruction set is quite obscure, having been designed for maximum flexibility in only 12 bits. It will be quite familiar to anyone who has programmed a narrow-word microprogrammable computer before.

There have been persistent rumors that the semiconductor house that makes the Mini-D for Burroughs is negotiating for sales rights; however, it appears that Burroughs will not permit any marketing of the product by any third party. The Mini-D would probably be especially attractive to the consumer and entertainment markets.

The Mini-D is a good model to study because it is likely that custom processors for extremely high-volume applications will be, in some ways,

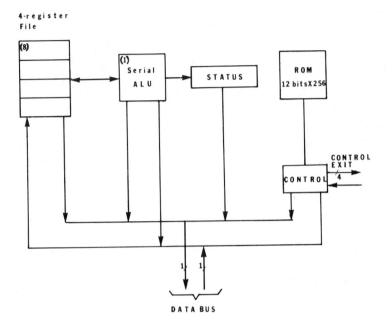

Fig. 2–3. Burroughs Mini-D (Courtesy of Burroughs Corp.)

similar. Intel, for instance, has designed and built a custom special-purpose CPU chip with an electrically reprogrammable ROM on-board.

2.4 ELECTRONIC ARRAYS

The Electronic Arrays' (EA) microprocessor is an 8-bit computer with 16 data registers and a unique kind of stack (Figure 2-4).

The programmer has use of 16 general-purpose 8-bit registers, one 16-bit index register, and an eight-place stack that is unique among microprocessors. One of the 16 data registers is the accumulator, and it alone may be shifted; it is probably treated as a special register by the user.

The uniquely organized push down stack has eight levels; a 3-bit pointer (P) selects the current entry. Subroutine calls are made by incrementing the P register, and returns decrement it. The particular stack item that is indexed by the P register holds the current program location counter and a data page pointer.

The EA microprocessor's storage addressing scheme arbitrarily divides a 16-bit address into two 8-bit halves. The most significant bits select one 256-byte page, and the least significant 8 bits select 1 byte of that page. In the currently selected pushdown stack item, 16 bits hold the program location counter (page and byte). The extra 8-bit entry in each stack item,

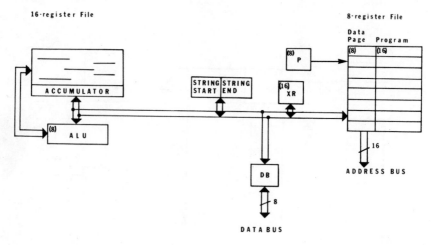

Fig. 2–4. Electronic Arrays Microprocessor (Courtesy of Electronic Arrays)

called *data page,* is used to select a default page at which data is stored; it typically points to locations in RAM.

Instructions that refer to data in main storage may have 8- or 16-bit addresses; that is, these instructions are either 2 or 3 bytes long. The 3-byte instructions have a 1-byte operation code and a 2-byte, 16-bit address. The shorter instructions use the currently selected data page register contents to select a page, and the instruction supplies the byte address within that page. In other words, the 8 bits from the stack are "laminated" with the 8 bits from the instruction to form a full 16-bit datum address.

This is one of the neater solutions to the addressing problem, allowing short addresses but with a variable range. It is fairly easy to arrange the bulk of data for a suite of subroutines in a 256-byte area; contrary to popular opinion among some designers, data are not generally accessed from contiguous locations.

The EA microprocessor is the first attempt to provide an array processor. A pair of 4-bit registers (string-start and string-end) are used to select a sequence of 1 to 16 registers to be treated as an array. From the sparse information available now, it appears that an array of up to 16 bytes in memory and an array in the on-chip registers may be added, subtracted, AND-ed, OR-ed, and XOR-ed, with results sent to the register array. The registers can be loaded and stored as arrays which should simplify interrupt servicing.

The pointer to the stack can be program or hardware controlled, so vectored interrupts via the stack are possible. The stack is said to be accessible, so software can be used to extend its depth.

2.5 FAIRCHILD

F-8

Fairchild's new F-8 microprocessor is a unique architecture; the CPU has no program location counter. Much more logic is packed on the CPU chip itself than in other micros, and some other important registers are duplicated on each and every memory chip in the set (Figure 2-5).

The F-8 family consists of a CPU and a RAM chip, a mask-programmed ROM chip, and a general memory interface chip. The RAM and ROM chips also provide I/O paths at chip's edge. The 1024 X 8 ROM provides two bidirectional 8-bit channels and the 256 X 8 RAM has one. The addresses are programmed into ROM I/O ports when the mask is cut.

Each memory chip accepts one interrupt signal (therefore, there may be as many different interrupts as there are memory chips), and each chip connects to two neighbors in order to accomplish chaining of interrupt priorities. Each chip also has a timer that can be programmed to interrupt; timers count in 15.5 μs increments.

The most important feature of the memory chips is that they each have two program location counters and a data address register; like registers in all chips all contain the same value. There are two program location counters on each chip so that interrupts and single-level subroutine calls can be performed quickly. All reference to data in RAM and ROM is made through the 16-bit data counter (memory address register) on the memory chips. Each of the three registers may be read into predetermined registers in the CPU's register file, modified, and sent back out to the storage chips.

One major disadvantage of the F-8 storage addressing scheme is the

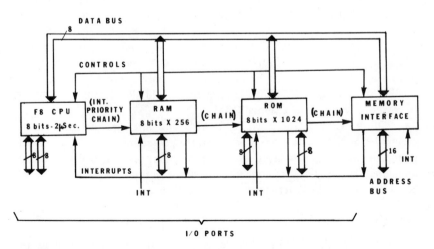

Fig. 2-5. FAIRCHILD F-8 (Courtesy of Fairchild Semiconductors)

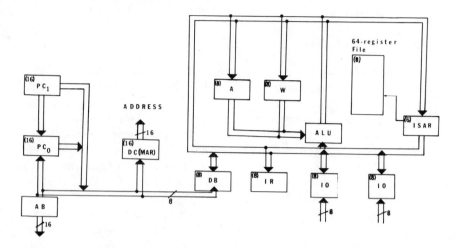

Fig. 2–6.

required use of the data counter. There are no instructions that explicitly refer to storage addresses, so that the global data counter must be loaded before referring to any data in RAM and ROM. This has been a serious programming disadvantage with the Intel 8008 which was rectified in the 8080 by adding instructions that have explicit storage addresses. Without these instructions, random references to main storage are complicated. For small applications and those possessing highly regularized and structured arrays, the F-8 CPU 64-word register file may alleviate the storage addressing problem.

The CPU also has two bidirectional I/O ports and a master clock on the single chip (Figure 2-6.) Duplicates of the program location counter(s) and storage address registers are not on the CPU chip. The master clock is controlled by a crystal or *RC* network connected to two pins; the maximum frequency is 2 megahertz (MHz). All this logic in one package means that some small applications can be designed with only one more chip (a ROM holding the program). The large register file should allow many applications to get along without any external RAM.

Of the CPU registers, W holds ALU and interrupt status. A is the accumulator, and ISAR is an indirect scratch-pad address register. The ISAR points to one of the 64 registers in the file; that register, and the lowest-numbered 12 registers, are accessible from instructions. Registers 9 through 15 have access to the W-register status bits and the external program counters.

PPS-25

Actually, the Fairchild PPS-25 is not nearly as complicated as the available documentation appears to make it (Figure 2-7).

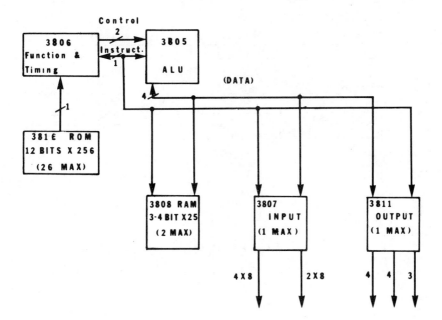

Fig. 2–7.

The PPS-25 chip set includes a two-chip CPU and ROM, RAM, and I/O chips. However, internally the PPS-25 is different from other processors (except MAPS from National). To begin with, the RAM module is organized as three 25-digit registers. Now, this seems to be an odd way to organize storage for a microprocessor, but it is most appropriate for numeric processors found in navigation instruments and calculators. However, few applications really require 25 digits of precision. In fact, the PPS-25 design allows the different parts of a 25-digit register to be used in different ways.

The use of the parts of a 25-digit register is the most confusing part of the system, and the literature is less than lucid. The "time enable" notion is the culprit; it is so poorly explained that most potential customers have simply dropped any consideration of the product. Perhaps the following, clearer explanation will help.

Data travels between RAM and CPU on a 4-bit bus. During a basic 62.5-μs machine cycle, there are 25 minicycles of 2.5 μs each. During each minicycle, a new digit is presented to the CPU from the selected register in the RAM, and an old digit is replaced. Therefore, the 25 digits are presented in 25 time-sequential "nibbles." Inside the PPS-25's CPU, there is a 6 × 25-bit ROM that represents six masks. Each mask is 25 bits long—the same as the number of digits in a RAM register. Each bit in the mask specifies whether the corresponding digit from the RAM register is to be operated upon by

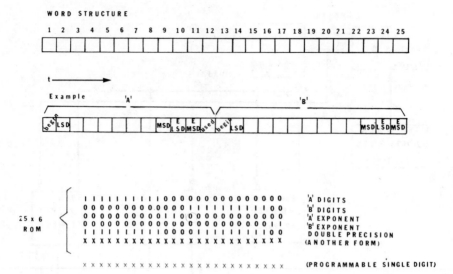

Fig. 2-8.

the current instruction. In most cases, the mask is all zeros except for a "burst" of one bits, defining that part of the data to be used. The example shown in Figure 2-8 illustrates how the 6 × 25 ROM might be specified for an application that uses 9-digit floating-point quantities. Two of the masks select the actual digits of significance (left and right half, so two numbers can be packed into a single 25-digit register), and two masks select the exponent digits. For double-precision operations, another mask is specified that allows 18 decimal digits of precision. The sixth mask is not specified in this example. For manipulation of all data not explicitly covered by a ROM pattern, the PPS-25 provides a single register that can be programmed to hold a number in the range 0 through 24, so that any single digit can be selected and operated upon; this would be used to access and operate on the sign words, for example.

Each instruction has a 3-bit code that specifies one of the six masks that defines the data format. The seventh code causes the selection of one specified digit out of the 25 (based on a register that is under the programmer's control). (The eighth code—zero—is used to mark those instructions that do not refer to data in RAM registers.)

Summarizing, then, an instruction that manipulates data specifies one of six masks, the bits of which "enable" certain digits to be processed by the instruction. "Time enable" is just a complicated way of saying "AND-mask."

Once the serial 4-bit-wide data path and its method of control by the time enable is understood, the only remaining idiosyncracy is the instruction

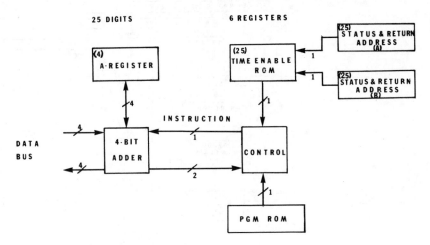

Fig. 2–9.

fetching sequence. Once that is explained, the rest of the architecture is conventional.

The instruction fetch uses the same 25 subcycles of 2.5 μs each (Figure 2-9). During the execution of one instruction, the next instruction is being fetched. The 25 time slots used during data operations on RAM are simultaneously used to send an address to ROM and then fetch an instruction. This transmission takes place on a 1-bit-wide path. During the fourth through twelfth time slots, a ROM instruction address is sent out; the least significant bit is sent first, and the last bit is always zero (this ninth bit was included in hopes that there might be a 512-word instruction ROM some day). During the fourteenth through twenty-fifth time slots, the instruction is serially transmitted from the ROM to the CPU.

Fairchild is deemphasizing the marketing of the PPS-25 in favor of the newer F-8.

2.6 GENERAL INSTRUMENTS CP-1600

The CP-1600 unit is a 16-bit, single-chip, high-speed MOS-LSI microprocessor. Employing a 5-MH$_z$, two-phase clock, the device completes a microcycle in 400 ns.

A basic block diagram of the CP-1600 is illustrated in Figure 2-10. It is noted that all data transfers within the machine are performed on 16-bit words processed in two 8-bit bytes. Internally, the architectural effect of this byte serial technique is to organize all data paths as 8 bits in width. In communicating with external devices, however, the CPU transfers 16 bits in parallel.

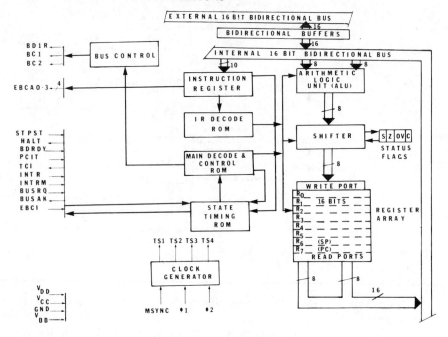

Fig. 2–10. GI CP-1600 (Courtesy of General Instrument, Inc.)

The major logic blocks through which all data flow are the arithmetic/ logic unit shifter, register array, and the internal 16-bit bus. The ALU is the primary data-processing element of the CPU. It accepts two data words, each 8 bits wide, from the internal 16-bit bus, and produces an 8-bit resultant.

The ALU passes the resultant to the shifter which is also 8 bits wide. The shifter can transfer data to the register array transparently, or can skew data one bit position right or left. The shifter, in combination with the ALU, can effect changes in the four status bits which monitor carry out from the most significant bit of the resultant, arithmetic overflow, sign detect, and zero detect.

The register array is comprised of the eight 16-bit registers with one 8-bit write port and two 8-bit read ports. The write port can direct data to any one of the eight registers and then either to that register's lower or upper 8-bit byte. The read ports can simultaneously output to the internal bus any two byte combinations, be they from the same register, different registers, or left or right byte.

The internal 16-bit bidirectional bus is the primary link for all information transfers between the CPU and the external world. Communications between the internal bus and the external bus are governed by the bus control signals BC1, BC2, and BDIR.

2.7 INTEL.

Intel has been the pioneer in the design and production of micro-processors and peripheral devices, and has generated nice original ideas.

3001/2

Intel's chip set ushers in a new era of performance in microprocessors. The 3000 family is a microprogrammable processor implemented in 2-bit slices. The Schottky TTL circuitry provides a "typical" microinstruction cycle of 160 ns. The architecture and microinstruction set has provisions for adding optional hardware to do almost anything, including even going faster. The product is aimed at replacing TTL controllers and processors, and Intel professes no plans to introduce a general-purpose macroinstruction set, even one like the immensely popular 8080.

The microprogram is stored in conventional bipolar ROMs, and RAMs can be easily substituted during development (Figure 2-11). The 40-pin 3001 microprogram control unit (MCU) generates the ROM address sequences by analyzing the current microinstruction, status flags, and up to 8 bits of the microinstruction fetched from main storage. Extensive control logic includes 4- and 16-way jumps that are steered by macroinstruction bits. The MCU also stores the ALU flag bits and selectively reinserts them on succeeding cycles to implement some functions.

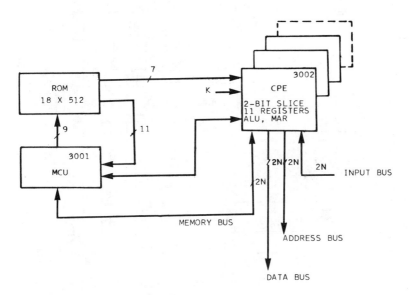

Fig. 2-11. Intel 3001 (Courtesy of Intel Corp.)

The MCU has no provisions for saving or restoring the current micro-instruction address. This weakness eliminates microlevel subroutines from the microprogrammer's arsenal; that is a serious inconvenience. Attempts to save the address externally will be hampered by the fact that only eight of the nine address bits can be loaded back into the chip. There are ways to implement microsubroutines with external hardware, but they all appear to be awkward.

The business end of the computer is built up with 28-pin 3002 central processing elements (CPE). Each CPE contains two bits of ALU, memory address register, an accumulator, and 11 general data registers (Figure 2-12). Carry propagate pins are provided for both ripple and look-ahead carry strategies; a compatible 8-bit look-ahead generator has been announced as part of the series. All paralleled inputs are specially buffered to permit a vast number of these chips to be stacked together (anyone need a 320-bit word?).

The CPE architecture is conceptually simple and is based on an ALU with three-way multiplexers on each of its data inputs. All chip inputs must pass through the ALU en route to the accumulator (AC) or register file. A memory address (MA) register is provided; memory and output data come directly from the AC. The 11 scratch-pad registers are organized as one temporary holding register and 10 general-purpose registers. The majority of the microinstructions perform functions on the accumulator and the

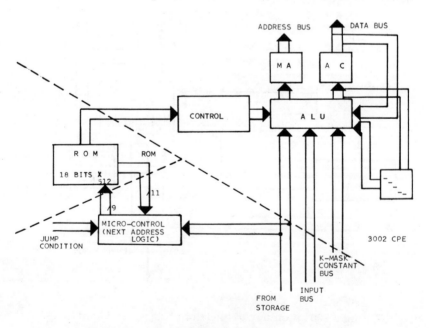

Fig. 2-12. Intel 3002 (Courtesy of Intel Corp.)

holding register in the scratch-pad file; this allows more function-control codes in these instructions.

An unusual feature of the CPE is the K input bus. On the way to the ALU, the accumulator and input bus are AND-ed with the K bus, which supplies a bit mask. The K bus can also feed microprogrammed constants directly into the ALU. A basic 18-bit-wide microprogram word must be extended, of course, to provide the desired number of K bits for generalized masking. Functions such as byte masking or swapping can be implemented with only a couple of K bits tied to the appropriate CPE pins.

Each microinstruction moves data from a specified source bus or register to a selected destination through the ALU. The microinstruction includes ALU function code, status flag control bits, and conditional jump fields, and is executed in a single clock cycle.

The announced chip set includes a priority interrupt control unit which can jam an address into ROM. The interrupt does not affect the microprogram address register, and the microprogram is written so that interrupts are recognized only at the time a macroinstruction fetch cycle is about to be initiated.

Microinstruction fetch and execute delays can be overlapped by providing latches between the ROM and CPEs.

4004

Intel's 4004 is the original microprocessor. It is a member of the MCS-4 family of parts based on a 4-bit word. The addressing structure is that of a "Harvard" class computer; data and program are not in the same storage medium or addressing system (Figure 2-13). Because of the unique RAM, the addressing arrangement, and the I/O port locations, the MCS-4 is sometimes difficult for neophytes to understand. However, once the Rubicon has

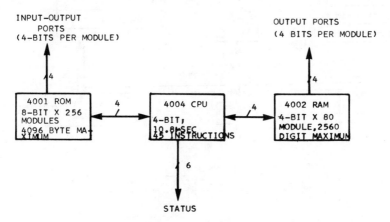

Fig. 2-13. Intel 4004 (Courtesy of Intel Corp.)

been crossed, the MCS-4 will be seen to be a powerful and quite complete chip set.

The MCS-4 set consists of chips that perform CPU functions, handle RAM and ROM storage (and input/output, coincidentally, on the same chips), and can be interfaced to a variety of main storage media. Recently added chips can handle generalized input and generate master clock signals. All interchip communication is through a single 4-bit bus (Figure 2-14). While this allows all parts to be designed into 16-pin DIPS, it does slow the system down. Instruction execution takes 10.8 or 21.6 μs.

The microprocessor has a 16-register file of general-purpose 4-bit digits, in addition to a 4-bit accumulator. Return addresses are stored into a four-place pushdown stack, the selected item of which is the current program location counter. With a 12-bit location counter, the 4004 may address up to 4096 8-bit words of program.

Since instructions cannot refer to data with explicit direct addresses, only register-indirect addressing is provided. Generally, an entire sequence of instructions is required to select a stored datum; careful allocation of data storage can make addressing less difficult.

Interrupts are not provided in the 4004. One unique pin at the edge of the chip (called TEST) is available to the conditional jump instructions to sense important external events. All input/output is performed through ports located in storage chips or accessed through storage interfacing chips. When the software is mask-programmed into type 4001 ROM chips, the four input/output bits can each be programmed for either input or output. The RAM modules provide only output ports.

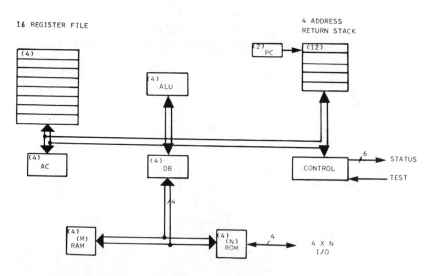

Fig. 2-14. Intel MCS-4 (Courtesy of Intel Corp.)

The MCS-4's head start in the industry and its 16-pin packages will make it an economical choice for some time to come.

4040

Just as Intel's experience with the 8008 led them to introduce an improved model (the 8080), their experience with the original microprocessor, the 4004, has produced specifications for the 4040. Most of the 4004's ills have been cured by the 4040. In a departure from the MCS-4 16-pin scheme, the 4040 has been packaged into a 24-pin DIP.

The 4040 can be best examined in relation to the 4004 (see Figure 2-15 also):

FEATURE	4004	4040
Program storage space (bytes)	4096	8192
Register file (4-bit digits)	16	24
Logic instructions (AND, OR)	No	Yes
Interrupt	No	Yes
Halt instruction	No	Yes
Return address stack	4 X 12	8 X 12

Communication between the two program banks is enhanced by the eight additional registers added to the 4040. However, use of subroutines in one bank by programs in the other is a software problem because the longer

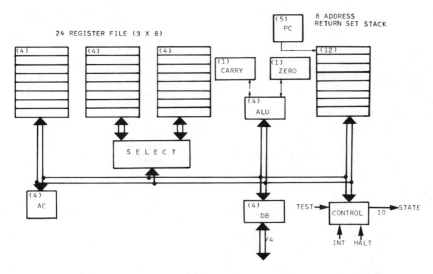

Fig. 2-15. Intel 4040 (Courtesy of Intel Corp.)

pushdown stack is still only 12 bits wide. Special interbank jump and call routines must be used to avoid losing the thirteenth bit of the return address.

Interrupts are handled by creating a subroutine call to a fixed 12-bit address, but the bank selection is not changed. Intel suggests duplicating the initial parts of the interrupt software in each bank of program storage.

The larger register files are necessary to support the kind of programs likely to be seen by the 4040. The return address stack has been lengthened to eight places, allowing up to seven subroutine levels. Usually, the programmer should leave one unused level so that interrupts can be serviced.

The data register file has been divided into two parts. Registers 0 through 7 are now duplicated; which register of the pair is selected is dependent upon the most recent register-bank select instruction issued. Registers 8 through 15 are not shared. Usually, the programmer will preserve one set of the 0-7 registers for use with subroutines in the first half of the ROM, and the other set will be selected prior to selecting the second half of ROM.

8008

The 8008 is an 8-bit microprocessor in a single 18-pin package. Two 8-bit numbers can be added in 20 μs; there is a grade-out known as the 8008-1 that can add in 12.5 μs (Figure 2-16).

Internally, the CPU is organized as a seven-register computer. One of those registers is the accumulator; nearly all arithmetic operation use it as well as all input/output. Because the 8008 does not have instructions that have direct addresses, two of the CPU registers are used for all references to

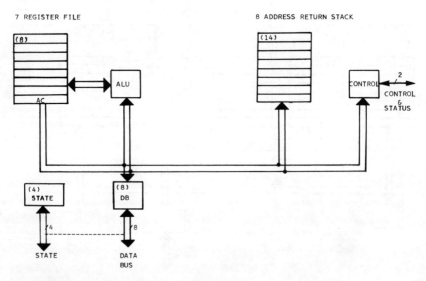

Fig. 2-16. Intel 8008 (Courtesy of Intel Corp.)

main storage. In order to fetch an operand from storage, the program must load an address into two (specific) registers of the file. This means, then, that at least three instructions must be used to refer to arbitrarily placed data. Furthermore, some common operations (such as moving data from one place in storage to another) are uncommonly complex.

Because of the small number of pin-outs, the 8008 requires that all data and addresses go through a single bidirectional 8-bit bus. Addresses up to 14 bits long require two sequential clock periods, and off-chip latches are required to hold the result.

The 8008 has an interrupt mechanism that is a model of simplicity. When the interrupt signal is raised, the processor inhibits incrementing of the program counter, issues an acknowledgment, and proceeds through a normal instruction fetch. The external interrupt hardware is expected to "jam in" a substitute instruction, usually a subroutine call that simultaneously saves the program counter and invokes the interrupt service routine.

When an interrupt strikes, it is always necessary to record something. In most computers, interrupts cause the CPU registers to be saved in main storage so they can be used for recording the fact of the interrupt and any essential processing can be done immediately. In the 8008, the register pair used for storage addressing may already contain values established by the interrupted program so they cannot be disturbed. The system designer can choose to reserve two of the general-purpose registers as interrupt registers (into which the storage addressing registers can be placed during interrupt processing), but this steals two of the seven registers available. In most cases, users avoid the interrupt mechanism except to start the processor at power-up.

A major disadvantage of the 8008 is the addressing scheme that requires programming addresses into a specific register pair. The interrupt handling problem is but one example of the side effects of that choice. Fortunately, the problem has been cured in the 8080.

A two-phase clock generator chip has been added to the 8008 family of parts. Many of the new parts for the newer 8080 will work with the 8008. Another component is rumored to be in design; it will replace the approximately 20 ICs necessary to interface the 8008 to storage and input/output.

8080

Intel's 8080 is an outgrowth of their experience with the 8008. Because of some of the idiosyncracies mentioned in the discussion of that older product, the 8080 was developed. Architecturally, the 8080 is significantly different from its predecessor (Figure 2-17). However, by design, there is major software compatibility; 8008 users have had little trouble upgrading to the 8080.

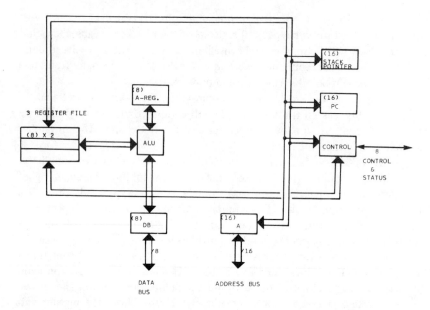

Fig. 2-17. Intel 8080 (Courtesy of Intel Corp.)

The most significant change between the 8008 and 8080 is the change from 18- to 40-pin packaging. This allows many formerly multiplexed data paths to be separated out and handled in parallel. This, as well as the change from PMOS to NMOS, has allowed a tenfold increase in processor speed. Furthermore, most of the external logic required to support the older processor is now on the 8080 CPU chip, and all the important interfacing signals appear on designated pins.

Architecturally, the 8080 has a three-register 16-bit file and an accumulator. For compatibility with the 8008, many instructions treat these as seven separate 8-bit registers. The 16-bit stack pointer is used to place all return addresses in RAM. Of course, this means the program counter has to be assigned a unique on-chip register. Note also that the storage addresses now extend over 16 bits and appear on a separate bus from the data and instruction bytes.

The stack, in RAM, can also be used to store data. It is of unlimited depth (to the limits of storage), although times for stack-referencing call instructions are slightly longer. Generality always exacts a toll in efficiency.

New instructions have been added to the set. The 8080 has instructions that permit explicit addressing of storage locations. Furthermore, where the 8008 only had a single pair of 8-bit registers allowed to address storage, the 8080 permits any of the three main registers to hold and output an address when using register-indirect addressing. This simplifies interrupt handling, too.

The pushdown stack can be used to hold the status bits and important register contents for interrupt servicing, avoiding another problem that was well known on the 8008.

The 8080 has two potential disadvantages: from a software standpoint, the lack of indexed addressing is serious in some applications; from a hardware view, the need for a third power supply must be considered.

The one recent study indicated the 8080 was a mere $20 more expensive than the 8008 when overall system costs were calculated. As industry pressure mounts, that gap will probably be reduced until the 8080 is cheaper to use than the 8008. With the introduction of a whole family of support parts for the 8080, Intel has opened the way toward the design of small systems with minimal outboard logic. Standard ROM and RAM chips from Intel's line graded out for appropriate speed, and some unique memory parts are assigned unique 8000-series part numbers. Other parts in the series include a three-state latch, a three-to-eight decoder, and drivers for clocks and buses. A universal synchronous–asynchronous interface chip is also available.

2.8   INTERSIL 6100

Intersil's approach to the market is based on two ideas: CMOS for low power drain and compatibility with DEC's PDP-8 to ease customer education. The 6100's instruction set is identical to that of the PDP-8; the speed is lower, but so is the power required (Figure 2-18). The wide operating temperature range and relaxed power-supply tolerances that are characteristic of CMOS apply to the 6100.

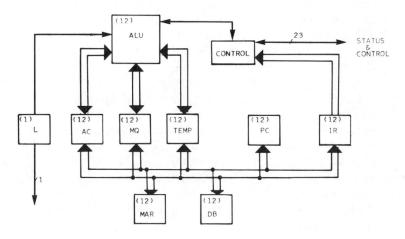

Fig. 2-18. Intersil 6100 (Courtesy of Intersil)

The usual PDP-8 architecture applies. There is a single accumulator, 12 bits long, extended at one end by a 1-bit link register. An accumulator extension, the MQ register, is included. All the PDP-8 instructions that use the MQ are provided, but not all the extended arithmetic element (EAE) instruction set is included. Because the chip is entirely static, the clock frequency can be reduced down to dc; while this is unimportant for production, it can be useful during software testing.

The PDP-8 is followed exactly, and this may present at least one problem. In the PDP-8, a subroutine call modifies the first word of the subroutine; the return address is stored there. This scheme will not work if subroutines are stored in ROM, as might be done in a microprocessor application. Dummy subroutines must be loaded in RAM (where they are subject to possible corruption) in order to link to and from subroutines in ROM.

Two package sizes for the 6100 are being implemented. The standard 40-pin package is intended for general use; a 28-pin version with reduced capabilities will also be available for dedicated minimum parts applications.

2.9 MONOLITHIC 6701

While the Monolithic Memories 6701 is not a complete microprocessor, it has all the essential features except instruction fetching and decoding. It might be considered as a register/ALU 4-bit slice as found in other architectures (Intel, National, and Raytheon, for instance). A rough schematic of the 6701 is shown in Figure 2-19. The 6701 makes no assumptions about sources of instructions and hence has no intrinsic provisions for referring to storage.

Historically, the 6701 has grown out of experience with the 74181 arithmetic logic unit. To the ALU, Monolithic has added a 16-register file and shift capabilities. There are two 4-bit address lines into the register file so that inputs to the ALU can be selected. The $\bar{Q}$ register is always available and is used as an accumulator outside the register file.

Control of data flow within the 6701 requires 16 bits. Two 4-bit groups are used to select the $\bar{A}$- and $\bar{B}$-register contents, and 8 bits are used to select the functional sequence inside the chip. The 8 function bits are fed into two read-only memories to derive 17 control signals. There are also 4-bit input and output ports for communicating with a bus system.

The 6701 can perform a register-to-register add in about 200 ns. When combined with instruction fetch and decode logic, a computer with a 400-ns cycle (plus main storage cycle time) could be created.

The bipolar processor is also available in the 5701 model; it is specified over the military temperature range.

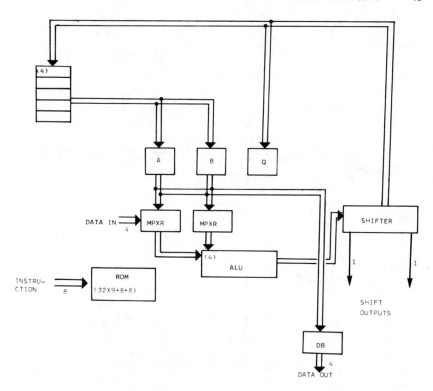

Fig. 2-19. Monolithic 6701 (Courtesy of Monolithic Memories, Inc.)

2.10 MOSTEK Z-80

A basic block Z-80 is illustrated in Figure 2-20a. The Z-80 CPU contains 208 bits of read/write memory that are accessible to the programmer. Figure 2-20b illustrates how this memory is configured into 18 8-bit registers and 4 16-bit registers. All Z-80 registers are implemented using static RAM. The registers include two sets of six general-purpose registers that may be used individually as 8-bit registers or in pairs as 16-bit registers. There are also two sets of accumulator and flag registers.

The Z-80 is fully software-compatible with the popular 8080A CPU offered from several sources.

2.11 MOTOROLA 6800

The Motorola 6800 is an integrated chip set with some special parts for input/output. Special ROM and RAM chips are included in the set so that

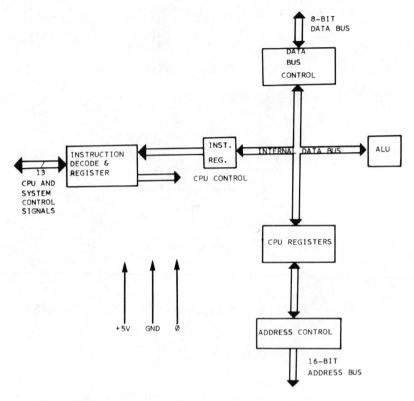

Fig. 2–20a. Mostek Z-80 (Courtesy of Mostek Corp.)

MAIN REG. SET		ALTERNATE REG. SET		
ACCUMULATOR A	FLAGS F	ACCUMULATOR A'	FLAGS F'	
B	C	B'	C'	
C	E	D'	E'	GENERAL
D	L	H'	L'	PURPOSE REGISTERS

INTERRUPT VECTOR I	MEMORY REFRESH R
INDEX REGISTER IX	
INDEX REGISTER IY	
STACK POINTER SP	
PROGRAM COUNTER PC	

SPECIAL PURPOSE
REGISTERS

Fig. 2–20b. CPU Register Configuration

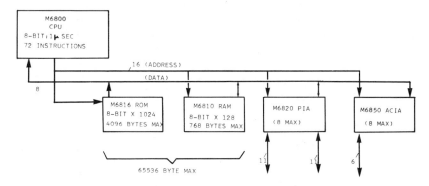

Fig. 2–21. Motorola 6800 (Courtesy of Motorola Semiconductors)

small applications can be supported with no external circuitry. Specifically, the system provides a 1024 × 8-bit ROM, a 128 × 8-bit RAM, a bidirectional peripheral interface adapter (PIA), and an asynchronous communications interface adapter (ACIA) (see Figure 2–21). The PIA offers bidirectional control on two 8-bit data buses in addition to control and interrupt lines for communication to and from peripheral devices. Peripheral controllers still need to be constructed, but the interfacing of these controllers to the CPU promises to be easier than with any other microprocessor. The ACIA includes parallel/serial conversion on the chip.

All these parts connect directly to one another. An early application of the 6800 with 2K × 8 ROM, 256 RAM, and five PIAs required no interface components between parts in the microprocessor family.

The CPU itself is organized as a conventional computer with an 8-bit data/instruction path. Instructions execute in 2 to 12 μs. There are two accumulators and a 16-bit index register. Return addresses are stored in a stack in RAM, and that stack is referenced via a pointer in the CPU.

Abbreviated addresses of 8 bits can be directed to refer to the first 256 bytes in main storage. Most programs are organized to refer to the locations for common work space. This abbreviated addressing is designed to compensate for the small number of CPU registers available.

Programming of the 6800 is relatively easy, but there are anomalies. There is, for example, no direct path from the two accumulators to the index register; to compute an index requires storing the 16-bit value into RAM, and then loading it into the index register. The choices of various addressing modes are somewhat arbitrary because only certain instructions admit certain modes; it is the programmer's responsibility to remember which addressing forms are valid for each instruction.

The 6800 provides for maskable interrupts at four levels. All the input/output devices appear on one interrupt level so that, once an interrupt is detected, polling must be used to isolate the device requiring attention.

When an interrupt occurs, the processor places status and register contents into the pushdown stack automatically. The interrupt return instruction refreshes the state of the machine from the stack. A software equivalent of the interrupt is provided also; the computer's state is pushed onto the stack and an interrupt service routine is invoked.

The PIA replaces the usual disorderly array of I/O circuitry with a single chip. Each PIA connects to the address and data buses and is treated in software just like storage locations. There are no special I/O instructions. The chip enable inputs are tied to memory address lines; this gives each PIA a unique set of addresses. Inside the PIA there are two independent halves. Each half can handle interrupts, generate control output levels or pulses, and transmit or receive up to 8 bits. Each port has an associated control register, an output word register, and a direction register, all accessible to the programmer.

To use the PIA, the direction register is loaded with 8 bits to establish each corresponding I/O line as an input or output. The output word register is loaded with the bits to be sent out, and input lines are read by simply reading from the storage address assigned to the PIA. In addition to the eight data lines, each port has an interrupt input and a multipurpose control line. Control register bits define the multipurpose line to be a second interrupt input, interrupt acknowledge output, control signal, or a pulse-generating output. Other control register bits provide masking for each interrupt line and for the interrupt flags required by the interrupt polling routine.

The ACIA is derived from the PIA design. It incorporates the essential features of a UART on-chip, but it does not handle a pair of data paths like the PIA. The ACIA can be easily interfaced with one of the popular odems.

2.12 NATIONAL

GPC/P

The GPC/P (general-purpose controller/processor) was the first micro-programmable microprocessor. Most users have avoided microprogramming, preferring to use National's own microprograms in either the 4-, 8-, or 16-bit sets. This may change with the introduction of National's FACE chip.

A rough schematic of the system is shown in Figure 2-22. A GPC/P is composed of two major components: CROM (control read-only memory), and RALU (register-ALU). The RALU is a 4-bit slice of the registers and arithmetic/logic unit, reminiscent of the internal organization of many minicomputers. The CROM contains microinstruction decoding control logic and a 100×23-bit ROM that contains the microprogram. A minimal system consists of one CROM and one RALU; that CROM must be suitably

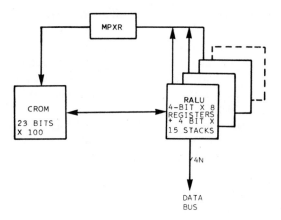

Fig. 2–22. National GPC/P (Courtesy of National Semiconductors)

microprogrammed to operate on 4-bit data quantities. In a minimum parts example, the 4-bit-wide registers are too small for some required facilities such as a program location counter, so that these must be added outboard of the GPC/P itself. This is, in fact, how the IMP-4 and IMP-8 operate.

In a larger configuration, four RALUs can be connected end-to-end to create a 16-bit word computer. One of two CROMs can be programmed to control this configuration. National supplies preprogrammed CROMs with the IMPs described below, and a five- or six-chip set (depending upon instruction set) comprises the basis of the IMP-16. Similarly, two RALUs and a CROM form the basis of the IMP-8. A CROM, a RALU, and a special interface chip (FILU) form the IMP-4. It appears to be possible to create word widths of up to about 24 bits without being affected by propagation delays.

More than one CROM can be connected to a system, and the CROMs may be individually selected by a small amount of outboard logic. In some applications then, available CROM chips may be used for most instructions and a custom CROM added to extend the instruction set. National is already doing this with an extended arithmetic set of instructions for the IMP-16. Each CROM holds one hundred 23-bit microinstruction words. There is a 4-bit path over which the CROM and RALUs communicate. The RALU contains multiplexing circuitry that allows external bus lines to appear like another register, and this permits input and output. To the microprogram, of course, main storage of the macromachine is just another peripheral device.

The RALU contains eight randomly accessible registers, a 16-word pushdown stack, and the ALU. Each microinstruction can specify any two registers as sources for the ALU and a register as destination for the result.

Sixteen bits of microcode are transmitted to the RALU on a four-wire multiplexed control bus. A four-phase clock is required.

Usually, one of the RALU registers is allocated as the program location counter for the macromachine. The other registers are used as programmer-accessible registers, memory address registers, RAM-stack pointers, and so on. The built-in pushdown stack can be used for data or return addresses, depending upon the microprogram.

The microinstruction language is rich and apparently well designed. The newest member of the GPC/P parts family allows microprograms to be stored in user-programmed RAM and ROM. Until now, microprogramming of the GPC/P has been made costly by mask changes to create new CROM chips; several interactions are usually required to work out all the bugs.

The FACE (field alterable control element) removes the ROM from CROM and allows the user to connect any available storage medium. Except for the outboard store, FACE appears to the GPC/P to be identical to CROM.

IMP-4

The IMP-4 is National's computer built with their GPC/P parts set. In order to build a cost-effective computer, however, a new part had to be introduced with wide registers for such elements as the program location counter. A minimum system consists of three chips: one RALU holds the 4-bit data registers, one CROM holds the microprogram, and the FILU (4-bit interface logic unit) adds all that logic necessary to make a 4-bit processor work with a 12-bit address bus.

A rough schematic of the system appears in Figure 2-23. In the IMP-4 three of the RALU's seven registers are reserved for constants. The other four random-access CPU registers are used as 4-bit accumulators in the user's program. The 16-place 4-bit pushdown stack is used for data in the IMP-4. The CROM is a standard GPC/P part and draws its instructions from the 4-bit instruction register that is physically located on the FILU chip.

The FILU is the entire interface to the rest of the computer, both storage and peripherals. On that chip are found a memory address register (MAR), instruction register, program location counter, and a seven-place return address pushdown stack. All the address registers are 12 bits wide.

The IMP-4 is somewhat slower than other 4-bit competitors, requiring 12 μs for a register-to-register binary addition. However, the added feature of microprogrammability could be exploited to compensate in many applications.

It is axiomatic that programming ease is inversely proportional to the number of different addressing schemes that have to be used with different register sizes. The IMP-4 suffers from this problem; it is difficult to program. The machine's language loosely follows Data General Nova style, but the inflexibility of the jump addressing and complicated way of loading the

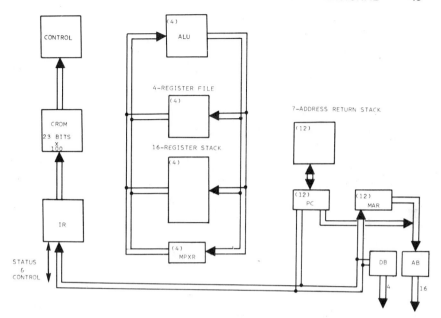

Fig. 2–23. National IMP-4 (Courtesy of National Semiconductors)

storage address (MAR) make practical programs relatively long and difficult to follow.

IMP-8

National's IMP-8 is the second most popular configuration designed around the GPC/P architectures. The basic system consists of one CROM and two RALU chips. Because all registers are only 8 bits wide, one additional external register is required to extend the program location counter. That external 8-bit register (see Figure 2-24) holds the most significant bits of the current program address and is called a *page-selection register (page counter)*.

The RALU's organization provides the user with four accumulators. The other three main registers are used for storage addressing (MAR and MDR) and, the least significant bits of the program location counter. The 8-bit MAR specifies the least significant bits of the address; the eight most significant bits come from the page counter or are set to zero. Data, therefore, can be addressed directly or indirectly via the current page or page zero.

Since indirect addressing is provided, most of the page zero is typically reserved for addresses to other pages in main storage; each indirect address occupies 2 bytes. Two of the accumulators can be used as index registers for addressing which alleviates many complexities in programming.

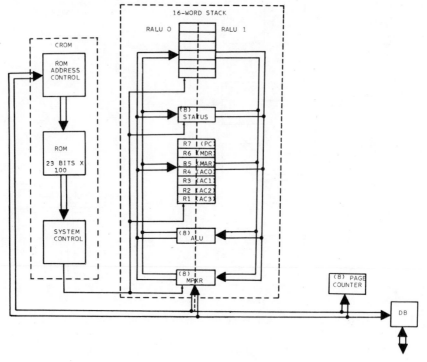

Fig. 2–24. National IMP-8 (Courtesy of National Semiconductors)

Jumps and subroutine calls affect both the internal and external halves of the program location counter. Subroutines put 2 bytes onto the RALU pushdown stack so that eight call levels can be used; the stack can also be used to store temporary data, 1 byte at a time.

IMP-16

The IMP-16 is, by far, National's most popular computer. It is significantly different from other designs, but its concepts are so fundamental that many of the microprocessors now being designed will look similar. The IMP-16 is made up of one or two CROM chips (depending upon whether the user selects the standard or the augmented instruction set) and four RALU chips (see Figure 2-25). The IMP-16 requires a significant amount of external hardware to make a complete computer; of course, it is the external hardware that allows flexibility. Instead of being "locked in" to a particular conditional jump structure, for example, the designer using the IMP-16 parts or boards can specify unique combinations; the block labeled MPXR is an example of that required circuitry.

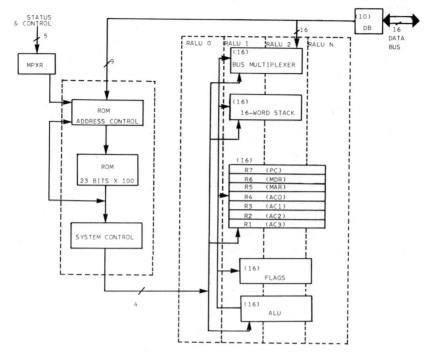

Fig. 2–25. National IMP-16 (Courtesy of National Semiconductors)

Since each register of the user's computer is 16 bits long, the architecture is quite easy to follow. The seven randomly accessible registers of the RALU are allocated by the microprogram so that the programmer has four accumulators. Two of the accumulators can be used as index registers; the other two have some special implications for certain instructions. The other three registers of the RALU are used by the microprogram for program counter (PC) and storage addressing (MAR and MDR).

The 16-place 16-bit pushdown stack is used for subroutine calls and interrupt handling; it can also be used for data storage under program control. The 16-bit "flags" register provides storage for such entities as carry and overflow conditions from the ALU—that requires 4 bits; the remaining 12 bits can be used by the programmer as status latches or as a way to communicate status to external devices.

The IMP-16 instruction set is vaguely modeled after the popular Data General Nova series. The instruction set is disorderly, and it takes some experience with the computer to be able to easily remember subtle differences among nearly identical instructions. Programming high–low equal tests is particularly difficult because of the unfortunate choice of jump conditions, SC/MP and PACE.

2.13 RAYTHEON RP16

Raytheon's RP16 uses 4-bit RALU slices built with bipolar technology to implement a 16-bit microprocessor. Three additional chips are included in the set, and all three are required to control the RALUs. The design uses ECL circuitry for some internal functions, but all interfaces are compatible with low-power Schottky TTL. The microcycle time is 200 ns, and the basic macroinstruction takes 1 μs. The RP16 appears in two slightly different models (see Figure 2–26): Model A has arithmetic features (a divide instruction, for example), and Model B is intended for byte-handling applications. Both models have multiply and double-precision add instructions and Model B includes byte-wise comparisons.

One major bus is the primary control route from the three control ROMs to the RALU chips. The eight 16-bit registers in the RALU file are mostly occupied with overhead functions. The following assignments are made in the microprogram that Raytheon supplies:

Stack pointer to RAM.

Program location counter.

*Base register (for base-displacement addressing).

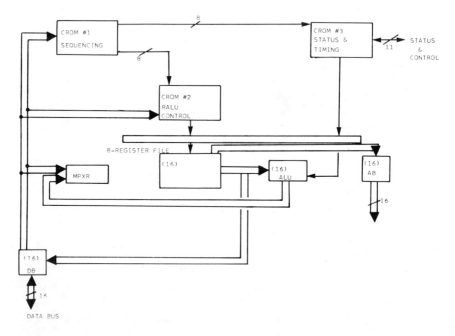

Fig. 2–26. Raytheon RP16 (Courtesy of Raytheon Corp.)

*Index register.

*Accumulator.

*Accumulator extension (for multiplication).

Working register (typically used as MDR).

Address register (MAR).

The four registers marked with asterisks are those that are useful to the programmer. The architecture that is microprogrammed in, then, is that of a two-address, one-accumulator machine.

A two-level interrupt scheme is included with both external- and program-initiated interrupts possible. This is also one of the few processors that offer a military operating temperature range.

2.14 RCA COSMAC

RCA has introduced an 8-bit microprocessor in the 6- to 8-μs speed range in CMOS. The basic system is shown in Figure 2-27. The COSMAC CPU has 16 general-purpose 16-bit registers. Each register may be used for data holding, as an index register, or as a program location counter.

Thus, the depth of an on-chip pushdown stack is limited by other uses of the registers as determined by the programmer. At any point in time, one register is the program location counter (as selected by a 4-bit P register)

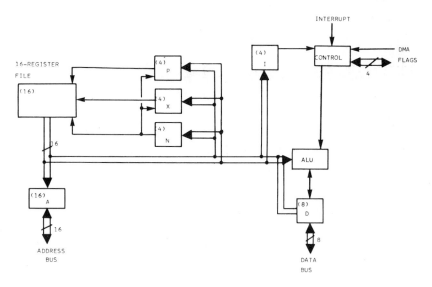

Fig. 2-27. RCA COSMAC (Courtesy of RCA Corp.)

and one is the current operand (as selected by a 4-bit N register). Since a program location counter in one program can be treated as an operand in another, the pushdown stack of return addresses can be extended at will by storing register contents (8 bits at a time) into main storage.

The register-indirect memory referencing scheme is similar to that used in other processors: instructions do not contain address operands, so all operands addressed first must be loaded into registers. COSMAC's register had been organized to largely ameliorate this problem by providing many wide registers, and allowing the programmer to use any one of them to address memory. In many applications, the net result is a shorter program store and, in many other applications, the necessity to continually load addresses becomes a tremendous burden. It all depends on the data structures of the application. COSMAC is built in a two-chip form at present, although future plans call for a one-chip version. A higher-speed version on a sapphire substrate is being investigated. RCA has been actively publicizing applications they have developed, but it will be toward the end of 1977 that samples will be available at large.

2.15 ROCKWELL PPS-8

Rockwell's experience with the PPS-4 has led them to expand the word size and develop the PPS-8. The newer microprocessor uses many of the same basic designs as the 4-bit computer, but more facilities for handling high-speed I/O problems are part of the set.

The PPS-8 parts set has a CPU, clock, ROM, RAM, and generalized I/O interfaces with a special DMA chip (see Figure 2-28). The DMA controller has the necessary storage address registers and CPU-inhibit lines to

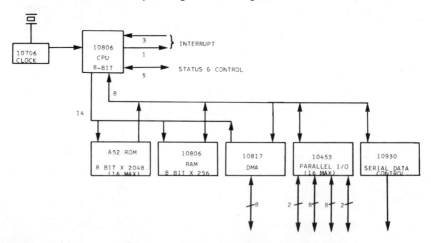

Fig. 2-28. Rockwell PPS-8 (Courtesy of Rockwell International)

allow peripheral devices to have direct access to the RAM via the data bus. The clock and ROM chips are the same ones used with the PPS-4. The 1200-bit/second serial data control chip is also common to both microcomputer sets.

The DMA controller has eight input lines that are connected to different peripheral device controllers. These eight DMA request lines are inherently priority-encoded; there are eight separate storage address registers in the DMA chip so that DMA requests can be interrupted. This may require some careful peripheral controller design to avoid timing problems. Also, the termination of a block transfer is controlled by the least significant 8 bits of the address, and a record length counter that is limited to 256 bytes; longer transfers require software intervention.

The CPU is obfuscated by its genesis (see Figure 2-29). In the translation of the PPS-4 design into an 8-bit computer, some unusual complications have been introduced. The A and W registers (accumulator and working, respectively) are used for most data manipulation. The X, Y, and Z registers are used for temporary storage; some instructions treat pairs of them as a single 16-bit register. The Z-X pair, for instance, is used as a storage address register for register-indirect addressing. The L register, on the other hand, is used to address bytes in program space (ROM). Each time L is used to fetch from ROM, it is automatically incremented by 1.

The L register is also used for subroutine return addresses, and so

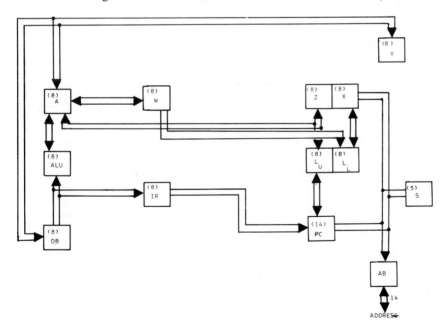

Fig. 2-29. PPS-8 CPU (Courtesy of Rockwell International)

forms a one-level pushdown stack for the program counter. Since L can be accessed from the program, the stack depth can be extended as necessary by software; for brief routines that call no other subroutines, the L register need not be preserved in RAM.

The 5-bit stack register (S) allows reference to the first 32 bytes of RAM. The X, Y, Z, A and L registers can be pushed onto the data stack; this is particularly useful during interrupt servicing. Each time the state of the machine is saved, seven words are required in the stack.

Three levels of priority interrupts are handled by the CPU by creating subroutine calls in the hardware. Interrupts must be disabled in order to use the L register as a data-reference register (as might be expected when indexing across an array), so that an interrupt does not destroy the address in the L register. Since the highest priority interrupt cannot be disabled, the L register must be used with caution.

In general, the PPS-8 is probably an efficient computer. It suffers from a lack of consistency in architecture, and many people will find it hard to program.

2.16 SIGNETICS 2650

The 2650 is Signetic's first venture into the microprocessor market-place. The computer is organized for 8-bit data, and a 32,768-word maximum program size. A rough sketch of the system is shown in Figure 2-30.

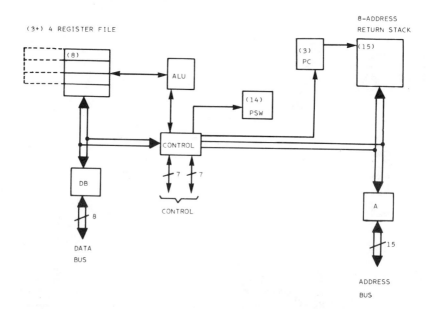

Fig. 2–30. Signetics 2650 (Courtesy of Signetics Corp.)

The central processor chip has a split register file and an eight-address return stack, the topmost item of which holds the current program location counter. The processor is controlled by the 14-bit program status word (PSW).

The register file is divided into three pairs of 8-bit registers and a common register. The selection of which half of the register file is used by instructions is dependent upon a bit in the PSW. A program, then, will normally have four registers to operate on. When a subroutine is called, or when an interrupt strikes, the register selection bit in the PSW can be changed to provide three preserved and three working registers.

Other PSW bits control the significance of the carry bit in shifts and computations, whether the sign enters into comparisons or not, and (in general) extend the properties of classes of instructions.

2.17   TEXAS INSTRUMENTS

One of the popular microprocessors introduced by this company is the 8080, details of which have been given in the Intel paragraph.

EXERCISES

2-1.   What is the time required to add two 8-bit numbers using an 8008?

2-2.   How many parts does the data register file have in a 4040?

2-3.   What are the main differences between the 4004 and the 4040?

2-4.   Give a block diagram of the 6100 and briefly describe its function.

2-5.   What is the memory capability of the Z80?

2-6.   Compare the 6800 and the 8080 and describe any differences, advantages, and/or disadvantages.

2-7.   Briefly describe the IMP-8.

2-8.   Which microprogram assignments are made in the RP16?

2-9.   Provide a block diagram of the PPS-8.

2-10.   Should you have to design a microprocessor-based system for general-purpose use, which of the microprocessors described thus far would you use? Why?

3

Terms Used in the World of Microprocessors

Throughout the chapters that follow you will encounter certain technical terms which describe the operation of a microprocessor system as well as the functions of the components that comprise it. It is a good idea at this point to give a short description of those terms so that you will not be surprised by them when they appear later.

Access Time. The time interval between the request for information and the instant the information is available.

Accounting Machine.

1. A keyboard-actuated machine that prepares accounting records.

2. A machine that reads data from external storage media, such as cards or tapes, and automatically produces accounting records or tabulations, usually on continuous forms.

Accumulator. A device that stores a number and which, on receipt of another number, adds the two and stores the sum.

Accuracy. The degree of freedom from error, that is, the degree of conformity to truth or to a rule. Accuracy is contrasted with precision. For example, four-place numerals are less precise than six-place numerals; nevertheless, a properly computed four-place numeral might be more accurate than an improperly computed six-place numeral.

ACK. Acknowledge message sent upon a communication link to indicate the reception of correct data. Used with error detectors in block and tree codes.

Adder. Switching circuit that combines binary bits to generate the sum and carry of these bits.

Address. An expression, usually numerical, which designates a specific location in a storage or memory device.

Address Format.

1. The arrangement of the address parts of an instruction. The expression "plus-one" is frequently used to indicate that one of the addresses specifies the location of the next instruction to be executed such as one-plus-one, two-plus-one, three-plus-one, four-plus-one.

2. The arrangement of the parts of a single address such as those required for identifying channel, module, track, and so on, in a disk system.

Address Register. A register in which an address is stored.

Algorithm. A term used by mathematicians to describe a set of procedures by which a given result is obtained.

Alphanumeric Code. A code whose code set consists of letters, digits, and associated special characters.

ALU. Arithmetic logic unit, a computational subsystem that performs the mathematical operations of a digital system.

Analog Representation. A representation that does not have discrete values but is continuously variable.

Arithmetic Shift.

1. A shift that does not affect the sign position.

2. A shift that is equivalent to the multiplication of a number by a positive or negative integral part of the radix.

Array Logic. A logic network whose configuration is a rectangular array of intersections of its input–output leads, with elements connected at some of these intersections. The network usually functions as an encoder or decoder.

ASCII. American National Standard Code for Information Interchange. The standard code, using a coded character set consisting of 7-bit coded characters (8 bits including parity check), used for information interchange among data-processing systems, communication systems, and associated equipment. The ASCII set consists of control characters and graphic characters. Synonymous with USASCII.

Assemble. To prepare a machine-language program from a symbolic-language program by substituting absolute operation codes for symbolic operation codes and absolute or relocatable addresses for symbolic addresses.

Assembler. A computer program that assembles.

Asynchronous Device. A device in which the speed of operation is not related to any frequency in the system to which it is connected.

Baud. A unit of signaling speed equal to the number of discrete conditions or signal events per second. For example, 1 baud equals ½ dot cycle/second in Morse Code, 1 bit/second in a train of binary signals, and one 3-bit value/second in a train of signals each of which can assume one of eight different states.

Baudot Code. Information code used in data transmission.

Benchmark Problem. A problem used to evaluate the performance of hardware or software, or both.

Block.

1. A set of things, such as words, characters, or digits handled as a unit.

2. A collection of contiguous records, recorded as a unit. Blocks are separated by block gaps and each block may contain one or more records.

3. A group of bits, or binary digits, transmitted as a unit. An encoding procedure is generally applied to the group of bits or binary digits for error purposes.

4. A group of contiguous characters recorded as a unit.

Block Diagram. A diagram of a system, instrument, or computer in which the principal parts are represented by suitable associated geometrical figures to show both the basic functions and the functional relationships among the parts.

Bootstrap. A technique or device designed to bring itself into a desired state by means of its own action (e.g., a machine routine whose first few instructions are sufficient to bring the rest of itself into the computer from an input device).

Borrow. An arithmetically negative carry.

Branching. A method of selecting, on the basis of results, the next operation to execute while the program is in progress.

Buffer. An isolating circuit used to avoid reaction of a driven circuit on the corresponding driver circuit. Also, a storage device used to compensate for a difference in the rate of flow of information or the time of occurrence of events when transmitting information from one device to another.

Bus. One or more conductors used for transmitting signals or power.

Call.

1. To transfer control to a specified closed subroutine.

2. In communications, the action performed by the calling party, or the operations necessary in making a call, or the effective use made of a connection between two stations.

Carry.

1. One or more digits, produced in connection with an arithmetic operation on one digit place of two or more numerals in positional notation, that are forwarded to another digit place for processing there.

2. The number represented by the digit or digits in definition 1.

3. Most commonly, a digit as defined in definition 1 that arises when the sum or product of two or more digits equals or exceeds the radix of the number-representation system.

4. Less commonly, a borrow.

5. To forward a carry.

6. The command directing that a carry be forwarded.

Carry-Look-Ahead. A type of adder in which the inputs to several stages are examined and the proper carries are produced simultaneously.

Cascade Connection. Two or more similar component devices arranged in tandem, with the output of one connected to the input of the next.

Central Processor Unit (CPU). Part of a computer system which contains the main storage, arithmetic unit, and special register groups. It performs arithmetic operations, controls instruction processing, and provides timing signals and other bookkeeping operations.

Channel.

1. A path along which signals can be sent (e.g., data channel, output channel).

2. The portion of a storage medium that is accessible to a given reading or writing station (e.g., track, band).

Character. A letter, digit, or other symbol that is used as part of the organization, control, or representation of data. A character is often in the form of a spatial arrangement of adjacent or connected strokes.

Check Bit. A binary check digit (e.g., a parity bit).

Code.

1. A set of unambiguous rules specifying the way in which data may be represented (e.g., the set of correspondence in the standard code for information interchange). Synonymous with coding system.

2. In data processing, to represent data or a computer program in a symbolic form that can be accepted by a data processor.

Combinatorial Logic System. Digital system not utilizing memory elements.

Compile. To prepare a machine-language program from a computer program written in another programming language by making use of the overall logic structure of the program, or generating more than one machine instruction for each symbolic statement, or both, as well as performing the function of an assembler.

Compiler. A program that compiles.

Complement Notation. A system of notation where positive binary numbers are identical to positive numbers in sign and magnitude notation, but where negative numbers are the exact complement of the magnitude of the corresponding positive value.

Conditional Jump. A jump that occurs if specified criteria are met.

Control Character. A character whose occurrence in a particular context initiates, modifies, or stops a control operation (e.g., a character that controls carriage return, a character that controls transmission of data over communication networks). A control character may be recorded for use in a subsequent action. It may in some circumstances have a graphic representation.

Control Hierarchy. Design development responsible for implementing "how" a system is to function. Not to be confused with "timing," as timing tells the system "when" to perform its function.

Counter. A circuit that counts input pulses and will give an output pulse after receiving a predetermined number of input pulses.

CRC. The cyclic redundancy check character.

Critical Race. Timing situation related to a synchronous operation. A "race" can occur when two variables are asked to change states simultaneously. "Critical" refers to the outcome that will determine the state of the machine.

Crosstalk. Interference that appears in a given channel but has its origin in another channel.

Cycle.

1. An interval of space or time in which one set of events or phenomena is completed.

2. A set of operations that is repeated regularly in the same sequence. The operations may be subject to variations on each repetition.

Data.

1. A representation of facts, concepts, or instructions in a formalized manner suitable for communication, interpretation, or processing by humans or automatic means.

2. Any representations such as characters or analog quantities to which meaning is or might be assigned.

Data Bus. One method of input/output for a system where data are moved into or out of the digital system by way of a common bus connected to several subsystems.

Data Processing. The execution of a systematic sequence of operations performed upon data. Synonymous with information processing.

Data Processor. A device capable of performing data processing, including desk calculators, punched card machines, and computers. Synonymous with processor.

Debug. To detect, locate, and remove mistakes from a routine or from malfunction of a computer. Synonymous with troubleshoot.

Decimal.

1. Pertaining to a characteristic or property involving a selection, choice, or condition in which there are 10 possibilities.

2. Pertaining to the number-representation system with a radix of 10.

Decimal Digit. In decimal notation, one of the characters 0 through 9.

Decoder. A conversion circuit that accepts digital input information—in the memory case, binary address information—that appears as a small number of lines and selects and activates one line of a large number of output lines.

Device Control Character. A control character intended for the control of ancillary devices associated with a data-processing or telecommunication system, usually for switching devices on or off.

Diagnostic. Pertaining to the detection and isolation of a malfunction or mistake.

Digit. A symbol that represents one of the nonnegative integers smaller than the radix. For example, in decimal notation, a digit is one of the characters from 0 through 9. Synonymous with numeric character.

Digitize. To use numeric characters to express or represent data (e.g., to obtain from an analog representation of a physical quantity, a digital representation of the quantity).

Direct Access.

1. Pertaining to the process of obtaining data from, or placing data into, storage where the time required for such access is independent of the location of the data.

2. Pertaining to a storage device in which the access time is effectively independent of the location of the data.

3. Synonymous with random access.

Direct Addressing. Method of programming that has the address pointing to the location of data or the instruction that is to be used.

Direct-Memory Access Channel (DMA). A method of input/output for a system that uses a small processor whose sole task is that of controlling input/output. With DMA, data are moved into or out of the system without program intervention.

Dot Matrix. A matrix of dots that is used to identify alphanumeric characters.

Double Precision. Pertaining to the use of two computer words to represent a number.

Dump.

1. To copy the contents of all or part of a storage, usually from an internal storage into an external storage.

2. A process as in definition 1.

3. The data resulting from the process as in definition 1.

Duplex. The method of operation of a communication circuit in which each end can simultaneously transmit and receive.

Dynamic Storage Elements. Storage elements which contain storage cells that must be refreshed at appropriate time intervals to prevent the loss of information content.

EBCDIC. Extended binary-coded decimal interchange code. An 8-bit, 256-character code used in transmission of binary data.

ECL Circuits. Bipolar emitter-coupled logic circuits; also called current-mode logic circuits.

Edge Triggering. Activation of a circuit at the edge of the pulse as it begins its change. Circuits then trigger at the edge of the input pulse rather than sensing a level change.

Edit. To modify the form or format of data (e.g., to insert or delete characters such as page numbers or decimal points).

Electrostatic Storage. A storage device that stores data as electro-statically charged areas on a dielectric surface.

Emulate. To imitate one system with another such that the imitating system accepts the same data, executes the same programs, and achieves the same results as the imitated system.

Encode. To apply a set of unambiguous rules specifying the way in which data may be represented such that a subsequent decoding is possible. Synonymous with code.

End-Around Carry. A carry generated in the most significant digit place and sent directly to the least significant place.

Entry Point. In a routine, a place to which control can be passed.

Erase. To obliterate information from a storage medium (e.g., to clear, to overwrite).

Error. Any discrepancy between a computed, observed, or measured quantity and the true, specified, or theoretically correct value or condition.

Execute. That portion of a computer cycle during which a selected control word or instruction is accomplished.

Exponent. In a floating-point representation, the numeral, or a pair of numerals representing a number, that indicates the power to which the base is raised.

Fetch. That portion of a computer cycle during which the next instruction is retrieved from memory.

Field. In a record, a specified area used for a particular category of data (e.g., a group of card columns used to represent a wage rate, a set of bit locations in a computer word used to express the address of the operand).

Fixed-Point Binary Number. A binary number represented by a sign bit and one or more number bits with a binary point fixed somewhere between two neighboring bits.

Flag.

1. Any of various types of indicators used for identification (e.g., a word mark).

2. A character that signals the occurrence of some condition, such as the end of a word.

3. Synonymous with mark, sentinel, tag.

Floating-Point Binary Number. A binary number expressed in exponential notation; that is, a part of the binary word represents the mantissa and a part represents the exponent.

Flowchart. A graphical representation for the definition, analysis, or solution of a problem in which symbols are used to represent operations, data, flow, equipment, and so on.

Format. The arrangement of data.

Function.

1. A specific purpose of an entity, or its characteristic action.

2. In communications, a machine action such as a carriage return or line feed.

Hamming Code. An error-correction code system used in data transmission. This code uses a parity check matrix in its operation.

Hardware. Physical equipment, as opposed to the computer program or method of use (e.g., mechanical, magnetic, electrical, or electronic devices).

Hazard. Transient output of a circuit that allows an undesired output value to appear during transition from one state to another

Immediate Address. Pertaining to an instruction in which an address part contains the value of an operand rather than its address. Synonymous with zero-level address.

Indexed Address. An address that is modified by the content of an index register prior to or during the execution of a computer instruction.

Indexing. In computers, a method of address modification that is implemented by means of index registers.

Index Register. A register whose content may be added to or subtracted from the operand address prior to or during the execution of a computer instruction. Synonymous with box.

Indirect Addressing. Programming method that has the initial address being the storage location of a word that contains another address. This indirect address is then used to obtain the data to be operated upon.

Information Feedback System. In telecommunications, an information transmission system that uses an echo check to verify the accuracy of the transmission.

Input/Output (I/O) Devices. Computer hardware by which data are entered into a digital system or by which data are recorded for immediate or future use.

Instruction. A statement that specifies an operation and the values or locations of its operands.

Instruction Counter. A counter that indicates the location of the next computer instruction to be interpreted.

Instruction Register. A register that stores an instruction for execution.

Interface. A shaped boundary. An interface might be a hardware component to link two devices or it might be a portion of storage or registers accessed by two or more computer programs.

Interleave (or Interlace). To assign successive storage location numbers to physically separated memory storage locations. This serves to reduce access time.

Interrupt. To stop a process in such a way that it can be resumed.

Jump. A departure from the normal sequence of executing instructions in a computer.

Jump Conditions. Conditions defined in a transition table that determine the changes of flip flops from one state to another state.

Label. One or more characters used to identify a statement or an item of data in a computer program.

Language. A set of representations, conventions, and rules used to convey information.

Level. The degree of subordination in a hierarchy.

Logic Shift. A shift that affects all positions.

Loop. A sequence of instructions that is executed repeatedly until a terminal condition prevails.

Machine Code. An operation code that a machine is designed to recognize.

Machine Language. A language that is used directly by a machine.

Macroinstruction. An instruction in a source language that is equivalent to a specified sequence of machine instructions.

Macroprogramming. Programming via macroinstructions.

Mainframe. Same as central processing unit.

Mask.

1. A pattern of characters that is used to control the retention or elimination of portions of another pattern of characters.

2. A filter.

Matrix.

1. In mathematics, a two-dimensional rectangular array of quantities. Matrices are manipulated in accordance with the rules of matrix algebra.

2. In computers, a logic network in the form of an array of input leads and output leads with logic elements connected at some of their intersections.

3. By extension, an array of any number of dimensions.

Microprogramming. Control technique used to implement the stored program control function. Typically, the technique is to use a preprogrammed read-only memory chip to contain several control sequences which normally occur together.

Mnemonic Symbol. A symbol chosen to assist the human memory (e.g., an abbreviation such as "mpy" for "multiply").

Modem (*Modulator-dem*odulator). A device that modulates and demodulates signals transmitted over communication facilities.

Multiplex. To interleave or simultaneously transmit two or more messages on a signal channel.

NAK. Message sent over data communications links to indicate that received data have been checked, are incorrect, and should be retransmitted.

Negative Logic. Logic in which the more negative voltage represents the "1" state; the less negative voltage represents the "0" state.

Nondestructive Readout. A memory designed so that readout does not affect the content stored. It is not necessary to perform a write after every read operation.

Numerical Control. Automatic control of a process performed by a device that makes use of all or part of numerical data generally introduced as the operation is in process.

Object Code. The language to which a statement is translated.

Operand. That which is operated upon. An operand is usually identified by an address part of an instruction.

Operating System. Software that controls the execution of computer programs and which may provide scheduling, debugging, I/O control, accounting, compilation, storage assignment, data management, and related services.

Operation.

1. A defined action—the act of obtaining a result from one or more operands in accordance with a rule that completely specifies the result for any permissible combination of operands.

2. The act specified by a single computer instruction.

3. A program step undertaken or executed by a computer (e.g., addition, multiplication, extraction, comparison, shift, transfer). The operation is usually specified by the operator of an instruction.

4. The event or specific action performed by a logic element.

Operation Code. A code that represents specific operations. Synonymous with instruction code.

Optical Character Recognition (OCR). The machine identification of printed characters through use of light-sensitive devices.

Pack. To compress data in a storage medium by taking advantage of known characteristics of the data in such a way that the original data can be recovered (e.g., to compress data in a storage medium by making use of bit or byte locations that would otherwise go unused).

Parallel Operation. The organization of data manipulating within circuitry wherein all the digits of a word are transmitted simultaneously on separate lines in order to speed up operation.

Parameter. A variable that is given a constant value for a specific purpose or process.

Parity Bit. A check bit appended to an array of binary digits to make the sum of all the binary digits, including the check bit, always odd or always even.

Parity Check. The technique of adding 1 bit to a digital word to make the total number of binary ones or zeros either always even or always odd. This type of checking will indicate an error in data but will not indicate the location of the error.

Peripheral Equipment. Units that work in conjunction with a computer but are no part of it.

Positive Logic. Logic in which the more positive voltage represents the "1" state; the less positive voltage represents the "0" state.

Priority Interrupt. Designation given to method of providing some commands to have precedence over others, thus giving one condition of operation priority over another.

Problem-Oriented Language. A programming language designed for the convenient expression of a given class of problems.

Processor.

1. In hardware, a data processor.

2. In software, a computer program that includes the compiling, assembling, translating, and related functions for a specific programming language, COBOL processor, or FORTRAN processor.

Programmable Logic Array (PLA). An integrated circuit that employs ROM matrices to combine sum and product terms of logic networks.

Programmable Read-Only Memory (PROM). A fixed program, read-only, semiconductor memory storage element that can be programmed after packaging.

Propagation Delay. The time required for a change in logic level to be transmitted through an element or a chain of elements.

Pushdown List. A list that is constructed and maintained so that the item to be retrieved is the most recently stored item in the list (i.e., last in, first out).

Pushdown Stack. A register that implements a pushdown list.

Pushup List. A list that is constructed and maintained so that the next item to be retrieved and removed is the oldest item still in the list (i.e., first in, first out).

Random-Access Memory (RAM). A memory from which all information can be obtained at the output with approximately the same time delay by choosing an address randomly and without first searching through a vast amount of irrelevant data.

Read-Only Memory (ROM). A fixed program semiconductor storage element that has been programmed at the factory with a permanent program.

Real Time. Pertaining to the performance of a computation during the actual time that the related physical process transpires, in order that results of the computation can be used in guiding the physical process.

Redundancy. The technique of using more than one circuit of the same type to implement a given function.

Refresh. Method that restores charge on capacitance which deteriorates because of leakage.

Register. Temporary storage for digital data.

Relative Address. The number that specifies the difference between the absolute address and the base address.

Sample-and-Hold Circuit. A circuit that performs the operation of looking at a voltage level during a short time period and accurately storing the voltage level for a much longer time period.

Scratch-Pad Memory. A small local memory utilized to facilitate local data handling on a temporary basis.

Sequencing. Control method used to cause a set of steps to occur in a particular order.

Sequential Logic Systems. Digital system utilizing memory elements.

Serial Accumulator. A register that receives data bits in serial or sequence and temporarily holds the data for future use.

Serial Operation. The organization of data manipulation within circuitry wherein the digits of a word are transmitted one at a time along a single line. The serial mode of operation is slower than parallel operation but utilizes less complex circuitry.

Setup Time. The minimum amount of time that data must be present at an input to ensure data acceptance when the device is clocked.

Shift. A movement of data to the right or left.

Shift Register. A register in which the stored data can be moved to the right or left.

Sign and Magnitude Notation. A system of notation where binary numbers are represented by a sign bit and one or more number bits.

Silo Memory. Reads out stored data in a first in, first out mode. Also known as FIFO.

Simulate. To represent the functioning of a device, system, or computer program by another (e.g., to represent the functioning of one computer by another, to represent the behavior of a physical system by the execution of a computer program, to represent a biological system by a mathematical model).

Simulator. A device, system, or computer program that represents certain features of the behavior of a physical or abstract system.

Skip. To ignore one or more instructions in a sequence of instructions.

Software. A set of computer programs, procedures, and possibly associated documentation concerned with the operation of a data-processing system (e.g., compilers, library routines, manuals, circuit diagrams).

Source Language. The language from which a statement is translated.

Source Program. A computer program written in a source language.

State. The condition of an input or output of a circuit as to whether it is a logic "1" or a logic "0." The state of a circuit (gate or flip-flop) refers to its output. A flip-flop is said to be in the "1" state when its output is "1". A gate is the "1" state when its output is "1."

Static Storage Elements. Storage elements which contain storage cells that retain their information as long as power is supplied unless the information is altered by external excitation.

Stored Program. A set of instructions in memory specifying the operation to be performed.

Subroutine. A routine that can be part of another routine.

Synchronous Circuit. A circuit in which all ordinary operations are controlled by equally spaced signals from a master clock.

System.

1. An organized collection of men, machines, and methods required to accomplish a set of specific functions.

2. An assembly of methods, procedures, or techniques united by regulated interaction to form an organized whole.

Table Look-up. A procedure for obtaining the function value corresponding to an argument from a table of function values.

Temporary Storage. In programming, storage locations reserved for intermediate results. Synonymous with working storage.

Terminal. A point in a system or communication network at which data can either enter or leave.

Transfer. Same as jump.

Translate. To transform statements from one language to another without significantly changing the meaning.

Truth Table. A chart that tabulates and summarizes all the combinations of possible states of the inputs and outputs of a circuit. It tabulates what will happen at the output for a given input combination.

Two's (2's)-Complement Notation. A system of notation where positive binary numbers are identical to positive numbers in sign and magnitude notation, but where 1 must be added to 1's-complement notation to obtain negative numbers.

USASCII. United States of America Standard Code for Information Interchange. The standard code used in the United States for transmission of data. Sometimes simply referred to as the "as' ki" code.

Variable. A quantity that can assume any of a given set of values.

Volatile Storage. A storage device in which stored data are lost when the applied power is removed.

Word. A character string or a bit string considered as an entity.

Write Enable. Also called read/write or R/W. The control signal to a storage element or a memory that activates the write-mode operation. Conversely, when not in the write mode, the read mode is active.

Write Time. The time that the appropriate level must be maintained on the write-enable line and that data must be present to guarantee successful writing of data in the memory.

You will find that all the terms above have been pretty well standardized throughout the industry and computer world, and although it would be a time-consuming process to memorize all of them, you should try to remember the most significant ones.

4

Memories

4.1 INTRODUCTION

The memory devices added to a microprocessor system greatly improve its capabilities. The reader must become familiar with such devices as random-access memories (RAMs), read-only-memories (ROMs), and so on. The purpose of this chapter is to discuss these devices as well as other types of memory.

4.2 RANDOM-ACCESS MEMORY (RAM)

There are a number of techniques used to store the information used by a computer. Among the more familiar storage media are magnetic tape, paper tape, punched cards, magnetic disks, and drums; all of these are basically mass sequential storage forms. The information they store is organized into fairly large blocks, with the information within a block stored sequentially—the computer uses storage location 1 first, location 2 second, and so on through the block.

However, in the course of all those computations and manipulations that a computer does so quickly, the most efficient organization for data is not necessarily in sequential blocks. A more practical approach with a block of data is to allow the computer to write-into or read-out-of any storage location. Not so surprisingly this brings back the topic at hand—random-access memories.

Basically, a random-access memory requires that any location within it can be reached or accessed without regard to any other location. At the selected location, data may be written (stored) in the memory or read (retrieved) from it. Between the time data are written and read, they must be reliably stored.

Owing to its basic capacity to store data and retrieve them at will, the RAM is a popular system design tool. Categories such as scratch pads, buffers, main memories, and mass storage are all applications for RAMs.

A scratch-pad memory is a small, fast memory normally associated with the CPU of the computer. The scratch pad, which is used for temporary storage of interim calculation results, must operate at speeds comparable to those of the CPU. This speed requirement means that, with the exception of all MOS computers, scratch-pad operation is not a MOS storage point.

Buffer memories may be employed between sections of a computer, between a computer mainframe and peripheral equipment, or in any digital system where temporary storage is required between operating units. The speed of the buffer must be at least equal to that of the input/output rate of the faster of the operating units, and its information storage capability is related to the data rates of the units. MOS random-access memories are a logical choice for many buffer memory applications, particularly in computer peripherals.

The main memory, or mainframe memory, is the primary operational storage block of a general-purpose computer. In present computers, this role is rapidly filled by semiconductor mainframe memories, operating at speeds in the 100- and 500-μs region.

The features that render MOS circuitry so attractive for memory use are very high circuit density, low cost, and low power dissipation.

The typical MOS storage cell is a remarkably simple, effective, and low-cost design. A basic MOS storage cell is illustrated in Figure 4-1. The cell consists of only six P-channel enhancement-mode devices. Two of these, R_1 and R_2, act as resistors and are biased on by the V_{GG} supply. The two cross-coupled transistors, Q_1 and Q_2, act as a storage element, while Q_3 and Q_4 are switches that selectively connect or isolate the individual storage cell from the sense-digit lines. Two sense-digit lines are used, providing dual rail—signal and complement—drive to the cell. The word-select line drives the gates of Q_3 and Q_4 and operates as a single rail—signal only—input.

With the P-channel devices used, the V_{SS} power supply is the most positive voltage and V_{DD} is negative by 10 V or more. Depending on the particular processing technology used in the construction of the cell and the cell operating constraints, V_{GG} is better equal to, or more negative than, V_{DD}. Since P-channel enhancement-mode devices are turned on when the gate is sufficiently negative (relative to the substrate), the substrate is connected to the most positive system voltage (i.e., V_{SS}).

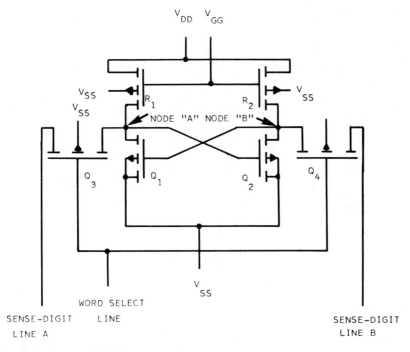

Fig. 4-1. The basic MOS storage cell

In the storage mode, the cell maintains one of its two stable states. The word-select line is in the high logic state (approaching V_{SS}), so transistors Q_3 and Q_4 are off. As a result, the storage cell is isolated from the sense-digit line. One of the possible stable states exists when the gate of Q_2 is low. This means that Q_2 is conducting so that its drain (node B) is at a high potential (approaching V_{SS}). The difference in potential between V_{DD} and the drain of Q_2 is dissipated across resistor R_2. The high potential on node B is coupled to the gate of Q_1. With this high potential on the gate, Q_1 is turned off. As a result, node A is at approximately V_{DD} since there is essentially no current flow through R_1. The drain of Q_1 (node A), which is connected to the gate of Q_2, provides the low or V_{DD} potential, which we define as being stable state 1.

In order to change the information stored in the basic cell, the sense-digit lines are appropriately biased and the word-selection line placed in the active or low state. Let us assume the sense-digit line condition shown in Figure 4-2. Sense-digit line A is at a high potential. The complementary signal is present on sense-digit line B, which is connected to a low potential. When the word-select line changes to a low potential, transistors Q_3 and Q_4 turn on, connecting the sense-digit lines to the cross-coupled transistors Q_1 and Q_2. In the example shown in Figure 4-2, Q_3 connects node A to the high level on sense-digit line A. This high potential is coupled to the

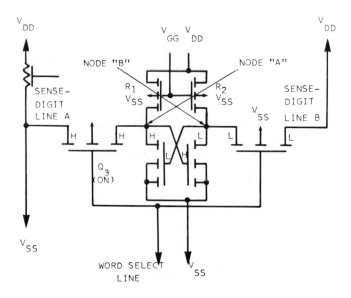

Fig. 4-2. Writing into the basic storage cell

gate of Q_2, and tends to turn Q_2 off. At the same time, because Q_4 is conducting, node B is coupled to the low supply. This low voltage is applied to the gate of Q_1 and tends to turn Q_1 on. This provides an additional path from V_{SS} to node A, further increasing the potential on the gate Q_2. Therefore, the indicated sense-digit line potentials in Figure 4-2 turn Q_1 on and Q_2 off. This is the alternate stable state of the storage element. Completing the write operation and raising the word-select line potential, turns off Q_3 and Q_4 and isolates the storage cell from the sense-digit lines.

Connecting sense-digit line B to V_{SS}, sense-digit line A to V_{DD}, and activating the word-select line will reverse the state of the flip-flop, turning Q_2 on and Q_1 off.

If complementary V_{SS} and V_{DD} signals are applied to the sense-digit lines while the word-select line is activated, the storage cell is placed into a writing mode. For reading, the word-select line is again activated, but this time both sense-digit lines are terminated with MOS resistors, as illustrated in Figure 4-3 (the portion of the circuit to the right of the dashed line is the simple MOS inverter used as the sense circuit).

The resistive terminations on the sense-digit lines do not change the state of the storage cell when Q_3 and Q_4 conduct the sense-digit lines to the storage cell. For the node that is in the high state, the sense-digit line resistor appears in parallel with the internal resistance (R_1 or R_2). For the drain node of the off-storage transistor, the sense-digit line terminating resistance appears as an additional source of V_{DD} potential, and, through the cross-coupling of Q_1 and Q_2, tends to keep the conducting transistor turned on.

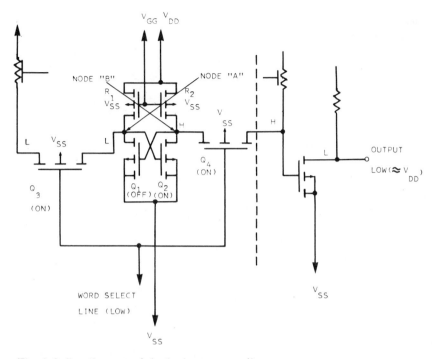

Fig. 4-3. Reading out of the basic storage cell

In addition to terminating resistors, at least one of the sense-digit lines must contain sensing circuitry to determine the state of the storage cell. At its simplest, this sense circuitry can be an MOS inverter, as illustrated in Figure 4-3.

The cell-sensing function is shown as a single-rail, or signal-only, operation. In an actual memory, sensing may be either single or dual rail. The decision is largely determined by the operating voltages and the processing of the MOS structures. As a generalization, low-voltage applications require double-rail operation for reliability, while single-rail operation is satisfactory at the higher voltages.

4.3 STATIC RAM

RAMs produced with MOS technology employ two different techniques to store information. Depending on the type of basic memory cell, MOS RAMs can be categorized as being either static or dynamic. Static MOS memories, which usually show poorer performance and higher costs, are easier to drive than the dynamic memories, which generally require clock signals in addition to power supplies.

Dynamic MOS circuits employ the very low leakage associated with the gate circuits and junctions of well-made MOS devices. These leakage currents are small enough to permit the parasitic capacitances of the circuit to exhibit time constants between milliseconds and seconds. These long time constants may be used to provide temporary storage, which may be made permanent by appropriate cycling or "refreshing" operations.

In the static RAM stage of Figure 4-4, two static inverters are wired together to make a flip-flop. Devices Q_5 and Q_6 are used as (two-way) transmission gates. In the reading mode, the conducting side of the flip-flop pulls the data line toward ground via these gates. Writing is accomplished by forcing the data lines to the value desired in the cell, thereby overriding the contents of the cell. Owing to the small current capability of devices Q_3 and Q_4, it is important that neither of the data lines be near ground when the transmission gates are turned on. With grounded data lines, the change associated with the capacitance of the data lines may flip the cell.

As a vehicle for comparison, let us consider a 256-bit static RAM constructed with P-channel, silicon-gate MOS technology, as illustrated in Figure 4-5. The memory is organized as one 256-bit plane, with full address decoding, and, with the exception of additional power supplies, is fully compatible with TTL logic levels. Typical access time is approximately 1 μs.

The memory chip is easily connected in an array to provide greater memory capacity. The illustration shows how the individual packages are connected to realize a 1024-byte memory. Address inputs, write gates (read/ write controls), and power leads are common to all packages in the array. Each row in the array corresponds to one plane of a ferrite-core memory (i.e., one row provides storage for 1 bit of each data word). All data inputs in a given row are connected together. All the data outputs in a given row are similarly connected. Each memory package realizes 1 bit from each of 256 bytes. Each column of packages in Figure 4-5 corresponds to 256 bytes of memory.

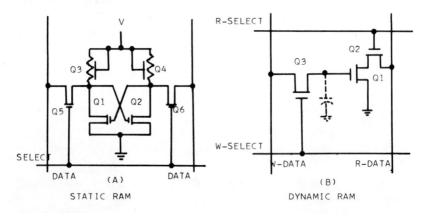

Fig. 4-4. Storage cells used in MOS RAMs

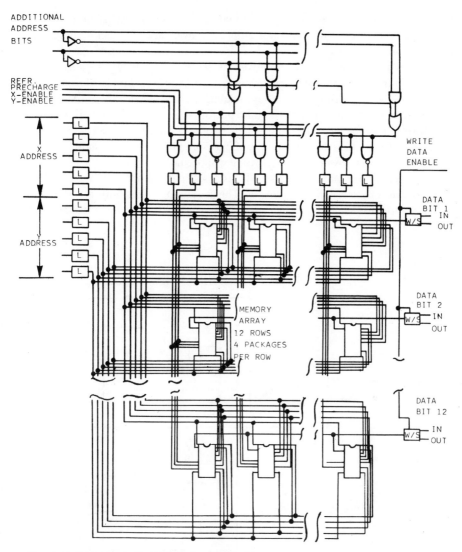

Fig. 4-5. 256-bit static RAM using MOS chips

Since it is produced with silicon-gate technology, this static memory provides easy interface to TTL logic levels. The section on interfacing below describes how RAMs are interfaced with TTL devices.

4.4 DYNAMIC RAM

The dynamic memory cell of Figure 4-4 may also be used as the basis of a MOS RAM. Unlike the memories constructed with the static cell, the data of these dynamic memories must be periodically refreshed to maintain their validity. Because of the small size of the cell, many more bits of memory may be produced on a chip of a given size than can be produced with static cells.

The dynamic cell is employed as the basis for RAM chips of up to 1024 bits. One possible organization of a 1024-bit chip is illustrated in Figure 4-6. With this organization, reading and writing occur simultaneously for all cells of one row. Because only one bit at a time is available for writing, an (internal) read operation must be performed prior to writing. This operation ensures that the refresh amplifiers contain data corresponding to the contents of the row into which writing will occur.

There are three clocklike signals associated with the dynamic RAM: *X-enable, Y-enable,* and *precharge.* The X- and Y-enable both act as a chip select for reading and writing. Several chips may have the input/output lead ORed to realize planes larger than 1024 bits.

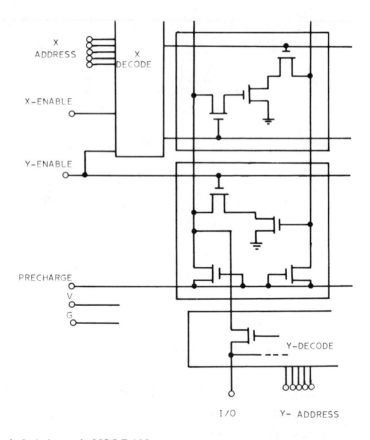

Fig. 4–6. A dynamic MOS RAM

Employing silicon-gate MOS technology, the clock signals and addresses are nominally 20 V peak to peak. These high voltages are necessary to obtain high-speed performance. The use of TTL-compatible levels would add significantly to the memory cycle and access times. Memory cycle times with the high levels are from 300 to 600 μs, depending upon chip organization, and drive signal rise and fall times.

To illustrate the use of the dynamic RAM of Figure 4-6 in a memory, consider the design of the 4096-word, 12-bit/word memory as illustrated in Figure 4-7. The devices are connected in an array. Each block labeled L is a level shifter to convert from logic levels to approximately 20-V levels. The blocks, labeled W/S, are word driver/sense amplifiers which sense the memory output currents when reading and perform level shifting when writing.

In the memory of Figure 4-7, the inputs to the X-enable, Y-enable, and precharge leads of the devices are individually decoded to provide chip selection. Decoding X-enable is sufficient for this function; however, the use of the extra decoders reduces the power dissipation of the memory. A major portion of the memory power dissipation is derived from energy associated with changing the device capacitances. The additional decoding reduces the amount of capacitance charged and discharged in each memory cycle.

The memory shown in Figure 4-7 realizes a 4096-word-by-12-bit memory with 22 level shifters. However, given a particular clock driver (level shifter), some other configuration may require additional peripheral components. Typical input capacitances of a single device are listed here:

1024-Bit Dynamic MOS RAM Capacitances	
Address (X or Y)	5 pF
X-enable	10 pF
Y-enable	30 pF
Precharge	30 pF

4.5 BUFFER CIRCUITS FOR RAMS

TTL to P-Channel MOS

As an example of interfacing TTL to *P*-channel static MOS circuitry let us consider the input requirements of a memory which is realized with *P*-channel silicon-gate MOS technology. In this case, it is assumed that the inputs of the memory are purely capacitive, so that, when driving the memory arrays, the primary considerations involve: (1) the effects of significant capacitive loads on address and data line buffers, and (2) guaranteeing proper voltage levels on these lines.

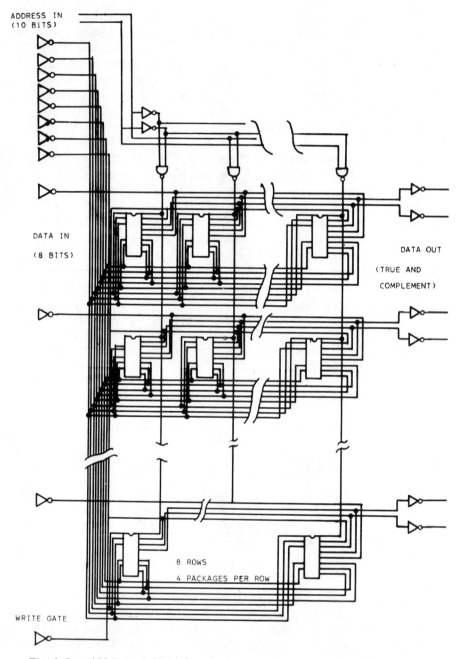

Fig. 4–7. A 4096 word, 12 bit/word memory

Figure 4-8 illustrates the nature of the TTL/static MOS interface. In Figure 4-8, Q conducts when the TTL gate output is sufficiently negative with respect to V_{CC} (at least 4.5 V below V_{CC}). The ratio of geometrics between Q_1 and Q_2 is chosen so that when Q_1 conducts, the internal MOS signal line is brought within 1-2 V of V_{CC}. When the TTL gate output is high, Q_1 does not conduct, and the internal MOS line is drawn toward the voltage supply by Q_2. The high level must be no lower than V_{CC} (-2 V). The purpose of resistor R is to guarantee proper operating levels, as TTL outputs without the resistor are only guaranteed to reach V_{CC} (-2.35 V) (7400 series). Note that the input signal voltage is referenced to V_{CC}. It is, therefore, important that V_{CC} is adequately bypassed to the TTL ground line. V_{CC} is normally the same supply as used for the TTL logic. When driving P-channel MOS, it is undesirable to allow this voltage to fall too low, for noise immunity may suffer. Owing to the fact that the MOS input draws no dc current for normal bias, a very large number of devices may be driven by a single TTL gate, although the capacitive loading in large arrays may cause some speed degradation.

The output of the P-channel MOS circuit can be designed to drive a TTL or low-power TTL gate.

Figure 4-9 illustrates the nature of the P-channel MOS/TTL interface. Parts that are not enabled by chip select have neither Q_1 nor Q_2 conducting. For a logic "1," Q_1 conducts, providing a one level approaching V_{CC}. However, for a logic "0," Q_2 conducts. In the particular device under discussion, Q_2 sinks at least 2.0 milliamperes (mA) when the output is at 0.45 V above ground, thus exceeding the minimum TTL sinking requirement of 1.6 mA.

TTL to N-Channel MOS

Figure 4-10 illustrates the nature of the input and output interfaces. Within the N-channel circuit, the signal voltage levels are very similar to

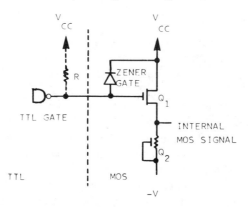

Fig. 4–8. TTL to p-channel MOS interface

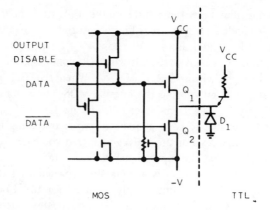

Fig. 4–9. P-channel MOS to TTL interface

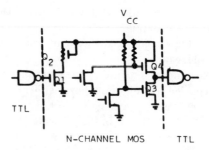

Fig. 4–10. N-channel TTL interface

TTL levels. When the TTL output is high, Q_1 conducts, producing a low internal level. When the TTL output is low, Q_1 is off, and Q_2 produces a high internal level. Input requirements are for high input levels of 2.2 V or greater and input levels of 0.65 V or less. As a result, noise margins are somewhat less than those of TTL circuitry. However, the slower N-channel circuits do not respond as rapidly to noise as bipolar TTL circuits. This slower response somewhat compensates for the reduced noise margins.

The output circuit is capable of driving one 1.6-mA TTL load with 0.3 mA in reserve. However, when OR-tying several devices in an array, this 0.3 mA is needed to compensate for output leakage currents. These output leakages (100 mA maximum) are equivalent to conduction currents in output transistor Q_4 of disabled devices. As a result, no more than four devices should be OR-tied when driving a standard TTL load. For larger arrays, OR-tie capability can be increased by a low-power TTL buffer stage, or by organizing the memory in 4K word modules, each with its own output buffer. These output buffers could be open-collector TTL gates, enabling data onto a bus, or could be designed by the use of multiplexers.

4.6   READ-ONLY MEMORIES (ROMS)

A read-only memory is an array of selectively open and closed uni-directional contacts, as illustrated in Figure 4–11. In the 16-bit array example, half of the address lines are decoded and used to energize one of the four row lines. This, in turn, activates those column lines which have a close contact to the one selected row line. The remaining address lines are decoded and enable one of the column sense amplifiers. If chip select is true, the data are gated to the output pin by the output driver.

The primary differences in ROMs is in the forming of the open or closed contact, that is, in the design of the cell. In mask-programmable ROMs, the contact is made by selectively including or excluding a small conducting jumper during the final phase of semiconductor manufacture. In bipolar-programmable ROMs, the contact is made with a fusible material such that the contact can later be opened, allowing the data pattern to be configured by the user after the device has been manufactured.

Once programmed, erasable programmable read-only memories (EP-ROMs) allow the programmed contacts to be restored to their initial state such that they can be reprogrammed as often as desired.

Types of ROMs

There are two basic PROM/ROM technologies (i.e., bipolar and MOS). The primary difference between the two types lies in the access time, that is, 50-90 ns for bipolar and about an order of magnitude higher for MOS. Bipolar ROMs are available in 1K, 2K, and 4K bit sizes, while MOS ROMs

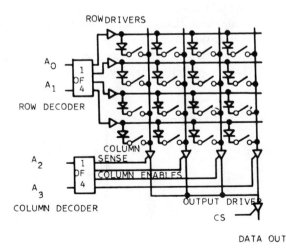

Fig. 4–11. 16-bit array

are available in 2K through 16K bit sizes. Although PROMs and ROMs are available from both technologies, EPROMs are available only with MOS technology.

Mask-Programmable ROMs. Integrated circuits are fabricated from a wafer of silicon through a number of processing steps, including photo-masking, etching, and diffusing, in order to create a pattern of junctions and interconnections across the surface of the wafer. One of the final steps in the manufacturing process is to coat the entire surface of the silicon wafer with a layer of aluminum, and then to selectively etch away portions of the aluminum, leaving the desired interconnecting pattern.

In the manufacture of mask-programmed read-only memories or commonly called ROMs, the row-to-column contacts are selectively made by the inclusion or exclusion of aluminum connections in the final aluminum etch process.

Electrically Programmable ROMs (EPROMs). Electrically program-mable ROMs allow the data pattern to be defined after final packaging rather than when the device is manufactured. Three types of electrically programmable PROMs are discussed below.

Nichrome Fuse. The first PROMs were made with a nichrome-fuse technology. Nichrome, an alloy of nickel and chrome, is deposited as a very thin film link to the column lines of the PROM. Heavy currents cause this film to "blow," opening the connections between the row and column lines. The cell is actually constructed of a transistor switch and the nichrome fuse, as shown in Figure 4-12. When the row is selected, the transistor Q_{xy}, is turned on, and, if the fuse is intact, the column bus is pulled toward V_{CC} (+5 V). If the fuse is "blown" or open, the column bus is left open.

Problems with nichrome fuses are all related to the technology. The selection of aluminum as the conductive material in integrated circuits and transistors did involve some serious metallurgical considerations. Of major importance is the fact that aluminum readily adheres to silicon dioxide but

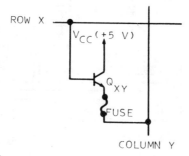

Fig. 4-12. Fuse cell

does not rapidly diffuse through it. In addition, aluminum forms ohmic contacts with silicon. Still, the formation of good silicon-to-aluminum contacts has always been a problem; the formation of good, reliable nichrome contact is a greater problem.

In addition, nichrome is not the easiest material to work with, especially considering the extremely thin layer (about 200 angstroms) that must be deposited to achieve the desired resistance in the fuse. This deposition is very hard to control and the nichrome is additionally subject to corrosion.

The most serious problem associated with nichrome-fuse technology is probably the phenomenon commonly referred to as "growback," the reversal of the programming process such that a single bit, after some time, will go from the programmed state back to the unprogrammed state. Considerable analysis has been carried out to investigate this growback phenomenon in nichrome-fuse PROMs to understand how the nichrome fuse blows to determine the location and movement of the metals before and after fusion, and to determine the reason for which a small number of these fuses (once blown) appear to reconnect.

Fusion occurs under a layer of glass which has been added to the entire wafer to provide scratch protection and to minimize electron migration in the metal. Since fusion takes place without oxygen or any other atmosphere, oxidation cannot play an important part in the fusing. It appears, rather, that the nichrome heats up under heavy current and becomes molten, forming a very narrow gap. The additional property of nichrome is that it forms fingerlike, or dendrite, structures. Studies indicate that it is dendritic relinking that causes the fuse to begin reconduction after some period of time.

Silicon Fuse. Bipolar PROMs operate in the same manner as do the nichrome fuses, with the exception that the fuse material is polycrystalline silicon, which is deposited in a thick layer at the appropriate stage in the manufacturing process.

During manufacturing of some PROMs, a test row and column are included on the die and are blown at wafer sort. The extra row and column are incorporated primarily to improve the programming yield of the final end product. By addressing this test row, the functionality of the decoders and the programmability of the fuses can be verified. The test-fuse circuitry is designed such that arrays with unusual fuses that could cause programming yield problems can be screened at electrical test.

Shorted Junction. A third type of bipolar PROM implementation is the shorted junction. The shorted junction cell is shown in Figure 4–13. In this cell, diode Q_1 is reverse-biased and the heavy flow of electrons in the reverse direction causes aluminum atoms from the emitter contact to migrate

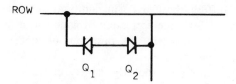

Fig. 4–13. Shorted junction cells

through the emitter to the base, causing an emitter-to-base short. Although the shorted junction PROM does not have the reliability problems associated with the nichrome fuse, programming is greatly complicated by the fact that underprogramming results in insufficient or intermittent contact with the base, and overprogramming results in possible internal shorts.

The problem of distributing heavy currents around the chip requires the use of multiple-layer metalization, and, as a result, no major semiconductor company has committed to the shorted-junction technology.

MOS Technology

As mentioned earlier, it is possible to produce PROMs and ROMs using MOS technology. Figure 4-14 shows a MOS storage element. The operation of the cell depends on charge transport to the floating gate by avalanche injection of electrons. The device is essentially a silicon-gate MOS-FET in which no connection is made to the silicon gate. Operation of the memory structure depends on charge transport to the floating gate by avalanche injection of electrons from either the source or drain.

A junction voltage in excess of -30 V applied to a P-channel device will result in the injection of high-energy electrons from the P–N junction surface avalanche region to the floating silicon gate. The amount of charge transferred to the floating gate is a function of amplitude and duration of the applied junction voltage, as shown in Figure 4-15. The presence or absence of charge can be sensed by measuring the conductance between the source and drain.

Once the applied junction voltage is removed, no discharge path is available for the accumulated electrons since the gate is surrounded by thermal oxide, which is a very low conductivity dielectric. The electric field in the structure after the removal of junction voltage is due only to the accumulated electron charge and is not sufficient to cause charge transport across the polysilicon/thermal oxide energy barrier.

Since the gate electrode is not electrically accessible, the charge cannot be removed by an electrical pulse. However, the initial condition of no electronic charge on the gate can be restored by illuminating the device with ultraviolet light, which results in the flow of a photo current from the floating gate back to the silicon substrate, thereby discharging the gate to its

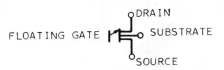

Fig. 4–14. MOS storage cell

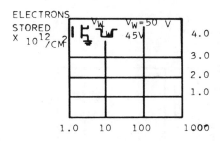

Fig. 4–15. Charge transfer vs. Programming pulse width

initial condition. This erase method allows complete testing of a complex programmable ROM array.

4.7 OPERATION AND PROGRAMMING OF A ROM

The logic symbol of a typical 1K PROM/ROM is illustrated in Figure 4-16. The device is organized as 256 4-bit words. A more functional diagram of the device is shown in Figure 4-17. The top six buffers (A_3-A_7) activate 1 of 32 decoders, which, in turn, select 1 of 32 rows in the 32 × 32 array. Buffers A_0-A_2 enable the 1 of 8 decoders, multiplexing 1 of 8 bits to the appropriate sense amplifier. The logical AND of $\overline{CS}_2 \circ \overline{CS}_1$ energizes all the columns in the array and provides a programming path. $\overline{CS}_1$, which is also active low, enables each of the four output buffers.

The outputs (Q_1-Q_4) are open-collector and thus may be OR-connected for memory expansion. The capacitance of the data-out pins is typically 7 pF.

One method of programming the device above is illustrated in Figure 4-18. Address inputs are at standard TTL levels. Only one output may be programmed at a time. The output to be programmed must be connected to V_{CC} through a 300-ohm resistor. This will force the proper programming current (3-6 mA) into the output when the V_{CC} supply is later raised to 10 V. All other outputs must be held at a TTL low level (0.4 V maximum).

The programming pulse generator produces a series of pulses to the

Fig. 4-16. Logic symbol of AK ROM

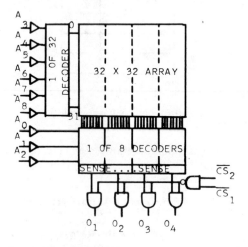

Fig. 4-17. Functional diagram of ROM

V_{CC} and $\overline{CS}_2$ leads. V_{CC} is pulsed from a low of 4.5 V (±0.25 V) to a high of 10 V (±0.25 V), while $\overline{CS}_2$ is pulsed from a low of ground (TTL logic O) to a high of 15 V ± 0.25 V. It is important to accurately maintain these voltage levels; otherwise, improper programming may result.

The pulses applied must maintain a duty cycle of 50 percent (±10 percent) and increase linearly over a period of approximately 100 ms to a maximum width of 8 μs (±10 percent). Typical devices have their fuse blown within 1 ms, but occasionally a fuse may take up to 400 ms to blow.

4.8 SHIFT REGISTERS

The MOS shift register has been one of the first semiconductor memory devices to find wide application. Two properties of MOS IC technology are uniquely compatible with the design of shift registers: the high impedance associated with the gate circuit permits temporary storage of charge on the

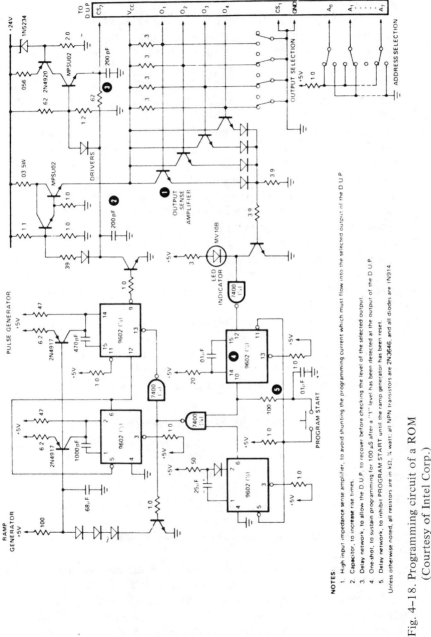

Fig. 4-18. Programming circuit of a ROM
(Courtesy of Intel Corp.)

95

parasitic capacitances, and MOS technology permits realization of bidirectional transmission gates that have zero dc offset. With the transmission gate, a gate node may easily be connected to, or disconnected from, other points in the circuit.

The shift register structure offers layout economies as well. Few interconnections are required, basic shift register stages may be made using little silicon area, and no decoding or other "overhead" circuits may be placed on the chip.

A dynamic shift register which employs only capacitive storage is illustrated in Figure 4-19. Each bit of the register requires six MOS devices, such as bit 1, which consists of MOS devices Q_{1A} through Q_{1F}. The input to this bit is the charge on the gate of Q_{1A} (IN1). When clock $\emptyset2$ goes negative (for P-channel devices), devices Q_{1A} and Q_{1B} form an inverter stage. If the charge on the gate of Q_{1A} is adequately negative to cause this device to conduct strongly, the node common to Q_{1A}, Q_{1B}, and Q_{1C} will approach V_{CC} (a positive level). On the other hand, if the charge is positive enough to leave Q_{1A} at cut off, when $\emptyset2$ becomes negative, the common node will approach V_{DD}, the negative supply.

At the same time, when $\emptyset2$ goes negative, Q_{1C} conducts, charging the parasitic gate capacitance of Q_{1D} (shown as capacitor in the illustration) to the same potential as the node common to Q_{1A}, Q_{1B}, and Q_{1C}. When $\emptyset2$ is removed, the gate of Q_{1D} retains its potential. Pulsing $\emptyset1$ negative then transfers and inverts the datum, depositing it at the input to the next stage.

In the circuit shown, an output device is provided so that charge need not be retained on external leads. This output buffer also acts as an inverter. To make input and output levels compatible, an input inverter is provided. In Figure 4-19, the data are available during clock phase 2. Data at the input must be available prior to and during phase 2.

4.9 CONTENT ADDRESSABLE MEMORY (CAM)

The RAMs previously discussed employ a fixed address structure. At the time of storage, data are assigned an address in memory. To retrieve the data, that address must be supplied. Content addressable memories, or CAMs, retrieve data based on content rather than address. When data are entered, they may be assigned to the first available locations. For such data to be retrievable, they must contain "keys", or identifiers, to aid in their location.

One realization of content addressable memory utilizes a memory cell which combines a basic random-access memory cell and a comparator. A Schottky technology bipolar realization of such a cell is shown in Figure 4-20. In Figure 4-20, transistors Q_1 and Q_2 form a memory flip-flop while transistors Q_3 and Q_4 and the four Schottky diodes form a comparator.

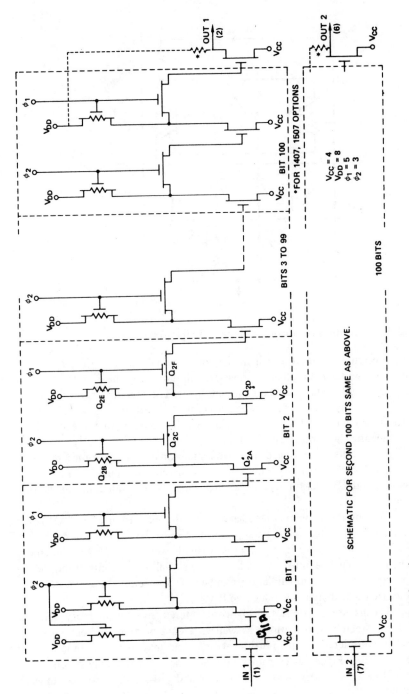

Fig. 4-19. MOS shift register

97

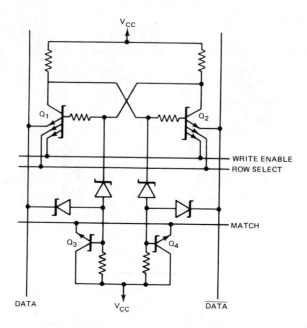

Fig. 4–20. Content Addressable Memory Cell (CAM)

Data are entered into the cell in the conventional way using the row-select data and write-enable lines. However, all data may be nondestructively compared with data placed on the data lines. The match line will be drawn positive by any mismatch between a connected cell and data line data. If both DATA and DATA lines are held low, the contents of the cell will not influence the signal on the match line.

CAM cells are arranged in a two-dimensional array to form a memory. To expand such a memory, row select and match lines must be extended in the horizontal direction and data lines must be extended in the vertical direction.

One of the problems associated with the expansion of a CAM is the connection of match lines. Each match line must be individually connected to all cells in its row. If a row must extend over more than one memory chip, its match line must be made common to all chips contributing to the row. As a result, a much larger number of connections are required in a given size CAM than in the same size RAM.

During use of a CAM, each word entered into the memory contains a "key" (search information) as well as a data portion. In some systems, what is considered a data portion at one time may at a later time be used for searching. Figure 4–21 shows how an array of CAMs may be organized in an 8-word memory with a 4-bit key and a 4-bit data portion to each word.

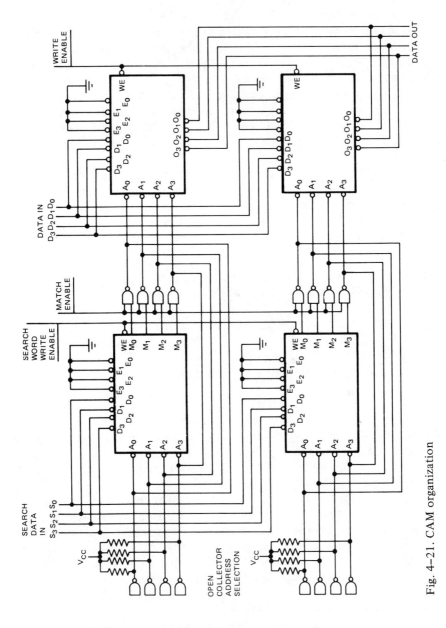

Fig. 4-21. CAM organization

Some organizations may permit multiple matches when searching a CAM. For example, the search may be equivalent to the question, "How many entries do I have which used X as the key?" The organization of Figure 4-21 would result in simultaneous selection of several data words if several such entries were found. To resolve multiple finds, a priority encoder may be used. The encoder selects only one of the several addresses. The addresses selected by the search may be polled in sequence to determine the various data items. Some IC priority encoders give binary addresses as output. In order to use these with the CAM of Figure 4-21, use of a decoder that would generate the linear select addresses for the CAM is required.

Small, fast CAMs find application in buffer memory control and certain types of parallel processors. Possible applications are found in pipeline processors and the implementation of some functions, such as sorts and searches.

CAM function may also be realized, with much longer effective access times, by actually searching the memory. For example, a shift register memory may be designed to include the comparison function as part of the recirculation logic. The data are completely searched in one circulation of the memory.

4.10 PROGRAMMABLE AND FIELD-PROGRAMMABLE LOGIC ARRAYS

A programmable logic array, or PLA, has definite advantages over a ROM. A PLA requires fewer logic levels than a ROM to produce the same control function, thus improving the dynamic performance of a system. The more efficient memory use of a PLA, as compared to rectangular ROM, could reduce the overall parts cost of a system. Finally, the use of PLAs offers lower systems manufacturing costs.

From a logical standpoint, a PLA is an assembly of AND gates that may be ORed at any of its outputs. With a greater number of possible inputs than a ROM, the former offers greater flexibility than the latter. As an example, a commercially available PLA has 14 inputs and 8 outputs, equivalent to a ROM with 2^{14}, or 16,384 words.

Even though a PLA can decode any input code to any output code, not all possible input combinations are allowed in the same device. Referring again to the commercial device mentioned above, we may find 96 equivalent words, or partial product terms, each of which is a logical AND function which relates to a portion of the total output terminal solution. Each of these terms may be programmed to any complexity up to the input limit of the PLA. Each of the outputs then becomes a logical sum (OR) of any combination of the partial product terms.

Figure 4-22 illustrates the logical data flow from the 14 address input terminals of the PLA, through the AND and OR gates, to the outputs.

The PLA may be treated as a limited-capability ROM, and thus can be suitable employed as a code converter. The success of the application requires that all the partial product terms for a particular code conversion be limited to the 96 available in the PLA.

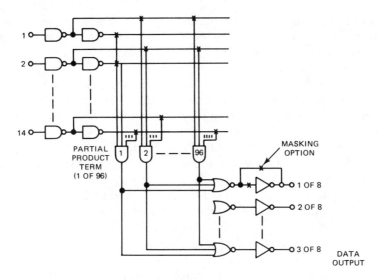

Fig. 4–22. Logic flow of PLA

For example, let us assume that a 12-line Hollerith is to be converted to an 8-line ASCII. In theory, 12-line input requires 4K words. However, seven of the 12 Hollerith lines are decimally coded, not binary coded, and, if the conversion were to be effected with an 8-input ROM, the seven lines would first have to be encoded to three binary lines, thus requiring additional logic elements. The three lines, in addition to the five that are already binary, could then input the ROM.

If the additional logic were dispensed with, and, instead a 12-input ROM were used, provisions would have to be made for this device to decode all nonexistent input possibilities into "don't care" or error output stages. On the other hand, a PLA accepts all 12 inputs, and, because it provides selective decoding, no provision is required for preencoding the inputs.

Because many processor-oriented systems have control instruction codes wider than conventional ROMs can accommodate, PLAs find a use in this area. Most processors have from 9 to 11 logical control code inputs, and, because each input instruction code must be logically ANDed with timing to form an output control signal, the timing code of the processor is also critical. Thus, most processors require a total input control group of from 11 to 13 bits to achieve output control. Standard ROMs can achieve this result at the cost of component expense and reduced dynamic performance. The solution requires two levels of logic to decode the proper ROM element group and allow the input data word to propagate to the output terminals.

Because in actual use not all combinations of instructions and timing data are used, data-compression techniques can reduce the number of ROMs required by this system. The technique most often used involves multiplexing the required codes into the ROMs. This technique cuts the number of ROMs, but at the expense of increased delay times in order to achieve the proper output levels.

The PLA-based solution to the problem, as shown in Figure 4-23, requires generation of logic equations for the output of the processor, isolating the common product terms, and implementing the design in a masked PLA.

Another application area for PLAs is that of controllers. A sequential controller usually requires that a random set of input variables occur simultaneously in order to satisfy the condition of a particular state. Attaining this condition allows the controller to advance to its next state.

In a traffic controller, for example, let us assume that traffic can flow at high rates in any of four directions. Let us further assume that the controller must accept manual inputs, and that its timing interval must be modified as traffic flow changes.

The state diagram of the controller, shown in Figure 4-24, indicates that a maximum time interval, X, must be checked against the current value of the controller's state A counter. If X is greater, the counter indexes to the next machine state (state B). The control coding allows the interval of each state to be shortened if traffic develops in another state. Furthermore, the controller can lengthen the interval of a particular state if no cross or left-turn signal is detected.

The PLA-based implementation of the controller, as shown in Figure 4-25, incorporates four traffic counters whose outputs are multiplexed sequentially into a PLA sequencer controller. There, the outputs are logically ANDed with current state timing, and with this information the sequencer modulates its period according to its state equations. One holding memory for each traffic counter receives the output data and stores control information for the traffic indicators. The scan decoder for the remote traffic counters also sequentially updates each holding memory.

Each of the examples above illustrates how a PLA can make system designs more economical by reducing circuit complexity and, occasionally, increasing dynamic performance.

FPLAs

The reader may have noticed that the PLA was described above as employed in a system, and no particulars as to its internal circuit design or electrical specifications have been given. Although PLAs have been available for several years, their introduction to the electronics market caused hardly a stir. The reason can be primarily attributed to the dampening of user enthusiasm, following the realization that, in most cases, mask charges and weeks of turnaround time imparted by factory programming created as

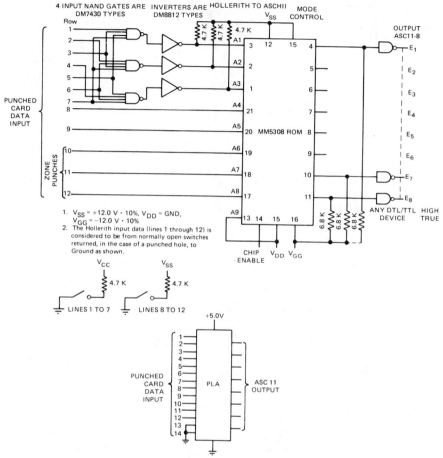

Fig. 4-23. PLA application

many problems as it solved and quickly eroded initial usage gains. The inevitable programming changes resulting from either user inexperience with the device or system evolution implied an intolerably long design cycle and, most important, no custom design flexibility and slow recovery from marginally hidden faults detected after system release in the field.

The preceding considerations rendered field programmability a mandatory feature for design economy and provided impetus to the industry to develop field-programmable logic arrays (FPLAs) which could be easily programmed by the *user*. With the growing availability of these devices, now for the first time the user can utilize the associative and logic compression properties of FPLAs as cost-effective design tools. Moreover, when accompanied by a few storage elements (flip-flops), the FPLA becomes a powerful logic machine for the design of finite-state sequential controllers

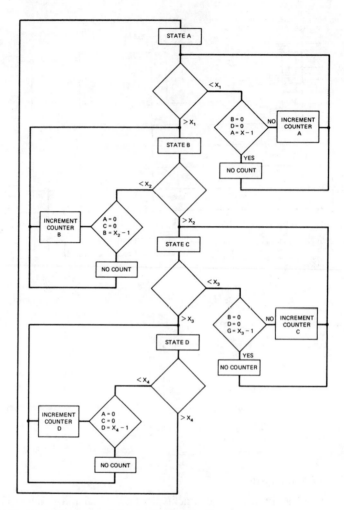

Fig. 4–24. State diagram of the traffic controller

for traffic processing, peripheral devices, and similar applications.

The internal structure of a typical FPLA is illustrated in Figure 4-26. The device is constructed with the nichrome-fuse technique previously described, and consists of an upper AND matrix containing 48 product term rows (P-terms) and a lower OR matrix containing 8 sum-term columns (5-terms), one for each output function. Each P-term in the AND matrix is initially coupled to each of 16 input variables via two Schottky diodes for programming the desired input state, and to each 5-term in the OR matrix through an emitter follower with an emitter fuse, for pulling the summing node to a high level when the P-term is activated. Each 5-term, in turn, is coupled to its respective output via an EX-OR gate which has pro-

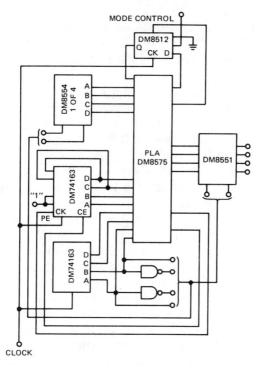

Fig. 4–25. PLA-based implementation of the controller

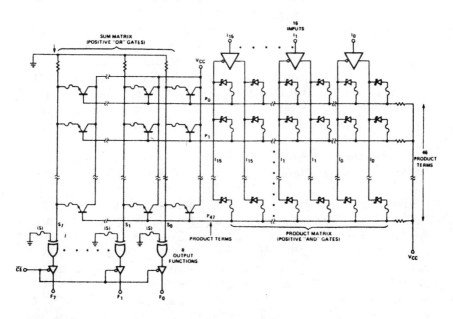

Fig. 4–26. Logic structure of a field programmable logic array

grammable transmission polarity by means of an input to ground through a fusible link.

The basic operation of an FPLA is as follows:

Since in a blank device all P-terms are in a logic "O" state, any unused P-terms require no programming at all and can be skipped during a programming sequence. Each P-term is programmed with the desired logic state of each input variable by fusing the appropriate link in the pair which couples each P-term to each input variable. If Pn contains Im, the $\overline{\text{Im}}$ link is fused, and vice versa. If Im is a "don't care" in Pn, both the Im and $\overline{\text{Im}}$ links must be fused. If fewer than 16 variables are used, the unused variables represent "don't care" conditions for all used P-terms, and their corresponding Im and $\overline{\text{Im}}$ links must be fused.

The response of each output function to programmed P-terms is assigned in the OR matrix. If any product term Pn activates an output function, the link coupling that output function to the P-term(s) must be fused, and vice versa. No programming is required of OR matrix links coupling used or unused P-terms to S-terms servicing any unused output functions. Finally, to program an output function true active-low when logically selected by any P-term, the corresponding link (S) must be fused.

The FPLA is programmed with the desired program table in three successive steps involving the AND matrix, OR matrix, and the transmission polarity of the output EX-OR gates. Automatic programming equipment is commercially available at present for this purpose.

The peripheral fusing internal to the FPLA, as well as the basic terminal requirements that must be provided to fuse the three sectors of the FPLA, are shown in Figures 4-27 and 4-28, respectively. Each P-term, 0 through 47, is individually addressed by applying a binary code to outputs F_0 through F_7, while all internal output buffers are disabled via the $\overline{\text{CE}}$ input. The address is steered by the AND-matrix select line through AND gates to the demultiplexer, selecting the P-term to be programmed. All input variables are initially disconnected from the P-term by applying a positive voltage (normally +10 V) to all inputs.

Links are set to blow one at a time by applying a TTL logic high or low level to each variable, depending on whether a high or low logic state is contained in the P-term. Actual fusing of the link is accomplished by raising the fuse enable input to +17 V, and by pulsing the $\overline{\text{CE}}$ input from a high level to a +10 V for approximately 1 ms. If an input variable is a "don't care" in the P-term, both fuses are successively blown.

To program the OR matrix, inputs I_0 through I_5 are now used to address each P-term, also by means of a binary input code. The demultiplexer steering network is correspondingly reversed by enabling the OR-matrix select line. All input buffers are simultaneously disabled by raising V_{CC} to +8.5 V, effectively disconnecting all inputs from the P-terms. For

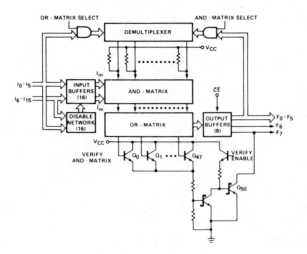

Fig. 4–27. Functional FPLA blocks

PROGRAM ⟶	'AND' MATRIX	'OR' MATRIX	OUTPUT ACT LEVEL
V_{CC}	+5.0 V	+8.75 V	LOW
INPUT(S) (Program) I_m	HIGH	ADDRESS P-TERM WITH $I_0 \sim I_5$	HIGH
INPUT(S) (Program) $\overline{I}_m$	LOW		
OTHER INPUTS	+10.0V		
OUTPUT(S) Contains P_n	ADDRESS P-TERM WITH $F_0 \sim F_5$	LOW	HIGH / LOW
OUTPUT(S) Excludes P_n		+10.0 V	LOW
Fuse Enable	+17.0 V	+17.0 V	LOW
$\overline{CE}$	+10 V / HIGH — 1MS	+10 V / HIGH — 1MS	HIGH

Fig. 4–28. Summary of FPLA programming requirements

each P-term, the emitter links coupling the P-term to each S-term are set to be fused one at a time as required. If the P-term appears in the logic expression of an output function, the corresponding S-term link is left intact, *regardless of the chosen output polarity.* Conversely, if the P-term is not contained in the output function, the S-term link is set to be fused by applying +10 V to that output. Again, actual fusing of the link occurs by applying +17 V to the fuse enable, and by pulsing the $\overline{CE}$ input from a high level to +10 V for 1 ms.

Finally, to program any output to active-low (F_p^* function, whereby the output switches from high to low logic level in response to an activated P-term), the link grounding the input to the EX-OR gate is fused by applying +17V to that output pin for approximately 1 ms with no V_{CC} power to the device.

EXERCISES

4-1. Name the clocklike signals associated with the dynamic RAM.

4-2. What is the primary advantage of MOS memory over bipolar memory?

4-3. Can data be shifted in both directions through a shift register? Explain.

4-4. Give the advantages or disadvantages of a PLA over a ROM.

4-5. Name a method used to expand the memory of a CAM. Are there any problems associated with such a method? Explain.

4-6. Briefly describe the silicon-fuse fabrication method.

4-7. Briefly describe the FPLA.

4-8. Describe the advantages or disadvantages of dynamic and static RAMs.

4-9. Describe mask-programmable ROMs.

4-10. What is the difference, if any, between ROMs and RAMs?

4-11. What is important in a memory?

5

Microprogramming

5.1 INTRODUCTION

Soon after a microprocessor system has been designed and constructed, it must be properly programmed to produce the desired results. However, prior to forming some sort of a program for the system, the problem must be identified, and a series of events must be placed in the proper sequence so that one may arrive at the solution.

The purpose of this chapter is to provide basic guidance to flow-charting and microprogramming so that basic software operation of the designs that follow may be more clearly understood.

5.2 PROBLEM DEFINITION

Prior to flowcharting, one must define the problem, carefully examine it, and determine which questions must be answered. As an example, let us say that automation is required of a traffic control system at the intersection of a main highway and a side street so that the control is sensitive to traffic conditions. These conditions are to be sensed by in-the-road vehicle detectors. Traffic-light commands will be based upon a combination of (closed-loop) feedback from these sensors and programmed (open-loop) sequences. Observations of traffic at the intersection have indicated that the controller should control the lights in the following manner:

1. Light should be normally green to the main highway.

2. If a vehicle is sensed on the side street, the controller must first check that 30 seconds have elapsed since the light last favored the side street.

3. If the check indicates that traffic has been flowing on Main Street for 30 seconds or longer, the controller should change the lights to green for Side Street, passing through the usual 4-second amber or caution interval.

4. Once Side Street has been given green, the controller should time out 30 seconds to limit the time it will favor Side Street.

5. At the same time, the controller should monitor the number of vehicles that are passing on Main Street. If seven vehicles approach the intersection (meaning that seven cars have queued up), change the lights without waiting the full 30 seconds.

Thus, the problem has been defined and properly sequenced. A flow-chart may follow. To facilitate idea transfers and to avoid confusion, certain flowchart standard symbols have been adopted as follows:

1. BEGIN-START OR END:

These symbols indicate where a flowchart begins and ends. The BEGIN-START symbol is normally located in the upper left-hand corner of the flowchart.

2. INPUT/OUTPUT:

This symbol is used to indicate the reading of input data or the printing of answers.

3. DECISION DIAMOND:

A question is asked that is usually answered yes or no. At least two lines must exist from a decision diamond. One is usually labeled yes, the other no.

4. ASSIGNMENT:

This symbol indicates values to be assigned to memory cells; or it may indicate that a calculation and assignment is to be made.

5. CONNECTION: ◯

This symbol permits the linking of one portion of a flowchart with another.

6. Arrows link various flowchart symbols together.

5.3 TYPES OF FLOWCHARTS

There are three basic types of flowcharts (i.e., the system flowchart, the general flowchart, and the detailed flowchart).

A *system flowchart* identifies the devices to be employed in the solution of a problem. Normally, the standard symbols used in this type of flowchart pertain to each particular type of device or machine. This type of chart is more-or-less a parts list required to construct a program.

A *general flowchart,* such as the one formed during the first portion for the solution of the problem above, indicates in general terms what is to be achieved by the program. Since a computer cannot understand any procedure or make any assumptions, the programmer must guide the machine through every step of the sequence to produce the desired solution.

A *detailed flowchart,* as the term implies, is a more explanatory version of the general flowchart.

Figure 5-1 illustrates the general and detailed flowchart for the traffic control system described above.

5.4 PROGRAMMING AND NUMBER SYSTEMS

Upon completion of the flowchart, the program must be organized. The various computers on the market at present are equipped with different input switches and displays for feeding the program into the machine, but the basic principle of operation in all of them is essentially the same.

Computers have been taught to recognize and freely manipulate a number system which is known to humans as decimal or base 10. The system, as we all know, employs 10 symbols, from 0 through 9, to represent the values or numbers. Various combinations of these symbols are employed to form other numbers. Each number or digit position is assigned a value equal to its position in the number sequence. For example, the number 15,342 is:

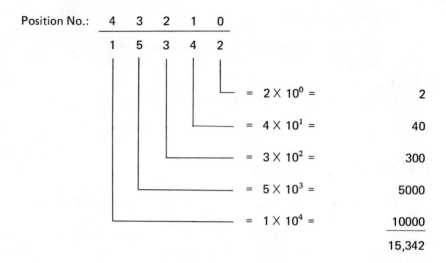

Position No.: 4 3 2 1 0

1 5 3 4 2

$= 2 \times 10^0 =$ 2

$= 4 \times 10^1 =$ 40

$= 3 \times 10^2 =$ 300

$= 5 \times 10^3 =$ 5000

$= 1 \times 10^4 =$ 10000

15,342

10 is the base value of the number system and 0, 1, 2, 3, and 4 indicate the position or weighted value.

Computers, being the simple machines that they are, employ a base 2 numbering system and use only zeros and ones to represent a value. By employing groups of ones and zeros and assigning values to the bit positions, large numbers may be represented. The computer "observes" the groups of ones and zeros and determines their value. The least significant bit would have a value of 2^0, the next bit would be 2^1, then 2^2, and so on. Let us use a group of 5 bits and assign bit 0 as the least significant bit in the following example:

Bit No.					
0		1	1×2^0		1
1		0	0×2^1		0
2	=	1	= 1×2^2	=	4
3		0	0×2^3		0
4		1	1×2^4		16
					21_{10}

Here, 21 is the sum of the value of the bit positions.

It can also be seen that by using larger groups of bits, larger numbers may be represented. An 8-bit computer that can handle 8-bit positions in parallel can represent numbers from 0 to 255_{10}.

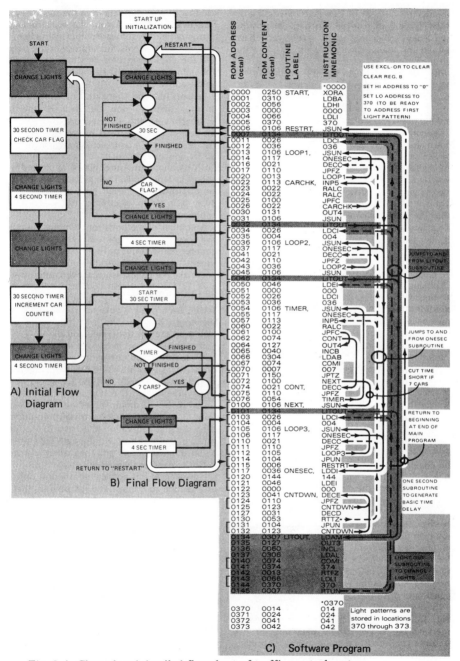

Fig. 5-1. General and detailed flowchart of traffic control system

The diagram contains the following labeled elements:

Initial Flow Diagram (A):
- START
- CHANGE LIGHTS
- 30 SECOND TIMER CHECK CAR FLAG
- CHANGE LIGHTS 4 SECOND TIMER
- CHANGE LIGHTS
- 30 SECOND TIMER INCREMENT CAR COUNTER
- CHANGE LIGHTS 4 SECOND TIMER

Final Flow Diagram (B):
- START UP INITIALIZATION
- RESTART
- CHANGE LIGHTS
- 30 SEC — NOT FINISHED / FINISHED
- CAR FLAG? — NO / YES
- CHANGE LIGHTS
- 4 SEC TIMER
- CHANGE LIGHTS
- START 30 SEC TIMER
- TIMER — FINISHED / NOT FINISHED
- 7 CARS? — NO / YES
- CHANGE LIGHTS
- 4 SEC TIMER
- RETURN TO "RESTART"

Software Program (C):

ROM ADDRESS (octal)	ROM CONTENT (octal)	ROUTINE LABEL	INSTRUCTION MNEMONIC
0000	0250	START,	*0000 XORA
0001	0310		LDBA
0002	0056		LDHI
0003	0000		0000
0004	0066		LDLI
0005	0370		370
0006	0106	RESTRT,	JSUN
0007	0134		LITOUT,
0011	0026		LDCI
0012	0036		036
0013	0106	LOOP1,	JSUN
0014	0117		ONESEC
0016	0021		DECC
0017	0110		JPFZ
0020	0013		LOOP1
0022	0113	CARCHK,	INP5
0023	0022		RALC
0024	0022		RALC
0025	0100		JPFC
0026	0022		CARCHK
0030	0131		OUT4
0031	0106		JSUN
0032	0134		LITOUT,
0034	0026		LDCI
0035	0004		004
0036	0106	LOOP2,	JSUN
0037	0117		ONESEC
0041	0021		DECC
0042	0110		JPFZ
0043	0036		LOOP2
0045	0106		JSUN
0046	0134		LITOUT,
0050	0046		LDEI
0051	0000		000
0052	0026		LDCI
0053	0036		036
0054	0106	TIMER,	JSUN
0057	0117		ONESEC
0056	0113		INP5
0060	0022		RALC
0061	0100		JPFC
0062	0074		CONT
0064	0127		OUT4
0065	0040		INCB
0066	0304		LDAB
0067	0074		COMI
0070	0007		007
0071	0150		JPTZ
0072	0100		NEXT
0074	0021	CONT,	DECC
0075	0110		JPFZ
0076	0054		TIMER,
0100	0106	NEXT,	JSUN
0101	0134		LITOUT,
0103	0026		LDCI
0104	0004		004
0105	0106	LOOP3,	JSUN
0106	0117		ONESEC
0110	0021		DECC
0111	0110		JPFZ
0112	0105		LOOP3
0114	0104		JPUN
0115	0006		RESTRT,
0117	0036	ONESEC,	LDDI
0120	0144		144
0121	0046		LDEI
0122	0000		000
0123	0041	CNTDWN,	DECE
0124	0110		JPFZ
0125	0123		CNTDWN
0127	0031		DECD
0130	0053		RTTZ
0131	0104		JPUN
0132	0123		CNTDWN
0134	0307	LITOUT,	LDAM
0135	0127		OUT3
0136	0060		INCL
0137	0306		LDAL
0140	0074		COMI
0141	0374		374
0142	0013		RTFZ
0143	0066		LDLI
0144	0370		370
0145	0007		RTUN
0370	0014		*0370 014
0371	0024		024
0372	0041		041
0373	0042		042

Annotation boxes:
- USE EXCL-OR TO CLEAR / CLEAR REG. B / SET HI ADDRESS TO "0" / SET LO ADDRESS TO 370 (TO BE READY TO ADDRESS FIRST LIGHT PATTERN)
- JUMPS TO AND FROM LITOUT SUBROUTINE
- JUMPS TO AND FROM ONESEC SUBROUTINE
- CUT TIME SHORT IF 7 CARS
- RETURN TO BEGINNING AT END OF MAIN PROGRAM
- ONE SECOND SUBROUTINE TO GENERATE BASIC TIME DELAY
- LIGHT OUT SUBROUTINE TO CHANGE LIGHTS
- Light patterns are stored in locations 370 through 373.

A) Initial Flow Diagram
B) Final Flow Diagram
C) Software Program

ALL BITS EQUAL 0					ALL BITS EQUAL 1				
Bit No.				Bit No.					
0	0	0×2^0	0	0	1	1×2^0	1		
1	0	0×2^1	0	1	1	1×2^1	2		
2	0	0×2^2	0	2	1	1×2^2	4		
3	= 0	0×2^3 = 0		3	= 1 =	1×2^3 =	8	=	255
4	0	0×2^4	0	4	1	1×2^4	16		
5	0	0×2^5	0	5	1	1×2^5	32		
6	0	0×2^6	0	6	1	1×2^6	64		
7	0	0×2^7	0	7	1	1×2^7	128		

A computer that has 16-bit positions may represent numbers with values from 0 to 65,535.

Another consideration in computers is the representation not only of numbers but of both positive and negative values. This may be accomplished by assigning one of the bits in a group as a plus/minus indicator. The normal method is to assign the most significant bit position to this task. If it is a logic 0, the value is positive. If it is a logic 1, the value is minus. Assuming a maximum group of 8 bits and using the eighth position as the sign, the following numbers may be represented:

	Bit No.					
	0	1	1×2^0		1	
	1	1	1×2^1		2	
	2	1	1×2^2		4	
	3	1	= 1×2^3	=	8	
	4	1	1×2^4		16	
	5	1	1×2^5		32	
	6	1	1×2^6		64	
Sign bit	7	0	= +		+127	

If bit 7 is equal to a 1, then the number above would be a negative, or –127. It should be noted that, by using the most significant bit for the sign, the maximum number that may be represented is only ±127. In a 16-bit computer, this number would be ±32,767.

Human beings have difficulty in visually converting the above ones and zeros to their represented value. Because of this, other methods of representing or reading these numbers have been implemented.

5.5 BINARY-CODED DECIMAL

Binary-coded decimal (BCD) employs groups of 4 binary bits or positions and uses only those combinations that add up to 0, 1, 2, 3, 4, 5, 6, 7, 8, or 9. For example:

BIT POSITION					
3	2	1	0		
0	0	0	0	=	0
0	0	0	1	=	1
0	0	1	0	=	2
0	0	1	1	=	3
0	1	0	0	=	4
0	1	0	1	=	5
0	1	1	0	=	6
0	1	1	1	=	7
1	0	0	0	=	8
1	0	0	1	=	9

The other binary combinations possible in the 4-bit positions are not allowed in the BCD method:

1	0	1	0	
1	0	1	1	
1	1	0	0	
1	1	0	1	— not valid
1	1	1	0	
1	1	1	1	

In an 8-bit computer, the decimal numbers 00 through 99 may be represented as follows:

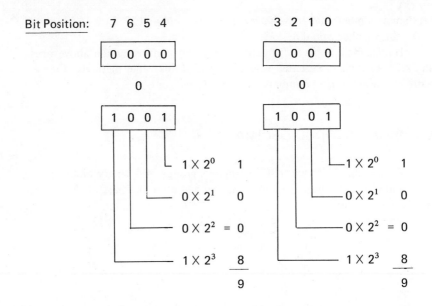

Note that the binary weighting system repeats for each 4-bit group. It is then compensated for by applying the decimal or base 10 rules to the converted numbers:

$$
\begin{array}{ll}
9 \times 10^0 & = \quad 9 \\
9 \times 10^1 & = \quad \underline{90} \\
& \quad \quad 99
\end{array}
$$

By only having to weigh up to four binary bits, one may easily become efficient at converting binary to decimal, and vice versa.

The maximum numbers, therefore, that 255_{10} represented in an 8-bit machine are then only 99_{10} in decimal versus 225_1 in binary.

As may be seen, the efficiency of a computer is restricted, owing to the illegal combination in each 4-bit group. Another representation in binary numbers allows for all combinations of the 4 group bits. This method is called hexadecimal.

5.6 HEXADECIMAL SYSTEM

The *hexadecimal* system (hex) employs a numbering system of base

16. Hex allows for all combinations of the 4-bit binary groups as follows:

BIT POSITION				BINARY	HEX SYMBOL
3	2	1	0		
0	0	0	0	0	0
0	0	0	1	1	1
0	0	1	0	2	2
0	0	1	1	3	3
0	1	0	0	4	4
0	1	0	1	5	5
0	1	1	0	6	6
0	1	1	1	7	7
1	0	0	0	8	8
1	0	0	1	9	9
1	0	1	0	10	A
1	0	1	1	11	B
1	1	0	0	12	C
1	1	0	1	13	D
1	1	1	0	14	E
1	1	1	1	15	F

The alphanumeric notation, A through F, is used to allow for a single-character representation of the 4-bit group without duplication.

The hexadecimal system may be used to represent all 16 combinations of binary weights possible in a group of 4-bit positions. An 8-bit computer may then represent the numbers 00 through FF, these numbers being equivalent to binary 0 through 255.

Bit Position: 7 6 5 4   3 2 1 0

                 0 0 0 0   0 0 0 0

                      :   :
                      :   :

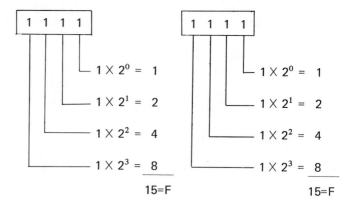

Applying the same rules as for decimal, with the exception of using base 16 instead of base 10, we obtain

As may be seen, binary numbers, regardless of the number of positions, may easily be converted by simply dividing them into groups of 4 bits. For example, in a 16-bit computer:

Hex	F	E	9	A
Binary	1111	1110	1001	1010
Hex	F	E	9	A

Furthermore, it becomes obvious that the use of a hex symbol to represent an equivalent for 4 binary bits requires fewer printed symbols. Most all computer documentation is at present using the hexadecimal representation of computer code.

5.7 POSITIVE AND NEGATIVE NUMBERS

In the hexadecimal system, the method of representing positive and negative numbers is the same as for binary. The most significant bit of the most significant group is set to a zero for positive and a one for negative. If a 16-bit computer has four groups of 4 bits each, then:

Hex	7	F	F	F
Binary 1 sign bit	0111	1111	1111	1111

This number is equivalent to a positive (+) 32,767. By using the most significant bit as a logic "1," the number becomes:

Hex	F	F	F	F
Binary 1 sign bit	1111	1111	1111	1111

This number is equivalent to a minus (-) 32,767.

5.8 PROGRAMMING FUNDAMENTALS

Two types of computer instructions and the way in which they are used in computer programs are described in this section. The first type of instruction operates on data stored in a memory location and must instruct the computer where the data are located so that the machine can find it. This type of instruction is said to *reference* a location in memory; therefore, these instructions are often called *memory reference instructions* (MRIs).

When speaking of memory locations, it is very important that a clear distinction be made between the address of a location and the contents of that location, as follows:

A memory reference instruction refers to a location by a 16-bit *address;* however, the instruction causes the computer to take some specific action with the *content* of the location. Thus, although the address of a specific location in memory remains the same, the content of the location is subject to change. In summary, a memory reference instruction uses a 16-bit address value to refer to a memory location, and it operates on the 16-bit binary number stored in the referenced memory location.

The second type of instructions are the *operate* instructions which perform a variety of program operations without the need for reference to a memory location. Instructions of this type are used to perform the following operations:

Clean the accumulator, test for negative accumulator, halt program execution, etc.

5.9 PROGRAM CODING

Binary numbers comprise the only language the computer can understand. Numbers are stored in binary form and all arithmetic operations are performed in binary. More important to the programmer, however, is the fact that, for the computer to understand an instruction, the instruction must be represented in binary. The computer cannot understand instructions that use the English language.

5.10 BINARY CODING

The computer has a set of instructions in binary code which it "understands." In other words, the circuitry of the machine is wired to react to these binary numbers in a certain manner. These instructions have the same appearance as any other binary number; the computer can interpret the same binary configuration of zeros and ones as data or as an instruction. The programmer instructs the computer whether to interpret the binary configuration as an instruction or as data by the way in which the configuration is encountered in the program. Let us assume that the computer has the following binary instruction set:

| Instruction A | 1110 | 0000 | 0001 | 0010 | This binary number instructs the computer to add the contents of location 0000 0000 0001 0010 to accumulator 0. |
| Instruction B | 1110 | 0000 | 0001 | 0111 | This binary number instructs the computer to add the contents of location 0000 0000 0001 0111 to accumulator 0. |

If instruction B is contained in a memory location with an address of 0000 0000 0001 0010 and the binary number 0000 0001 1111 1111 is stored in location with an address of 0000 0000 0001 0111, the following program could be written:

LOCATION				CONTENT			
0000	0000	0001	0010	1110	0000	0001	0111
0000	0000	0001	0111	0000	0001	1111	1111

If this program were to be executed, the number 0000 0001 1111 1111 would be added to the accumulator.

5.11 HEXADECIMAL CODING

Most programmers seldom use the binary number system in actual practice because binary configurations appear cumbersome and confusing. Instead, the binary system is substituted by the hexadecimal system. It is very important that the conversion method between the two systems be thoroughly understood.

When the conversion to hex is performed, instruction B becomes $E017_{16}$, and the previous program is changed as follows:

LOCATION	CONTENT
0012_{16}	$E017_{16}$
0017_{16}	$01FF_{16}$

In order to demonstrate the fact that the computer cannot distinguish between a number and an instruction, let us consider the following program:

LOCATION	CONTENT	
0011	E012	(instruction A)
0012	E017	(instruction B)
0017	01FF	(the number $01FF_{16}$)

Instruction A, which adds the contents of location 0012 to the accumulator, has been combined with the previous program. Upon execution of the program, assuming the initial accumulator value = 0, the computer will execute instruction A and add $E017_{16}$ as a number to the accumulator, obtaining a result of $E017_{16}$. The computer will then execute the next instruction, which is E017, causing its internal architecture to add the contents of 0017 to the accumulator. After the execution of the two instructions, the number E216 is in the accumulator. Thus, the program above caused the number $E017_{16}$ to be used as an instruction and as a number by the computer.

5.12 MNEMONIC CODING

Coding a program in hex numbers, although an improvement upon binary coding, is nevertheless very inconvenient. The programmer must learn a complete set of hex numbers which have no logical connection with the operations they represent. The coding is difficult for programmers when they are writing programs, and this difficulty is compounded when they attempt to debug or correct a program. There is no easy way to remember the correspondence between a hex number and a computer operation.

In order to simplify the process of writing or reading a program, each instruction is often represented by a simple three- or four-letter *mnemonic symbol.* These mnemonic symbols are considerably easier to relate to a computer operation because the letters often suggest the definition of the instruction. The programmer is now in a position to program in a language of letters and numbers which suggests the meaning of each instruction.

The computer still does not understand any language except binary numbers. Now, however, a program can be written in a symbolic language and translated into the binary code of the machine as a result of the one-to-one comparison between the binary instructions and the mnemonics. This translation could be done by hand, defeating the purpose of mnemonic instructions, or the computer could be used to do the translation for the programmer. Using a binary code to represent alphabetic characters, the programmer is in a position to store alphabetic information in the computer memory. By instructing the computer to perform a translation, substituting binary numbers for the alphabetic characters, a program is generated in the binary code of the computer. This process of translation is called *assembling* a program. The program that performs the translation is called an *assembler.* At this point, it is rather essential that certain observations be made about the assembler as follows:

1. The assembler itself must be written in binary, not mnemonic, code.

2. The assembler performs a one-to-one translation of mnemonic codes into binary numbers.

3. The assembler allows programs to be written in a symbolic language which is easier for the programmer to understand and remember.

5.13 ELEMENTARY PROGRAMMING TECHNIQUES

Thorough understanding of the instruction set of a particular microprocessor system is the first step the programmer must take. The next step is to learn to use the instruction set to obtain correct results, and to obtain them efficiently. This is done by studying the following programming techniques. Examples, which should further familiarize the reader with the instructions and their uses, are given to illustrate each technique.

The modern digital computer is capable of storing information, performing calculations, making decisions based on the results, and arriving at a final solution to a given problem. Each step that the computer is to perform must first be worked out by the programmer.

The programmer must write a program which is a list of instructions for the computer to follow in order to arrive at a solution to a given problem. This list of instructions is based on a computational method, sometimes called *algorithm,* to solve the problem. The list of instructions is placed in the computer memory to activate the applicable circuitry so that the computer can process the problem.

5.14 CODING A PROGRAM

The introduction of an assembler enabled the programmer to write a symbolic program, employing meaningful mnemonic codes rather than the octal representation of the instructions. The programmer may now write mnemonic programs such as the following example which multiplies 18_{10} by 36_{10} using successive addition:

020	LIO,0	(initialize)
021	LIO-18	(set up a CNTR)
022	STO,212	(count the additions of 36)
023	ADDO,211	(add 36)
024	ISZ 212	(skip if CNTR is 0)
025	JMP 204	(add another 36 if not done)
026	HALT	(stop after 18 times)
027	0012	(equal to 18_{16})
028	0024	(equal to 36_{16})
029	0000	(holds the tally)

Organization of the program above was greatly simplified because mnemonic codes were used for the hex instructions. However, organizing the absolute address of each instruction is clearly an inconvenience. If the programmer later adds or deletes instructions, plus altering the location assignments of the program, he/she must rewrite those instructions whose operands refer to the altered assignments. If the programmer wishes to move the program to a different section of memory, she/he must rewrite the program. Since such changes must be made often, particularly in larger programs, a better means of assigning locations is required. The assembler does just that.

Location Assignment

As in the previous program example, most programs are written in successive memory locations. If the programmer assigned an absolute location to the first instruction, the assembler could be instructed to assign the next instructions to the following locations in order. The assembler maintains a *current location counter* by which it assigns successive locations to instructions.

Symbolic Addresses. The programmer does not, at the outset, know which locations will be used to store constants or the tally. Therefore, he/she must leave blanks after each MRI and return to fill these in after locations have been assigned to these numbers. In the previous program, the number of locations after the assigned initial address must be counted in order to assign the correct values to the MRI operands. Actually, this is not necessary because symbolic names may be assigned to the locations to which she/he must refer, and the assembler will assign address values for the programmer. The assembler maintains a symbol table in which it records the hex values of all symbolic addresses. With symbolic address nomenclatures, the program is as follows:

020	LIO,0
021	GO:LIO-18
022	STO,CNTR
023	MULT:ADDO,B
024	ISZ CNTR
025	JMP MULT
026	HALT
027	A:
028	B:
029	CNTR:

(*Note:* The ":" after a symbol (e.g., GO:) indicates to the assembler that the symbol is a symbolic address.)

Symbolic Programming Conventions. Any sequence of letters (A, B, C, ..., Z) and digits (0, 1, ..., 9) beginning with a letter and terminated by a delimiting character (: or =) is a *symbol*.

User-Defined Symbols. User-defined symbols (stored in the external symbol table) must be four characters in length. The colon after a symbol in a line of coding (e.g., MULT:LDO) indicates to the assembler that the value of MULT is the address of the location in which the instruction is stored. When an instruction that references MULT (now a *symbolic address*) is encountered, the assembler supplies the correct address value for MULT. Care must be taken that a symbolic address is never used twice in the same program, and that all locations referenced by an MRI are identified somewhere in the program.

5.15   MACHINE CODE

Each of the 72 executable instructions of the source language assembles into 1 to 3 bytes of machine code. The number of bytes depends on the particular instruction and on the addressing mode. The addressing modes that are available for use with the various executive instructions are indicated in Figure 5-2.

The coding of the first (or only) byte, corresponding to an executable instruction, is sufficient to identify the instruction and the addressing mode. The hexadecimal equivalents of the binary codes, which result from the translation of the 72 instructions, in all valid modes of addressing, are shown in Figure 5-3.

There are 197 valid machine codes, 59 of the 256 possible codes being unassigned. The octal and decimal equivalents of the machine-language codes are shown in Figures 5-4 and 5-5. The machine codes are listed alphabetically in Figure 5-5.

When an instruction translates into 2 or 3 bytes of code, the second byte, or the second and third bytes, contain(s) an operand, an address, or information from which an address is obtained during execution.

5.16   STACK AND STACK POINTER

The stack consists of any number of locations in RAM memory. The stack provides for temporary storage and retrieval of successive bytes of information, which may include any of the following items:

Current status of the CPU.

Return address.

Data.

The stack can be used for the following purposes:

Interrupt control.

Subroutine control.

Temporary storage of data (under control of the program).

Reentrant code.

The microprocessing unit includes a 16-bit stack pointer. This contains an address that enables the CPU to find the current location of the stack.

When a byte of information is stored in the stack, it is stored at the address contained in the stack pointer. The stack pointer is decremented

Mnemonic	*	Immediate	Direct	Extended	Indexed
ABA	1B	•	•	•	•
ADCA	•	89	99	B9	A9
ADCB	•	C9	D9	F9	E9
ADDA	•	8B	9B	BB	AB
ADDB	•	CB	DB	FB	EB
ANDA	•	84	94	B4	A4
ANDB	•	C4	D4	F4	E4
ASL	•	•	•	78	68
ASLA	48	•	•	•	•
ASLB	58	•	•	•	•
ASR	•	•	•	77	67
ASRA	47	•	•	•	•
ASRB	57	•	•	•	•
BCC	24	•	•	•	•
BCS	25	•	•	•	•
BEQ	27	•	•	•	•
BGE	2C	•	•	•	•
BGT	2E	•	•	•	•
BHI	22	•	•	•	•
BITA	•	85	95	B5	A5
BITB	•	C5	D5	F5	E5
BLE	2F	•	•	•	•
BLS	23	•	•	•	•
BLT	2D	•	•	•	•
BMI	2B	•	•	•	•
BNE	26	•	•	•	•
BPL	2A	•	•	•	•
BRA	20	•	•	•	•
BSR	8D	•	•	•	•
BVC	28	•	•	•	•
BVS	29	•	•	•	•
CBA	11	•	•	•	•
CLC	0C	•	•	•	•
CLI	0E	•	•	•	•
CLR	•	•	•	7F	6F
CLRA	4F	•	•	•	•
CLRB	5F	•	•	•	•
CLV	0A	•	•	•	•
CMPA	•	81	91	B1	A1
CMPB	•	C1	D1	F1	E1
COM	•	•	•	73	63
COMA	43	•	•	•	•
COMB	53	•	•	•	•
CPX	•	8C	9C	BC	AC
DAA	19	•	•	•	•
DEC	•	•	•	7A	6A
DECA	4A	•	•	•	•
DECB	5A	•	•	•	•
DES	34	•	•	•	•
DEX	09	•	•	•	•
EORA	•	88	98	B8	A8
EORB	•	C8	D8	F8	E8
INC	•	•	•	7C	67

Mnemonic	*	Immediate	Direct	Extended	Indexed
INCA	4C	•	•	•	•
INCB	5C	•	•	•	•
INS	31	•	•	•	•
INX	08	•	•	•	•
JMP	•	•	•	7E	6E
JSR	•	•	•	BD	AE
LDAA	•	86	96	B6	A6
LDAB	•	C6	D6	F6	E6
LDS	•	8E	9E	BE	AE
LDX	•	CE	DE	FE	EE
LSR	•	•	•	74	64
LSRA	44	•	•	•	•
LSRB	54	•	•	•	•
NEG	•	•	•	70	60
NEGA	40	•	•	•	•
NEGB	50	•	•	•	•
NOP	01	•	•	•	•
ORAA	•	8A	9A	BA	AA
ORAB	•	CA	DA	FA	EA
PSHA	36	•	•	•	•
PSHB	37	•	•	•	•
PULA	32	•	•	•	•
PULB	33	•	•	•	•
ROL	•	•	•	79	69
ROLA	49	•	•	•	•
ROLB	59	•	•	•	•
ROR	•	•	•	76	66
RORA	46	•	•	•	•
RORB	56	•	•	•	•
RTI	3B	•	•	•	•
RTS	39	•	•	•	•
SBA	10	•	•	•	•
SBCA	•	82	92	B2	A2
SBCB	•	C2	D2	F2	E2
SEC	0D	•	•	•	•
SEI	0F	•	•	•	•
SEV	0B	•	•	•	•
STAA	•	•	97	B7	A7
STAB	•	•	D7	F7	E7
STS	•	•	9F	BF	AF
STX	•	•	DF	FF	EF
SUBA	•	80	90	B0	A0
SUBB	•	C0	D0	F0	E0
SWI	3F	•	•	•	•
TAB	16	•	•	•	•
TAP	06	•	•	•	•
TBA	17	•	•	•	•
TPA	07	•	•	•	•
TST	•	•	•	7D	6D
TSTA	4D	•	•	•	•
TSTB	5D	•	•	•	•
TSX	30	•	•	•	•
TXS	35	•	•	•	•
WAI	3E	•	•	•	•

* Combines the Inherent, Relative, and Accumulator Addressing Modes.

Fig. 5-2. Machine codes

Code		Code			Code				Code			
00	*	40	NEG	A	80	SUB	A	IMM	C0	SUB	B	IMM
01	NOP	41	*		81	CMP	A	IMM	C1	CMP	B	IMM
02	*	42	*		82	SBC	A	IMM	C2	SBC	B	IMM
03	*	43	COM	A	83	*			C3	*		
04	*	44	LSR	A	84	AND	A	IMM	C4	AND	B	IMM
05	*	45	*		85	BIT	A	IMM	C5	BIT	B	IMM
06	TAP	46	ROR	A	86	LDA	A	IMM	C6	LDA	B	IMM
07	TPA	47	ASR	A	87	*			C7	*		
08	INX	48	ASL	A	88	EOR	A	IMM	C8	EOR	B	IMM
09	DEX	49	ROL	A	89	ADC	A	IMM	C9	ADC	B	IMM
0A	CLV	4A	DEC	A	8A	ORA	A	IMM	CA	ORA	B	IMM
0B	SEV	4B	*		8B	ADD	A	IMM	CB	ADD	B	IMM
0C	CLC	4C	INC	A	8C	CPX	A	IMM	CC	*		
0D	SEC	4D	TST	A	8D	BSR		REL	CD	*		
0E	CLI	4E	*		8E	LDS		IMM	CE	LDX		IMM
0F	SEI	4F	CLR	A	8F	*			CF	*		
10	SBA	50	NEG	B	90	SUB	A	DIR	D0	SUB	B	DIR
11	CBA	52	*		91	CMP	A	DIR	D1	CMP	B	DIR
12	*	52	*		92	SBC	A	DIR	D2	SBC	B	DIR
13	*	53	COM	B	93	*			D3	*		
14	*	54	LSR	B	94	AND	A	DIR	D4	AND	B	DIR
15	*	55	*		95	BIT	A	DIR	D5	BIT	B	DIR
16	TAB	56	ROR	B	96	LDA	A	DIR	D6	LDA	B	DIR
17	TBA	57	ASR	B	97	STA	A	DIR	D7	STA	B	DIR
18	*	58	ASL	B	98	EOR	A	DIR	D8	EOR	B	DIR
19	DAA	59	ROL	B	99	ADC	A	DIR	D9	ADC	B	DIR
1A	*	5A	DEC	B	9A	ORA	A	DIR	DA	ORA	B	DIR
1B	ABA	5B	*		9B	ADD	A	DIR	DB	ADD	B	DIR
1C	*	5C	INC	B	9C	CPX		DIR	DC	*		
1D	*	5D	TST	B	9D	*			DD	*		
1E	*	5E	*		9E	LDS		DIR	DE	LDX		DIR
1F	*	5F	CLR	B	9F	STS		DIR	DF	STX		DIR
20	BRA REL	60	NEG	IND	A0	SUB	A	IND	E0	SUB	B	IND
21	*	61	*		A1	CMP	A	IND	E1	CMP	B	IND
22	BHI REL	62	*		A2	SBC	A	IND	E2	SBC	B	IND
23	BLS REL	63	COM	IND	A3	*			E3	*		
24	BCC REL	64	LSR	IND	A4	AND	A	IND	E4	AND	B	IND
25	BCS REL	65	*		A5	BIT	A	IND	E5	BIT	B	IND
26	BNE REL	66	ROR	IND	A6	LDA	A	IND	E6	LDA	B	IND
27	BEQ REL	67	ASR	IND	A7	STA	A	IND	E7	STA	B	IND
28	BVC REL	68	ASL	IND	A8	EOR	A	IND	E8	EOR	B	IND
29	BVS REL	69	ROL	IND	A9	ADC	A	IND	E9	ADC	B	IND
2A	BPL REL	6A	DEC	IND	AA	ORA	A	IND	EA	ORA	B	IND
2B	BMI REL	6B	*		AB	ADD	A	IND	EB	ADD	B	IND
2C	BGE REL	6C	INC	IND	AC	CPX		IND	EC	*		
2D	BLT REL	6D	TST	IND	AD	JSR		IND'	ED	*		
2E	BGT REL	6E	JMP	IND	AE	LDS		IND	EE	LDX		IND
2F	BLE REL	6F	CLR	IND	AF	STS		IND	EF	STX		IND
30	TSX	70	NEG	EXT	B0	SUB	A	EXT	F0	SUB	B	EXT
31	INS	71	*		B1	CMP	A	EXT	F1	CMP	B	EXT
32	PUL A	72	*		B2	SBC	A	EXT	F2	SBC	B	EXT
33	PUL B	73	COM	EXT	B3	*			F3	*		
34	DES	74	LSR	EXT	B4	AND	A	EXT	F4	AND	B	EXT
35	TXS	75	*		B5	BIT	A	EXT	F5	BIT	B	EXT
36	PSH A	76	ROR	EXT	B6	LDA	A	EXT	F6	LDA	B	EXT
37	PSH B	77	ASR	EXT	B7	STA	A	EXT	F7	STA	B	EXT
38	*	78	ASL	EXT	B8	EOR	A	EXT	F8	ADC	B	EXT
39	RTS	79	ROL	EXT	B9	ADC	A	EXT	F9	ADC	B	EXT
3A	*	7A	DEC	EXT	BA	ORA	A	EXT	FA	ORA	B	EXT
3B	RTI	7B	*		BB	ADD	A	EXT	FB	ADD	B	EXT
3C	*	7C	INC	EXT	BC	CPX		EXT	FC	*		
3D	*	7D	TST	EXT	BD	JSR		EXT	FD	*		
3E	WAI	7E	JMP	EXT	BE	LDS		EXT	FE	LDX		EXT
3F	SWI	7F	CLR	EXT	BF	STS		EXT	FF	STX		EXT

Notes: 1. Addressing Modes: A = Accumulator A   IMM = Immediate   REL = Relative
B = Accumulator B   DIR = Direct   IND = Indexed
2. Unassigned code indicated by ''*''.   EXT = Extended

Fig. 5-3. Hexadecimal equivalents of machine codes

000	*		100	NEG	A	200	SUB	A	IMM	300	SUB	B	IMM
001	NOP		101	*		201	CMP	A	IMM	301	CMP	B	IMM
002	*		102	*		202	SBC	A	IMM	302	SBC	B	IMM
003	*		103	COM	A	203	*			303	*		
004	*		104	LSR	A	204	AND	A	IMM	304	AND	B	IMM
005	*		105	*		205	BIT	A	IMM	305	BIT	B	IMM
006	TAP		106	ROR	A	206	LDA	A	IMM	306	LDA	B	IMM
007	TPA		107	ASR	A	207	*			307	*		
010	INX		110	ASL	A	210	EOR	A	IMM	310	EOR	B	IMM
011	DEX		111	ROL	A	211	ADC	A	IMM	311	ADC	B	IMM
012	CLV		112	DEC	A	212	ORA	A	IMM	312	ORA	B	IMM
013	SEV		113	*		213	ADD	A	IMM	313	ADD	B	IMM
014	CLC		114	INC	A	214	CPX		IMM	314	*		
015	SEC		115	TST	A	215	BSR		REL	315	*		
016	CLI		116	*		216	LDS		IMM	316	LDX		IMM
017	SEI		117	CLR	A	217	*			317	*		
020	SBA		120	NEG	B	220	SUB	A	DIR	320	SUB	B	DIR
021	CBA		121	*		221	CMP	A	DIR	321	CMP	B	DIR
022	*		122	*		222	SBC	A	DIR	322	SBC	B	DIR
023	*		123	COM	B	223	*			323	*		
024	*		124	LSR	B	224	AND	A	DIR	324	AND	B	DIR
025	*		125	*		225	BIT	A	DIR	325	BIT	B	DIR
026	TAB		126	ROR	B	226	LDA	A	DIR	326	LDA	B	DIR
027	TBA		127	ASR	B	227	STA	A	DIR	327	STA	B	DIR
030	*		130	ASL	B	230	EOR	A	DIR	330	EOR	B	DIR
031	DAA		131	ROL	B	231	ADC	A	DIR	331	ADC	B	DIR
032	*		132	DEC	B	232	ORA	A	DIR	332	ORA	B	DIR
033	ABA		133	*		233	ADD	A	DIR	333	ADD	B	DIR
034	*		134	INC	B	234	CPX		DIR	334	*		
035	*		135	TST	B	235	*			335	*		
036	*		136	*		236	LDS		DIR	336	LDX		DIR
037	*		137	CLR	B	237	STS		DIR	337	STX		DIR
040	BRA	REL	140	NEG	IND	240	SUB	A	IND	340	SUB	B	IND
041	*		141	*		241	CMP	A	IND	341	CMP	B	IND
042	BHI	REL	142	*		242	SBC	A	IND	342	SBC	B	IND
043	BLS	REL	143	COM	IND	243	*			343	*		
044	BCC	REL	144	LSR	IND	244	AND	A	IND	344	AND	B	IND
045	BCS	REL	145	*		245	BIT	A	IND	345	BIT	B	IND
046	BNE	REL	146	ROR	IND	246	LDA	A	IND	346	LDA	B	IND
047	BEQ	REL	147	ASR	IND	247	STA	A	IND	347	STA	B	IND
050	BVC	REL	150	ASL	IND	250	EOR	A	IND	350	EOR	B	IND
051	BVS	REL	151	ROL	IND	251	ADC	A	IND	351	ADC	B	IND
052	BPL	REL	152	DEC	IND	252	ORA	A	IND	352	ORA	B	IND
053	BMI	REL	153	*		253	ADD	A	IND	353	ADD	B	IND
054	BGE	REL	154	INC	IND	254	CPX		IND	354	*		
055	BLT	REL	155	TST	IND	255	JSR		IND	355	*		
056	BGT	REL	156	JMP	IND	256	LDS		IND	356	LEX		IND
057	BLE	REL	157	CLR	IND	257	STS		IND	357	STX		IND
060	TSX		160	NEG	EXT	260	SUB	A	EXT	360	SUB	B	EXT
061	INS		161	*		261	CMP	A	EXT	361	CMP	B	EXT
062	PUL	A	162	*		262	SBC	A	EXT	362	SBC	B	EXT
063	PUL	B	163	COM	EXT	263	*			363	*		
064	DES		164	LSR	EXT	264	AND	A	EXT	364	AND	B	EXT
065	TXS		165	*		265	BIT	A	EXT	365	BIT	B	EXT
066	PSH	A	166	ROR	EXT	266	LDA	A	EXT	366	LDA	B	EXT
067	PSH	B	167	ASR	EXT	267	STA	A	EXT	367	STA	B	EXT
070	*		170	ASL	EXT	270	EOR	A	EXT	370	EOR	B	EXT
071	RTS		171	ROL	EXT	271	ADC	A	EXT	371	ADC	B	EXT
072	*		172	DEC	EXT	272	ORA	A	EXT	372	ORA	B	EXT
073	RTI		173	*		273	ADD	A	EXT	373	ADD	B	EXT
074	*		174	INC	EXT	274	CPX		EXT	374	*		
075	*		175	TST	EXT	275	JSR		EXT	375	*		
076	WAI		176	JMP	EXT	276	LDS		EXT	376	LDX		EXT
077	SWI		177	CLR	EXT	277	STS		EXT	377	STX		EXT

Notes: 1. Addressing Modes:
A = Accumulator A   IMM = Immediate   REL = Relative
B = Accumulator B   DIR = Direct   IND = Indexed
2. Unassigned code indicated by "*"
EXT = Extended

Fig. 5-4. Octal equivalents of machine codes

Code	Mnem	Acc	Mode	Code	Mnem	Acc	Mode	Code	Mnem	Acc	Mode	Code	Mnem	Acc	Mode
000	*			064	NEG	A		128	SUB	A	IMM	192	SUB	B	IMM
001	NOP			065	*			129	CMP	A	IMM	193	CMP	B	IMM
002	*			066	*			130	SBC	A	IMM	194	SBC	B	IMM
003	*			067	COM	A		131	*			195	*		
004	*			068	LSR	A		132	AND	A	IMM	196	AND	B	IMM
005	*			069	*			133	BIT	A	IMM	197	BIT	B	IMM
006	TAP			070	ROR	A		134	LDA	A	IMM	198	LDA	B	IMM
007	TPA			071	ASR	A		135	*			199	*		
008	INX			072	ASL	A		136	EOR	A	IMM	200	EOR	B	IMM
009	DEX			073	ROL	A		137	ADC	A	IMM	301	ADC	B	IMM
010	CLV			074	DEC	A		138	ORA	A	IMM	202	ORA	B	IMM
011	SEV			075	*			139	ADD	A	IMM	203	ADD	B	IMM
012	CLC			076	INC	A		140	CPX		IMM	204	*		
013	SEC			077	TST	A		141	BSR		REL	205	*		
014	CLI			078	*			142	LDS		IMM	206	LDX		IMM
015	SEI			079	CLR	A		143	*			207	*		
016	SBA			080	NEG	B		144	SUB	A	DIR	208	SUB	B	DIR
017	CBA			081	*			145	CMP	A	DIR	209	CMP	B	DIR
018	*			082	*			146	SBC	A	DIR	210	SBC	B	DIR
019	*			083	COM	B		147	*			211	*		
020	*			084	LSR	B		148	AND	A	DIR	212	AND	B	DIR
021	*			085	*			149	BIT	A	DIR	213	BIT	B	DIR
022	TAB			086	ROR	B		150	LDA	A	DIR	214	LDA	B	DIR
023	TBA			087	ASR	B		151	STA	A	DIR	215	STA	B	DIR
024	*			088	ASL	B		152	EOR	A	DIR	216	EOR	B	DIR
025	DAA			089	ROL	B		153	ADC	A	DIR	217	ADC	B	DIR
026	*			090	DEC	B		154	ORA	A	DIR	218	ORA	B	DIR
027	ABA			091	*			155	ADD	A	DIR	219	ADD	B	DIR
028	*			092	INC	B		156	CPX		DIR	220	*		
029	*			093	TST	B		157	*			221	*		
030	*			094	*			158	LDS		DIR	222	LDX		DIR
031	*			095	CLR	B		159	STS		DIR	223	STX		DIR
032	BRA	REL		096	NEG	IND		160	SUB	A	IND	224	SUB	B	IND
033	*			097	*			161	CMP	A	IND	225	CMP	B	IND
034	BHI	REL		098	*			162	SBC	A	IND	226	SBC	B	IND
035	BLS	REL		099	COM	IND		163	*			227	*		
036	BCC	REL		100	LSR	IND		164	AND	A	IND	228	AND	B	IND
037	BCS	REL		101	*			165	BIT	A	IND	229	BIT	B	IND
038	BNE	REL		102	ROR	IND		166	LDA	A	IND	230	LDA	B	IND
039	BEQ	REL		103	ASR	IND		167	STA	A	IND	231	STA	B	IND
040	BVC	REL		104	ASL	IND		168	EOR	A	IND	232	EOR	B	IND
041	BVS	REL		105	ROL	IND		169	ADC	A	IND	233	ADC	B	IND
042	BPL	REL		106	DEC	IND		170	ORA	A	IND	234	ORA	B	IND
043	BMI	REL		107	*			171	ADD	A	IND	235	ADD	B	IND
044	BGE	REL		108	INC	IND		172	CPX		IND	236	*		
045	BLT	REL		109	TST	IND		173	JSR		IND	237	*		
046	BGT	REL		110	JMP	IND		174	LDS		IND	238	LDX		IND
047	BLE	REL		111	CLR	IND		175	STS		IND	239	STX		IND
048	TSX			112	NEG	EXT		176	SUB	A	EXT	240	SUB	B	EXT
049	INS			113	*			177	CMP	A	EXT	241	CMP	B	EXT
050	PUL	A		114	*			178	SBC	A	EXT	242	SBC	B	EXT
051	PUL	B		115	COM	EXT		179	*			243	*		
052	DES			116	LSR	EXT		180	AND	A	EXT	244	AND	B	EXT
053	TXS			117	*			181	BIT	A	EXT	245	BIT	B	EXT
054	PSH	A		118	ROR	EXT		182	LDA	A	EXT	246	LDA	B	EXT
055	PSH	B		119	ASR	EXT		183	STA	A	EXT	247	STA	B	EXT
056	*			120	ASL	EXT		184	EOR	A	EXT	248	EOR	B	EXT
057	RTS			121	ROL	EXT		185	ADC	A	EXT	249	ADC	B	EXT
058	*			122	DEC	EXT		186	ORA	A	EXT	250	ORA	B	EXT
059	RTI			123	*			187	ADD	A	EXT	251	ADD	B	EXT
060	*			124	INC	EXT		188	CPX		EXT	252	*		
061	*			125	TST	EXT		189	JSR		EXT	253	*		
062	WAI			126	JMP	EXT		190	LDS		EXT	254	LDX		EXT
063	SWI			127	CLR	EXT		191	STS		EXT	255	STX		EXT

Notes: 1. Addressing Modes:
A = Accumulator A B = Accumulator B
IMM = Immediate DIR = Direct EXT = Extended
REL = Relative IND = Indexed

2. Unassigned code indicated by "*"

Fig. 5-5. Decimal equivalents of machine codes

(by one) immediately following the storage in the stack of each byte of information. Conversely, the stack pointer is incremented (by one) immediately before retrieving each byte of information from the stacks, and the byte is then obtained from the address contained in the stack pointer. The programmer must ensure that the stack pointer is initialized to the required address before the first execution of one instruction that manipulates the stack.

Normally, the stack will consist of a single block of successive memory locations. However, some instructions in the source language change the address contained in the stack pointer without storing information in or retrieving information from the stack. The use of these instructions may result in the stack being other than one continuous sequence of memory locations. In such a case it may alternatively be considered that there exist two or more stacks, each of which consists of a block of successive locations in the memory.

5.17 SAVING CPU STATUS

The status of the microprocessing unit is saved in the stack during the following operations:

1. In response to an external condition indicated by a negative edge on the "nonmaskable interrupt" control input signal to the CPU.

2. During execution of the machine code corresponding to either of the source-language instructions SWI (software interrupt) or WAI (wait for interrupt).

3. During servicing of an interrupt from a peripheral device, in response to a negative edge on the "interrupt request" control input signal to the CPU [provided that the interrupt mask bit (1) is clear] .

The status is stored in the stack in accordance with the scheme shown in Figure 5-6. Prior to storing the status, the stack pointer contains the address of a memory location represented in Figure 5-6 by "m." The stack, if any, extends from location m+1 to higher locations. The status is stored in 7 bytes of memory beginning with the byte at location m and ending with the byte at location m-6. The stack pointer is decremented after each byte of information is entered into the stack.

The information which is saved in the stack consists of the numerical content of all the registers of the programming model, except the stack pointer.

The value stored for the program counter (PCH and PCL) is in accordance with the following rules:

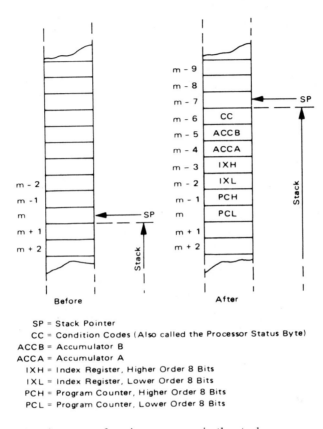

SP = Stack Pointer
CC = Condition Codes (Also called the Processor Status Byte)
ACCB = Accumulator B
ACCA = Accumulator A
IXH = Index Register, Higher Order 8 Bits
IXL = Index Register, Lower Order 8 Bits
PCH = Program Counter, Higher Order 8 Bits
PCL = Program Counter, Lower Order 8 Bits

Fig. 5-6. Saving the status of a microprocessor in the stack

1. If in response to a nonmaskable interrupt, or to an interrupt from a peripheral device, the value saved for the program counter is the address of that instruction which would be the next to be executed, if the interrupt had not occurred.

2. If, during execution of a SWI or WAI instruction, the value saved for the program counter is the address of that SWI or WAI instruction, plus one.

The values stored for the other registers (CC, ACCB, ACCA, IXH, and IXL) are in accordance with the following rules:

1. If, in response to a nonmaskable interrupt, or an interrupt from a peripheral device, the values saved are those which resulted from the last instruction executed before the interrupt was serviced.

2. If, during execution of a SWI or WAI instruction, the values saved

are those which resulted from the last instruction executed before the SWI or WAI instructions.

3. The condition codes H, I, N, Z, V, and C, in bit positions 5 through 0 of the processor condition codes register, are stored, respectively, in bit positions 5 through 0 of the applicable memory location in the stack. Bit positions 7 and 6 of that memory location are set (i.e., go to the 1 state).

5.18 INTERRUPT POINTERS

A block of memory is reserved for pointers, which provide for read-only storage of the addresses of programs that are to be executed in the event of a reset (or power-on), a nonmaskable interrupt signaled by a "low state" of the "nonmaskable interrupt" control input, a software interrupt, or a response to an interrupt signal from a peripheral device. Each of the respective pointers occupies two bytes of memory, and is disposed at locations from n-7 to n, as illustrated in Figure 5-7.

The location indicated in Figure 5-7 by n is that location that is addressed when all the lines of the address bus are in the high (i.e., 1) state. In most systems location n will be the highest address in the memory. However, the correspondence of n to a particular numerical value depends on the hardwired interconnections of the parts of the programmable system to the address bus.

5.19 RESET (OR POWER-ON)

The "reset" control input to the CPU starts the execution of the program, either for initial operation or from a power-down condition following a power failure. When a positive edge is detected on this input line, the program counter is loaded with the address stored in the restart pointer, at locations n-1 and n of memory. The CPU then proceeds with execution of a restart program, which begins with the instruction that is addressed by the program counter. The restart, and the continued execution, depends, however, on the "go/halt" control input being in the "go" condition.

When the go/halt control input is in the high state, the machine will fetch the instruction addressed by the program counter and start execution. When this line passes into a low state, execution will stop. The stop may become effective at the completion of execution of the current instruction. Alternatively, one more instruction may be executed before the stop becomes effective, due to the look-ahead capability described in more detail below. Execution of the program will not be resumed until the go condition is restored.

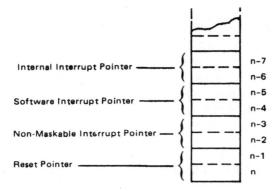

Internal Interrupt Pointer

Software Interrupt Pointer

Non-Maskable Interrupt Pointer

Reset Pointer

n-7
n-6
n-5
n-4
n-3
n-2
n-1
n

n = Memory Location Addressed When All Lines of
The Address Bus are in the High (1) State.

Fig. 5-7. Reset and interrupt pointers

The go/halt input must remain in the go condition for the interrupt sequences to be completed. Otherwise, the machine will stop execution at the end of an instruction. The following sections of this text, which describe the interrupt operations, assume that the go state is maintained.

5.20 NONMASKABLE INTERRUPT (NMI)

The sequence of operations that occurs following a nonmaskable interrupt is initiated by a negative edge on the nonmaskable interrupt control input to the CPU. Execution of the current instruction is completed. The response of the CPU to the nonmaskable interrupt signal may begin on the completion of execution of the current instruction. Alternatively, one more instruction in the program may first be executed, owing to the look-ahead capability of the CPU.

The status of the CPU is then saved in the stack. The program counter is then loaded with the address stored in the nonmaskable interrupt pointer, at locations n-3 and n-2 of memory. The CPU then starts execution of the nonmaskable interrupt program, which begins with the instruction now addressed by the program counter.

5.21 SOFTWARE INTERRUPT (SWI)

During execution of the SWI instruction, the status of the CPU is saved in the stack, as described previously. The value saved for the program counter is the address of the SWI instruction, plus 1.

After the status has been saved, the interrupt mask bit I is set (I = 1). The CPU will not respond to an interrupt request from a peripheral device while the interrupt mask bit is set.

The program counter is then loaded with the address stored in the software interrupt pointer, at locations n-5 and n-4 of memory. The CPU then proceeds with execution of a software interrupt program, which begins with the instruction used by the program counter.

The CPU will remain insensitive to an interrupt request from any peripheral device (signaled by a low state of the "interrupt request" control input signal to the CPU), until the interrupt mask bit has been reset by execution of the programmed instructions.

5.22 INTERRUPT REQUEST

A request for an interrupt by a peripheral device is signaled by a low state of the interrupt request control input to the CPU.

The CPU will not respond to an interrupt request while the interrupt mask bit is set ($I = 1$). Normal execution of the program would be continued until the interrupt mask bit is reset ($I = 0$), which then enables the CPU to respond to the interrupt request.

Execution of the current instruction will always be completed before the CPU responds to an interrupt request. The response of the CPU to the interrupt request may begin on the completion of the current instruction. Alternatively, one more instruction in the program may first be executed, owing to the look-ahead capability of the CPU. The response of the CPU to the interrupt request then proceeds as follows:

1. *Saving the status:* Provided the last instruction executed was not a WAI instruction, the status of the CPU will next be saved. The value saved for the program counter is the address of the instruction that would be the next to be executed if the interrupt had not occurred. This step is omitted if the last instruction executed was a WAI instruction. The reason for this is that the status was already saved by the WAI instruction in preparation for the interrupt.

2. *Interrupt mask:* The interrupt mask bit is then set ($I = 1$). This prevents the CPU from responding to further interrupt requests until the mask bit has been cleared by execution of programmed instructions.

3. *Internal interrupt pointer and program:* The program counter is loaded with the address stored in the internal interrupt pointer, at locations n-7 and n-6 of memory. The CPU then proceeds with execution of an internal interrupt program, which begins with the instruction now addressed by the program counter. The internal interrupt pointer is selected by logic, which is internal to the CPU. At the point when execution of the internal interrupt program

begins, no distinction will have been made regarding the source of the interrupt request.

In a system in which there is more than one possible source of interrupt request, the internal interrupt program must include a routine for identifying the origin of the request. As it applies to a system, the routine would consist of a programmed interrogation of the addressable registers of the PIAs and the ACIAs in order to identify the peripheral device that has requested the interrupt.

5.23 WAIT INSTRUCTION (WAI)

The status of the CPU is saved in the stack during execution of the WAI instruction. The value saved for the program counter is the address of the WAI instruction, plus 1.

Execution of the WAI instruction does not change the interrupt mask bit. If the interrupt mask bit is set (I = 1), the CPU cannot respond to an interrupt request from any peripheral device. Execution will stop after saving the status of the CPU. In this case, execution could be resumed only by a nonmaskable interrupt or a reset interrupt.

If the interrupt mask bit is in the reset state (I = 0), the CPU will service any interrupt request that may be present. If the interrupt request input is in the high state, execution will be suspended, and the CPU will wait for an interrupt request to be signaled. If an interrupt request is signaled by the interrupt request input passing to the low state, the interrupt will be serviced as described above. The interrupt mask bit will be set, the program counter will be loaded with the address stored in the internal interrupt pointer, and execution of the internal interrupt program will begin.

5.24 MANIPULATION OF THE INTERRUPT MASK BIT

The interrupt mask bit is affected by execution of the source language instructions SWI and RTI and by the servicing of an interrupt request from a peripheral device. The interrupt mask may also be manipulated by the use of any of the following instructions:

CLI—clear interrupt mask bit.

SEI—set interrupt mask bit.

TAP—transfer accumulator A to processor condition codes register.

The state of the interrupt mask bit will also affect the result of the following instruction: TPA transfer the processor condition codes register to accumulator A. During execution of the TPA instruction, the condition codes H, I, N, Z, V, and C, are in bit positions 5 through 0 of accumulator A. Bit positions 7 and 6 of accumulator A are set (i.e., go to the 1 state). After execution of the TAP instruction, the state of each of the condition codes H, I, N, Z, V, and C will be whatever is retrieved from the respective bit positions 5 through 0 of accumulator A.

5.25 SPECIAL PROGRAMMING REQUIREMENTS

A comprehensive program should make provision for the following special requirements:

1. *Pointers:* The program should place the addresses of the reset and interrupt routines in the respective pointers at the high-address end of memory. The addresses would usually be placed in the pointers by use of the FDB (form double constant byte) assembler directive in the source program.

2. *Reset and Interrupt Sequences:* The sequence of instructions to be addressed by the reset pointer, the nonmaskable interrupt pointer, the software interrupt pointer, and the internal interrupt pointer should be provided in the program.

3. *Input and Output:* The program would usually include provision for input and output relating to peripheral devices. In a programmable system, the input and output routines would involve reading and writing coded data from and into the addressable registers of the PIAs and ACIAs. The input and output routines would normally be reached via conditional branch instructions in the internal interrupt program.

5.26 LOOK-AHEAD FEATURE

At the completion of the instruction being executed, the CPU responds to any of the following signals:

1. Halt.

2. Nonmaskable interrupt.

3. Interrupt request (when the interrupt mask is in the reset state).

However, if the interrupt occurs during the last cycle of an instruction, look-ahead to the next instruction will mask the interrupt until the completion of the next instruction.

5.27 RETURN FROM INTERRUPT (RTI)

The source-language instruction RTI assembles into 1 byte of the machine code. Execution of this instruction consists of the restoration of the CPU to a state pulled from the stack.

Seven bytes of information are pulled from the stack and stored in respective registers of the CPU. The address stored in the stack pointer is incremented before each byte of information is pulled from the stack.

After execution of the RTI instruction, the state of each of the condition codes H, I, N, Z, V, and C will be whatever is retrieved from the respective bit positions 5 through 0 of the applicable memory location in the stack. In particular, it should be noted that the interrupt mask bit (I bit) may be either set or reset by execution of the RTI instruction.

5.28 SUBROUTINE LINKAGE

The stack provides an orderly method of calling a subroutine and returning from the subroutine. Use of a stack allows subroutine calls when in a subroutine (subroutine nesting).

5.29 CALL SUBROUTINE (BSR OR JSR)

A return address is saved in the stack during execution of the machine code corresponding to either of the source-language instructions BSR (branch to subroutine) or JSR (jump to subroutine).

The return address is stored in accordance with Figure 5-8. Before storing the address, the stack pointer contains the address of a memory location, represented in Figure 5-8 by m. The stack, if any, extends from memory location m+1 to higher locations. The return address is stored in 2 bytes of memory, at locations m-1 and m. The stack pointer is decremented after each byte of the return address is pushed into the stack.

For either of the instructions BSR or JSR, the return address which is saved in the stack is that of the next byte of memory following the bytes of code that correspond to the BSR or JSR instruction. Thus, for the BSR instruction, the return address is equal to the address of the BSR instruction, plus two. For the JSR instruction, the return address is equal to the address of the JSR instruction, plus three or plus two, according to whether the instruction is used with the extended or the indexed mode of addressing.

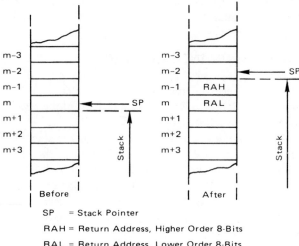

SP = Stack Pointer

RAH = Return Address, Higher Order 8-Bits

RAL = Return Address, Lower Order 8-Bits

Fig. 5-8. Saving and return address in the stack

5.30 RETURN FROM SUBROUTINE (RTS)

During execution of RTS instruction, the return address is obtained from the stack and is loaded into the program counter. The address stored in the stack pointer is incremented before each byte of the return address is pulled from the stack. This operation is the reverse of that represented in Figure 5-8.

5.31 DATA STORAGE IN THE STACK

The source-language instruction PSH is used for storing a single byte of data in the stack. This instruction addresses either register A or register B. The contents of the specified register is stored in the stack, in accordance with Figure 5-9. The address contained in the stack pointer is decremented.

Conversely, the source-language instruction PVL retrieves data from the stack. This instruction addresses either register A or register B. The addresses contained in the stack pointer is incremented. A single byte of data is then obtained from the stack and is loaded into the specified register. The operation is the reverse of that represented in Figure 5-9.

5.32 REENTRANT CODE

The reentrant code is an attribute of a program that allows the program to be interrupted during execution, to be entered by another user, and, subsequently, to be reentered at the point of interruption by the first user.

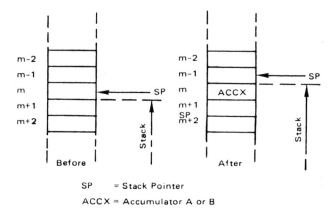

SP   = Stack Pointer

ACCX = Accumulator A or B

Fig. 5-9. Data storage in the stack

The reentrant code produces the desired results for all users, a program with an intermediate state of execution that is totally restorable when it is re-entered after an interruption.

The instruction TSX allows data on the stack to be manipulated by the indexed mode of addressing.

5.33 MANIPULATION OF THE STACK POINTER

The address saved in the stack pointer is affected by execution of the source-language instructions SWI, WAI, RTI, BSR, JSR, RTS, PSH, and PUL, as well as by the servicing of a nonmaskable interrupt or an interrupt request from a peripheral device, as has been described in previous paragraphs. In these operations, the stack pointer is coordinated with the storing and retrieval of information in the stack.

The address in the stack pointer may also be manipulated without storing or retrieving information in the stack. This is carried out by the following source-language instructions.

DES—decrement stack pointer.

INS—increment stack pointer.

LDS—load the stack pointer.

TXS transfer index register to stack pointer.

The use of any of these four instructions can result in the stack being other than a block of successive locations in memory.

The contents of the stack pointer is also involved in execution of the following instructions:

STS—store the stack pointer.

TSX—transfer stack pointer to index register.

The instruction TSX loads into the index register a value equal to the contents of the stack pointer, plus 1. The instruction TXS loads into the stack pointer a value equal to the contents of the index register, minus 1. This is in accordance with the operation of the stack pointer during execution of instructions SWI, WAI, BSR, JSR, or PSH, or during servicing of an interrupt from a peripheral device, in which the stack pointer is set to one less than the address of the last byte stored in the stack.

EXERCISES

5-1.   Give the various symbols used in flowcharting.
5-2.   Provide a flowchart for the sequence of events in leaving your residence by car, driving through town, and arriving at your work.
5-3.   Name the various types of flowcharts.
5-4.   Analyze bit position 11 and arrive at its hexadecimal equivalent.
5-5.   Describe mnemonic coding.
5-6.   What are symbolic addresses?
5-7.   Describe the functions of a stack pointer.
5-8.   What are interrupt pointers?
5-9.   How is the status saved in an interrupt request?
5-10.   What is a BSR or JSR? Describe.
5-11.   Describe data storage in the stack.

Peripheral Devices

6.1 INTRODUCTION

In addition to the CPU and memory devices, a microprocessor system must be equipped with some means of communicating with peripheral equipment such as audio cassette units, teletypes, CRT terminals, and keyboard/printers. The microcomputer manipulates parallel data byte information at high speeds relative to the slow-speed asynchronous data format required for communicating with peripherals. Therefore, an efficient interface adapter to convert the processor parallel data byte information into a serial asynchronous data format and vice versa is a highly desirable system function that relieves the microprocessor of this time-consuming task.

6.2 ASYNCHRONOUS COMMUNICATIONS INTERFACE ADAPTER

A device that provides the data formatting/interface function described above is the Asynchronous Communications Interface Adapter (ACIA) as illustrated in Figure 6-1. The asynchronous data format characteristics are used by this device to establish bit and character synchronization in the absence of a clock that has been presynchronized to the data. An asynchronous data format consists of a serial bit stream with the data bits preceded by a start bit and followed by one or more stop bits. The ACIA converts a character that was serially received from peripheral equipment to a parallel

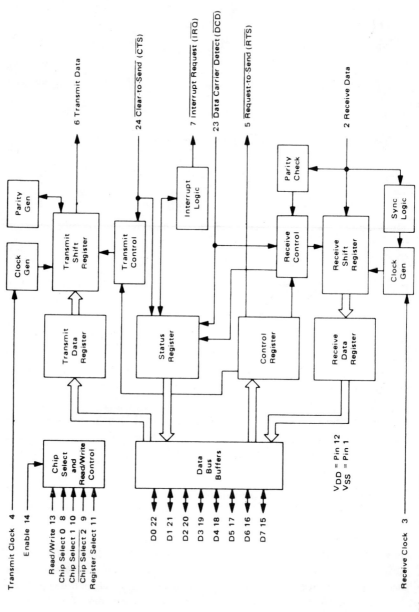

Fig. 6-1. Block diagram of an ACIA

142

byte with the start, stop, and parity bits deleted from the character. Furthermore, the parallel bytes from the microprocessor are converted to serial form with start, stops, and optional parity bits appended to the character. Performing these functions in hardware outside the processor enables the microprocessor to more efficiently communicate with peripheral equipment by using a minimum of software overhead.

The ACIA consists of control, status, transmit data, and receive data registers; data bus buffers; transmit and receive shift registers; and peripheral control.

Transmitter

In a typical transmitting sequence, a character is written into the transmit data register (TDR) if a status read operation indicated that the TDR was empty (TDRE). The write data command (trailing edge of the enable pulse) causes the TDRE status bit to go "low," indicating a transmitter data register full condition. During an idling condition (absence of data transmission), the transfer of data from the TDR to the transmit shift register will take place within one data bit time. This results in a delay (due to internal operation of the ACIA) in the transmission of the character from the transmit data output with respect to the write data command of one to two data bit times as illustrated in Figure 6-2. The trailing edge of the internal transfer signal returns the TDRE status bit to a "high" level, indicating a transmitter data register empty condition. The transmitter shift register

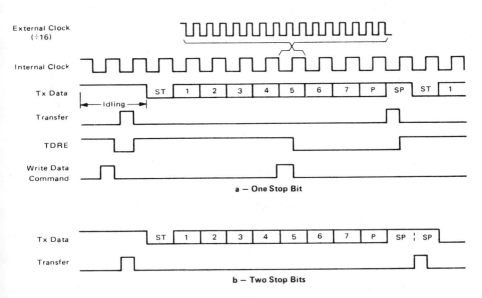

Fig. 6-2. Transmitter Asynchronous Operation

serializes the data and transmits the data bits, starting with data bit DO, preceded by a start bit and followed by 1 or 2 stop bits. Furthermore, internal parity (odd or even) can be optionally added by the ACIA, and will occur between the last data bit and the first stop bit.

The start, data, and stop bits are shifted out of the transmit shift register on the negative transition of the external transmit clock which is coincident with the negative transition of the internal clock. Selection of the external clock frequency is based on the data transmission rate and clock division ratio of the ACIA. For example, a data transmission rate of 300 bits/second (bps) requires an external clock frequency of 300 Hz in the ÷1 mode and 4800 Hz (16 times the data rate) in the ÷16 mode.

After the first character has been loaded into the TDR, the status register can be read again to check for a transmit data register empty condition and the current peripheral status. If the transmit data register is empty, another character can be written into the TDR, even though the first character is still being shifted out of the shift register, due to double buffering being used within the ACIA. Referring to Figure 6-2, the second character is transferred to the transmit shift register during the last stop bit time of the first character, resulting in a contiguous transmission of characters (isochronous transmission). If the second character is not written into the TDR prior to the last stop bit time of the character being transmitted, the transmitter will return to an idling condition at the end of that character time.

During the transmission operation, word length and stop bit select may be changed any time except during the internal transfer time without affecting the character being transmitted. The even/odd parity select will immediately affect the character presently being transmitted. Furthermore, changes in word length and parity select will affect the reception of data by the receiver.

Since the control register containing the functions above is common to both the transmitter and receiver sections, these functions for the transmitter must be changed when the receiver is not receiving data (i.e., idling). This control register consideration must also be adhered to for transmission between a local transmitter and a remote receiver.

Receiver

In many asynchronous data communications systems, the data are transmitted in a random manner without any additional synchronization signal. Therefore, the start and stop elements of the asynchronous characters are used to establish both bit and character synchronization. The receiver generates an internal clock that is synchronized to the data from an external clock source (Rx clock). As with the transmitter portion, the selection of the external clock frequency is based on the received data transmission rate and clock division ratio of the ACIA. For example, a data transmission rate of 300 bps requires an external clock frequency of 4800 Hz (16 times the data rate) in the ÷16 mode, and 19,200 Hz (64 times the data rate) in the ÷64 mode.

Bit synchronization in the ÷16 and ÷64 modes is initiated by the leading mark-to-space transition of the start bit. The start bit on the receiver data input is sampled during the positive transitions of the external clock as shown in Figure 6–3. If the input remains at a low level for a total of nine separate samplings in the ÷16 mode or 33 samplings in the ÷64 mode, which is equivalent to more than 50 percent of 8-bit times, the bit is assumed to be a valid start bit. This start bit is shifted into the shift register on the negative edge of the internal clock. Once a valid start bit has been detected, bit and character synchronization are obtained and the remaining bits are shifted into the shift register at their approximate midpoints.

If the receiver input returns to a mark state during the start-bit sampling period, this false start bit is ignored and the receiver resumes looking for the mark-to-space transition of a valid start bit; this technique is known as false start-bit deletion. The ACIA monitors the start bit on an incremental sampling basis rather than on a continuous sampling basis. This technique is a desirable feature for operation within a noisy environment and stems from the fact that a noise pulse occurring anywhere in a continuous sampling technique would initialize the monitoring logic; whereas in an incremental sampling technique, the noise pulse must occur during the sample to initialize the monitoring logic. The receiver will repeat this process for synchronization of each character in the message.

Divide-by-1 mode selection will not provide internal bit synchronization within the receiver. Therefore, the external receive clock must be synchronized to the data under the following considerations. The sampling of the start bit occurs on the positive edge of the external clock, and the start bit is shifted into the shift register on the negative edge of the external clock, as shown in Figure 6–4. For higher reliability of sampling, the positive transition of the external clock (sampling point) should occur at the approximate midpoint of the bit interval.

After the start bit has been detected, the remaining portion of the character being received is checked for parity, framing, and overrun errors.

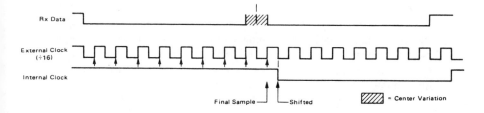

Fig. 6–3. Receiver Start Bit Detection (÷ 16 and ÷ 64 Modes)

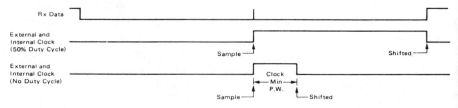

Fig. 6–4. Clock Requirement for ÷ 1 Mode

The complete reception of the character produces a high on the receiver data register full (RDRF) status bit, indicating that the receiver data register is full (Figure 6-5).

The received character is transferred to the receive data register (RDR) with the start, stop, and parity bits stripped from the character. At the same time, any receive data errors (parity, overrun, framing) are available in the status register in accordance with the status register definitions. The RDR is oriented such that the first data bit received is available on the DO output. The receiver is double buffered so that one character may be read from the data register as another character is being received in the shift register. During the reception of data characters, the absence of the first stop bit of the character will not result in the receiver losing character synchronization, but will indicate a framing error. This receive process is repeated for each character in the total message.

The ACIA contains an internal power-on reset circuit to detect the power line turn-on transition and to hold the ACIA in a reset state until initialization is complete to prevent the occurrence of any erroneous output transitions. In addition to the initialization of the transmitter and receiver sections, the power-on reset circuit holds the CR5 and CR6 bits of the control register at a logic 0 and logic 1, respectively. When CR5 = 0 and CR6 = 1, the $\overline{\text{Request-to-Send}}$ ($\overline{\text{RTS}}$) output is held high, and an interrupt from the transmitter is disabled. The power-on reset logic is sensitive to the shape of the V_{DD} power-supply turn-on transition. To ensure correct operation of the reset function, the power turn-on transition must have a positive slope throughout its transition. The conditions of the status register and other outputs during a power-on reset or software master reset are shown in Table 6-1.

The internal ACIA power-on reset logic must be released prior to the transmission of data by performing a software master reset function via the control register. Control register bits CR0 and CR1 are used to program a master reset condition while the remaining control register bits provide other functions.

The internal power-on reset logic will inhibit any change in bits CR5 and CR6 of the control register. Therefore, the control word that generates

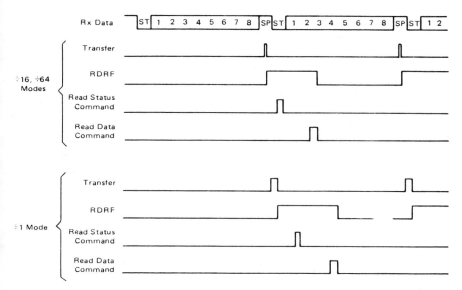

Fig. 6–5. Receiver Asynchronous Operation

the master reset function clearing the internal power-on reset will not change the RTS output or the internal transmit interrupt enable (TIE), as reflected in Table 6-1. Furthermore, the state of the receiver interrupt enable (RIE) bit of the control register has no external effect because the receiver is initialized by the master reset function.

After master reset of the ACIA, the programmable control register can be set for a number of options, such as variable clock divider ratios, variable word length, one or two stop bits, and parity (even, odd, or none). Furthermore, bits CR5 and CR6 of the control register are no longer inhibited and can now be programmed for several options.

During the initialization of the ACIA, the master reset function can be optionally used to establish a communications link without generating an interrupt from the transmitter or receiver sections. For example, the first control word, XXXXXX11-LSB (X = don't care), resets the power-on reset logic. To maintain a reset condition, the second control word, X01XXX11-LSB, holds the transmitter and receiver in a reset state and produces a low on the $\overline{\text{RTS}}$ output. The $\overline{\text{RTS}}$ output may be used to enable a local modem. The local modem, upon detection of a remote modem's carrier, will generate a low on the Clear-to-Send ($\overline{\text{CTS}}$) input of the ACIA. Since the $\overline{\text{CTS}}$ bit of the status register reflects the present status of the $\overline{\text{CTS}}$ input, the establishment of the communications link can be verified by reading the status register of the ACIA.

Table 6-1. Reset Functions

	POWER-ON RESET								MASTER RESET (Release Power-on Reset)								MASTER RESET (General)							
	b7	b6	b5	b4	b3	b2	b1	b0	b7	b6	b5	b4	b3	b2	b1	b0	b7	b6	b5	b4	b3	b2	b1	b0
Status register	0	0	0	0	x	x	0	0	0	0	0	0	x	x	0	0	0	0	0	0	x	x	0	0
IRQ Output				1								1								1				
RTS Output				1								1								x				
Transmit Break Capability			Inhibit								Inhibit								Optional					
Internal: RIE				0								x								x				
TIE				0								0								x				

Held by Power-on Reset

Defined by control register

(x = independent of reset function)

Status Register

ACIA status information is available to the CPU through the bus interface by means of the ACIA status register. Status information arrives from three sources: the receiving section, the transmitting section, and the peripheral status inputs.

Receiver Status

Receive Data Register Full (RDRF), Bit O. A logic high level on the RDRF bit indicates that data have been transferred to the receive data register and that the received data can be read from the ACIA. Reading the receive data register causes the RDRF status bit to go low. A low on the Data Carrier Detect ($\overline{\text{DCD}}$) input enables the RDRF status bit to be generated from a receive data register full condition. A high on the $\overline{\text{DCD}}$ input or a master reset condition will force the RDRF status bit to a low state until the $\overline{\text{DCD}}$ input returns to a low state. This is independent of the state of the status register $\overline{\text{DCD}}$ bit.

Transmitter Status

Transmit Data Register Empty (TDRE), Bit 1. The write data command causes the TDRE status bit to go low, indicating a data register full condition. An internal transfer signal transfers the data from the transmit data register to the transmit shift register and causes the TDRE bit to go high, indicating a transmit data register empty condition. The TDRE bit contains the present status of the transmit data register when the Clear-to-Send ($\overline{\text{CTS}}$) input is in a low state.

Peripheral Status

Data Carrier Detect ($\overline{\text{DCD}}$), Bit 2. A high level on the $\overline{\text{DCD}}$ input, indicating a loss of carrier, causes (1) the $\overline{\text{DCD}}$ status bit to go high; (2) the RDRF bit to be inhibited (low); and (3) immediate initialization of the receiver. When the receive interrupt enable (RIE) is set, a loss of carrier will cause (1) an interrupt to occur ($\overline{\text{IRQ}}$ output goes low), and, (2) the $\overline{\text{IRQ}}$ status register bit to go high. The characteristics of the $\overline{\text{DCD}}$ status bit and the associated $\overline{\text{IRQ}}$ status bit are as follows, with reference to the six segments in Figure 6–6, where each segment represents a specific condition. It is pointed out that the $\overline{\text{IRQ}}$ output is the inverse logic level of the $\overline{\text{IRQ}}$ status bit.

Segment 1: A master reset of the ACIA resets the interrupt status bit ($\overline{\text{IRQ}}$) generated by a loss of carrier.

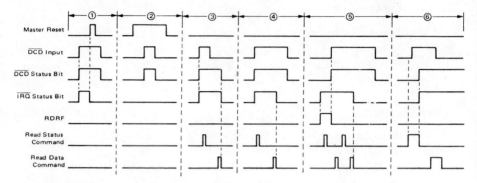

Fig. 6–6. Data Carrier Detect Variations

Segment 2: If the $\overline{DCD}$ input goes high during a master reset condition, the $\overline{DCD}$ status will reflect the state of the $\overline{DCD}$ input.

Segment 3: After an interrupt has occurred from a loss of carrier, the $\overline{IRQ}$ and $\overline{DCD}$ status bits are reset by first reading the status register and then reading the data register, provided the $\overline{DCD}$ input has returned to a low level.

Segment 4: If the $\overline{DCD}$ input remains high after a read status and a read data, the $\overline{IRQ}$ bit will be cleared, but the $\overline{DCD}$ status bit remains high and will follow the state of the $\overline{DCD}$ input.

Segment 5: If a read status occurs when the $\overline{DCD}$ input is low followed by a loss of carrier ($\overline{DCD}$ input goes high) prior to the read data command, this read data command will not reset either the $\overline{IRQ}$ or $\overline{DCD}$ status bits. The next read status followed by a read data will reset the $\overline{IRQ}$ status bit.

Segment 6: A transition of the $\overline{DCD}$ input during a read status or read data command is not recognized until the trailing edge of the read command. The $\overline{DCD}$ input to the ACIA must be tied low if it is not used.

Clear-to-Send ($\overline{CTS}$), Bit 3. The $\overline{CTS}$ status bit continuously reflects the state of the $\overline{CTS}$ input. A high on the $\overline{CTS}$ input will inhibit the TDRE status bit and associated interrupt status bit ($\overline{IRQ}$). The $\overline{CTS}$ input has no effect on a character being transmitted from the shift register or the character in the transmit data register (the transmitter is not initialized). Furthermore, the $\overline{CTS}$ bit is not affected by a master reset. The $\overline{CTS}$ input to the ACIA must be tied low if it is not used.

Framing Error (FE), Bit 4. A framing error indicates the absence of the first stop bit of a character, resulting from a loss of character synchronization, faulty transmission, or a "break" (all spaces) condition. If one of these conditions is present, the internal receiver transfer signal will cause the FE bit to go high. The next internal transfer signal will cause the FE status bit to be updated for the error status of the next character, as shown in Figure 6-7. A high on the $\overline{DCD}$ input or master reset will disable and reset the FE status bit.

Overrun Error (OVRN), Bit 5. A high state on the OVRN status bit indicates that a number of characters were received but not read from the receive data register, resulting in the loss of a character/or characters. The OVRN status bit is set when the last character prior to the overrun condition has been read. The read data command forces the RDRF and OVRN status bits to go high if an overrun condition exists. The next read data command causes the RDRF and OVRN status bits to return to a low level. During an overrun condition, the last character in the receive data register that was not read subsequent to the overrun condition is retained, since the internal transfer signal is retained. Figure 6-8 illustrates the timing events during an overrun error condition. A high state on the $\overline{DCD}$ input or a master reset disables and resets the OVRN status bit.

Parity Error (PE) Bit 6. If the parity check function is enabled, the internal transfer signal causes the PE status bit to go high if a parity error condition exists. The parity error status bit is updated by the next internal transfer signal, as shown in Figure 6-7. A high state on the $\overline{DCD}$ input or a master reset disables and resets the PE status bit.

Interrupt Request ($\overline{IRQ}$), Bit 7. A high level on the $\overline{IRQ}$ status bit may be generated from three sources: transmitter, receiver, and loss of carrier.

1. Transmitter—If the transmitter interrupt enable (TIE) is active, the state of the TDRE status bit is reflected by the $\overline{IRQ}$ status bit (see TDRE, bit 1).

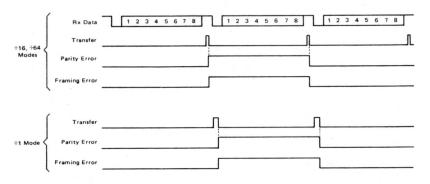

Fig. 6-7. Parity and Framing Errors

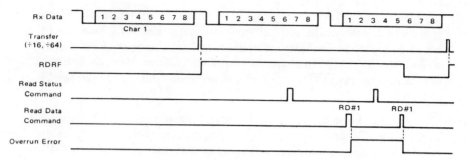

Fig. 6-8. Overrun Error

2. Receiver—If the internal receiver interrupt enable (RIE) is active, the state of the RDRF status bit is reflected by the $\overline{\text{IRQ}}$ status bit (see RDRF, bit 0).

3. Data carrier loss—a loss of carrier (logic high level) on the $\overline{\text{DCD}}$ input generates an interrupt on the $\overline{\text{IRQ}}$ status bit if RIE is active (see $\overline{\text{DCD}}$, bit 2).

The status information above is accumulated in a random asynchronous manner. Owing to the asynchronous nature of status updating, it is possible that the status word will change before or after the reading of the status register. This presents no problem during a status read cycle because no automatic status reset will occur. The response of the system to a status word will depend upon the status bit read. Should a status change not be registered, it can be read during the next read status cycle.

6.3 SYSTEM IMPLEMENTATION

In a microcomputer-based system, an address map of the system identifies the block of memory allocated for the system program, stack storage location, interrupt locations, peripheral addresses, and so on. The ACIA requires two addresses in the CPU system for addressing its four registers: control, status, transmit, and receive. To select a register within the ACIA requires the appropriate logic levels on the chip inputs (CS0, CS1, $\overline{\text{CS2}}$), register select input (RS), and read/write control input (R/W).

The R/W output line provided by the CPU is used to control writing into and reading from peripheral interface devices or memory. In addition, the R/W control selects one of the read or write registers in the ACIA. A combination of the chip selects and register select inputs can be used to minimize the amount of address decoding logic required for each peripheral. For example, the four Boolean combinations of address lines A14 and A15 select blocks of memory locations as shown in Figure 6-9. Assigning these blocks specif d functions, such as RAM, ROM, and peripheral devices, forms a memory ap of the system. In this example, the peripheral devices are assigned t addresses between 8000 and BFFF (hexadecimal notation). Assigning address bit A15 to CS0 and address bit A14 to $\overline{CS2}$ selects a peripheral device when A15 = 1 and A14 = 0. Since the ACIA requires two addresses, the use of address bit A0 for the RS input assigns two consecutive addresses for selection of the ACIA's four internal registers. Connecting the CS1 input to one of the other address lines allows the selection of 13 different peripherals without any additional decoding logic.

The peripheral side of the ACIA provides a means by which a microcomputer can efficiently control a peripheral device requiring an asynchronous serial data format. This format is generally used in, but not confined to, low and medium transmission rate systems—1800 bps and below. A teletype is an example system which has a transmission rate of 110 bps or 10 characters/second. An interface device is required between a teletype and an ACIA to convert the TTL compatible levels of the ACIA to the 20-mA current loop of the teletype. A noncomplemented data teletype interface requires an optical coupler with the addition of logic inverters, as shown in Figure 6-10.

The ACIA provides a means to control a modem for the transmission of data to and from a remote terminal, such as a teletype, over the telephone lines. The modem function can be implemented with a low-speed modem device, as shown in Figure 6-11. This device employs a frequency-shift keying (FSK) technique for the transmission of data up to a maximum data rate of 600 bps. A typical system consists of a local modem and a similar modem at the remote terminal. The local modem converts the digital data from the ACIA to analog form for transmission over the telephone lines. In a similar manner, analog data received from the remote modem is converted back to digital form by the local modem for use by the microcomputer system via the ACIA.

DEVICE	BLOCK OF MEMORY (Hexadecimal Notation)	ADDRESS															
		A15	A14	A13	A12	A11	A10	A9	A8	A7	A6	A5	A4	A3	A2	A1	A0
ROM	C000 – FFFF	1	1	x	x	x	x	x	x	x	x	x	x	x	x	x	x
Peripheral	8000 – BFFF	1	0	x	x	x	x	x	x	x	x	x	x	x	x	x	x
RAM	4000 – 7FFF	0	1	x	x	x	x	x	x	x	x	x	x	x	x	x	x
RAM	0000 – 3FFF	0	0	x	x	x	x	x	x	x	x	x	x	x	x	x	x
ACIA #1	8400 – 8401	CS0	$\overline{CS2}$	0	0	0	CS1	0	0	0	0	0	0	0	0	0	RS
ACIA #2	8020 – 8021	CS0	$\overline{CS2}$	0	0	0	0	0	0	0	0	CS1	0	0	0	0	RS

X = 1 or 0
CS0 = 1
$\overline{CS2}$ = 0
CS1 = 1
RS = 1 or 0

Fig. 6-9. Address Specification

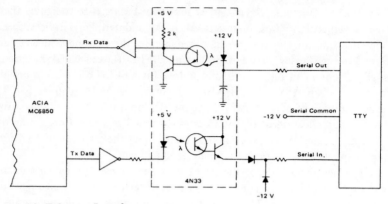

ı.g. 6–10. Teletype Interface
(Courtesy of Motorola Semiconductors)

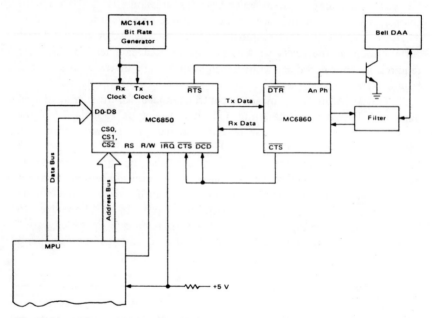

Fig. 6–11. ACIA to Modem Interface

Software

Since the internal registers of the ACIA and other CPU interface adapters appear as memory locations to the CPU, there is no need for special instructions in the CPU instruction set when interface adapters are employed. The CPU instructions most commonly used for writing information into the ACIA and reading information out of the ACIA are the store (STA) and load (LDA) instructions, respectively.

A store instruction causes the read/write (R/W) output of the CPU to go low, while a load instruction causes the R/W output to go high. Assigning consecutive addresses with address bus bit A0 tied to the ACIA register select input (RS) along with the R/W input allows access to one of the four ACIA internal registers, in accordance with Table 6-2. For example, an STA

Table 6-2. ACIA Register Selection

ADDRESS* LOCATION (Hexadecimal Notation)	STA INSTRUCTION (R/W = 0)	LDA INSTRUCTION (R/W = 1)
8400 RS = A0 = 0	Control register	Status register
8401 RS = A0 = 1	Transmit register	Receive register

*A0 tied to RS.

instruction to address 8400 (hexadecimal notation) performs a write to the ACIA control register, whereas an LDA instruction to the same address performs a read of the ACIA register.

The ACIA must be initialized prior to transmitting and receiving data. During a power-on transition, an internal power-on chip reset (latch) holds the $\overline{\text{IRQ}}$ output high to prevent the ACIA from interrupting the CPU or transmitting erroneous information. The power-on reset function is released by master-resetting the ACIA.

A master reset is accomplished by storing a word with bits B0 and B1 equal to 1 in the control register. After master resetting, the control register is programmed to set the counter divide ratio, word length, parity, interrupt control, and so on, which completes the initialization of the ACIA. After completion of initialization, the ACIA can then be used for transmitting and receiving data. Because of the length of data messages, the transmission of data is normally handled in subroutines to reduce the duplication of instructions.

6.4 PERIPHERAL INTERFACE ADAPTER (PIA)

Parallel-oriented peripherals can be connected to a CPU via the PIA. A basic block diagram is shown in Figure 6-12. The PIA contains two I/O circuit blocks, each capable of controlling an independent 8-bit peripheral I/O bus. Multiple PIAs can be used with a single system and selectively addressed by means of chip select inputs.

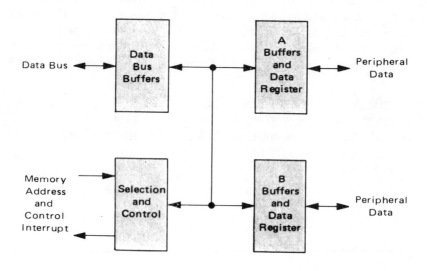

Fig. 6–12.

The PIA interfaces to the CPU with an 8-bit bidirectional data bus, three chip select lines, two register select lines, two interrupt request lines, read/write line, enable line, and reset line. These signals permit the CPU to have complete control over the PIA.

The various functions of the device are as follows:

Bidirectional Data (DO–D7). The bidirectional data lines (DO–D7) allow the transfer of data between the CPU and PIA. The data bus output drivers are three-state devices that remain in the high-impedance (off) state except when the CPU performs a PIA read operation. The read/write line is in the read (high) state when the PIA is selected for a read operation.

Enable (E). The enable pulse, E, is the only timing signal that is supplied to the PIA. Timing of all other signals is referenced to the leading and trailing edges of the E pulse. This signal will normally be a derivative of the CPU $\emptyset 2$ clock.

Read/Write (R/W). This signal is generated by the CPU to control the direction of data transfers on the data bus. A low state on the PIA read/write line enables the input buffers, and data are transferred from the CPU to the PIA on the E signal if the device has been selected. A high on the read/write line sets up the PIA for transfer of data to the bus. The PIA output buffers are enabled when the proper address and the enable pulse E are present.

$\overline{\text{Reset}}$. The active low $\overline{\text{Reset}}$ line is used to reset all register bits in the PIA to a logical "0" (low). This line can be used as a power-on reset and as a master reset during system operation.

Chip Select (CS0, CS1, and $\overline{\text{CS2}}$). These three input signals are used to select the PIA. CS0 and CS1 must be high and $\overline{\text{CS2}}$ must be low for selection of the device. Data transfers are then performed under the control of the enable and read/write signals. The chip select lines must be stable for the duration of the E pulse. The device is deselected when any of the chip selects are in the inactive state.

Register Select (RS0 and RS1). The two register select lines are used to select the various registers inside the PIA. These two lines are used in conjunction with internal control registers to select a particular register that is to be written or read.

The register and chip select lines should be stable for the duration of the E pulse while in the read or write cycle.

$\overline{\text{Interrupt Request}}$ ($\overline{\text{IRQA}}$ and $\overline{\text{IRQB}}$). The active low interrupt request lines ($\overline{\text{IRQA}}$ and $\overline{\text{IRQB}}$) act to interrupt the CPU either directly or through interrupt priority circuitry. These lines are "open drain" (no-load device on the chip). This permits all interrupt request lines to be tied together in a wire-OR configuration.

Each interrupt request line has two internal interrupt flag bits that can cause the $\overline{\text{Interrupt Request}}$ line to go low. Each flag bit is associated with a particular peripheral interrupt line. Furthermore, four interrupt enable bits provided in the PIA may be used to inhibit a particular interrupt from a peripheral device.

Servicing an interrupt by the CPU may be accomplished by a software routine that, on a prioritized basis, sequentially reads and tests the two control registers in each PIA for interrupt flag bits that are set.

The interrupt flags are cleared (zeroed) as a result of a CPU read peripheral data operation of the corresponding data register. After being cleared, the interrupt flag bit cannot be enabled to be set until the PIA is deselected during an E pulse. The E pulse is used to condition the interrupt control lines (CA1, CA2, CB1, CB2). When these lines are used as interrupt inputs, at least one E pulse must occur from the inactive edge to the active edge of the interrupt input signal to condition the edge sense network. If the inter-conditioned, the interrupt flag will be set on the next active transition of the interrupt input pin.

EXERCISES

6-1.   Explain the function of a UART (ACIA).

6-2.   Explain the function of a register select in a PIA.

6-3.   How can multiple PIAs be used with a single system?

6-4.   What is parity error? Explain.

6-5.   Provide a block diagram of a microprocessor system capable of receiving and transmitting data from/to a cassette recorder.

6-6.   Describe data carrier detect.

6-7.   What is an overrun error?

6-8.   Describe the master reset function during the initialization of an ACIA, and provide an example based on Table 6-1, other than the example described in the text.

6-9.   Name the various types of flowcharts and describe each of them.

7

Basic Microprocessor Design

7.1 INTRODUCTION

During the extensive research for the preparation of this text, it was discovered that, although the manufacturers' data books on CPUs and peripheral devices provide all the necessary electrical specifications, certain facts pertinent to actually connecting the various devices to obtain a desired result are not clearly explained. Unless one receives some sort of practical experience, the road to success will be a bit longer.

Although the purpose of this text is not to discuss "do-it-yourself" projects, the following practical example of a microprocessor system design explains step by step how the devices are interconnected and how one arrives at a result. The task of constructing the actual design must be left for the reader, but adequate information is given here as to past numbers and their value.

7.2 BASIC DESIGN

As stated previously, a basic microcomputer system requires the following units:

1. A central processing unit (CPU).

2. A read-only memory (ROM).

3. A random-access memory (RAM).

4. A peripheral interface adapter (PIA).

5. An asynchronous communications interface adapter (ACIA).

6. A clock generator.

7. Some sort of keyboard, display, and peripheral hardware.

The following Motorola devices have been selected for the present discussion:

1	MC6800	CPU
1	MCM6830	RDM with JBUG monitor
3	MCM6810	RAM (128 × 8)
2	MC6820	peripheral interface adapter (PIA)
1	MC6850	asynchronous communications interface adapter (ACIA)
1	MC6871B	clock generator
1		keyboard/display system

The basic block diagram of this system is shown in Figure 7-1. The detailed schematic diagrams of the microprocessor unit and the display unit are shown in Figures 7-2 and 7-3, respectively.

7.3 OPERATION OF THE SYSTEM

The system under discussion is equipped with a keyboard and display. Since all the devices have been chosen to operate at +5 V, a 5-V power supply is required. Choose a -2-A supply.

The keyboard has 16 keys, labeled 0 through F for entry of hexadecimal data, and 8 keys that command the following functions:

M: examine and change memory.

E: escape (abort) from operation in progress.

R: examine contents of CPU registers P, X, A, B, CC, S.

G: go to specified program and begin execution of designated program.

P: punch data from memory to magnetic tape.

L: load memory from magnetic tape.

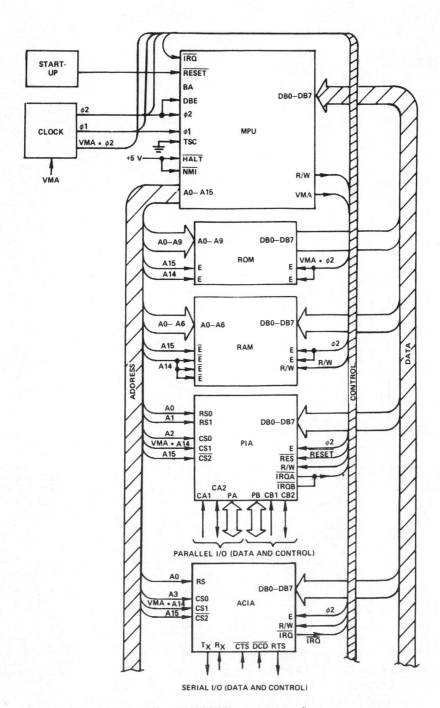

Fig. 7–1. Block diagram of an M6800 Microprocessor System
(Courtesy of Motorola Inc.)

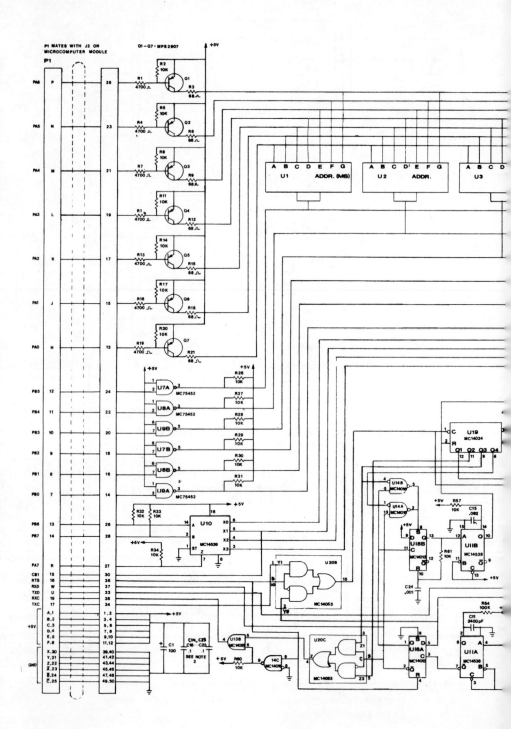

162

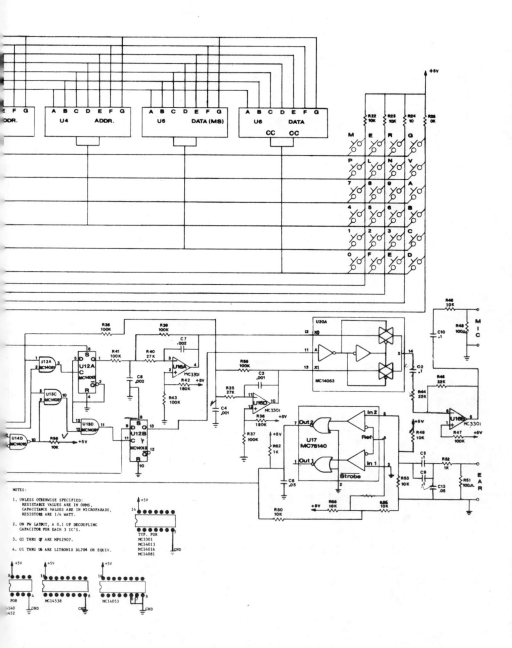

Fig. 7-2. Schematic diagram of the M6800 microprocessor system

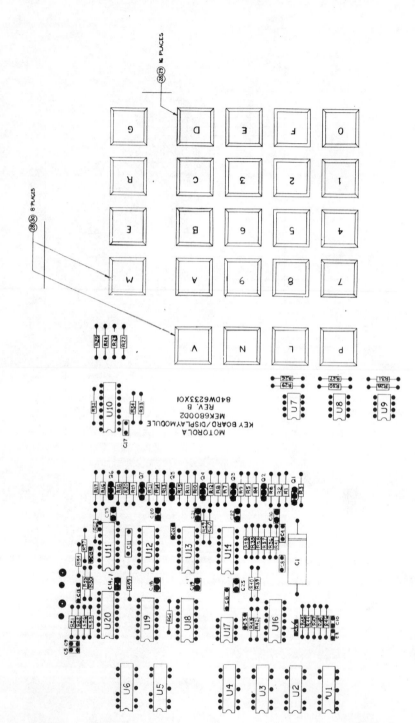

Fig. 7-3. M6800 display and Interface

N: trace one instruction.

V: set (and remove) breakpoints.

The operating procedures for each of these functions are described in the paragraphs that follow. If the reader has decided to actually construct the system under discussion, he should proceed as follows:

Apply 5-V dc power. When the reset switch is activated, the JBUG prompt symbol, a "dash," is displayed in the leftmost display indicator. The remaining five displays will be blanked. The JBUG control and monitor program is now in operation, and any of the functions described below may be invoked by means of the data and command keys. The display should indicate the prompt dash before any command is invoked.

7.4 MEMORY EXAMINE AND CHANGE (KEY M)

This function permits examination and, if required, change of memory locations. A map of the MC6800 instructions is shown in Table 7-1 and is useful in translating memory data to instruction mnemonics.

The memory location to be examined is opened by entering the address (as four digits of hex via the hex keyboard), followed by activation of the M key (hhhhM). The display will now show the address that was entered in its group of four displays on the left and the contents in the two displays on the right. At this point, the reader has the following three options:

1. Leave this location unchanged and move to the next location by depressing key G. The new address and its data would then be displayed.

2. Change the data by simply entering the new data via the hex keyboard (hh). In this case, the display would then be showing the new data that were entered. Any attempt to change the ROM would not affect the display from continuing to show the original data.

3. Activate the memory examine function by depressing the E key. This action will cause return of operation to the monitor, and the prompt will again be displayed.

7.5 ESCAPE (ABORT) FROM OPERATION IN PROGRESS (KEY E)

This function provides the proper exit from the other functions or programs. Examples of its use are included in the description of the other functions.

MSB\LSB	0	1	2	3	4	5	6	7	8	9	A	B	C	D	E	F
0	*	NOP (INH)	*	*	*	*	TAP (INH)	TPA (INH)	INX (INH)	DEX (INH)	CLV (INH)	SEV (INH)	CLC (INH)	SEC (INH)	CLI (INH)	SEI (INH)
1	SBA	CBA	*	*	*	*	TAB (INH)	TBA (INH)		DAA (INH)		ABA (INH)	*	*	*	*
2	BRA (REL)		BHI (REL)	BLS (REL)	BCC (REL)	BCS (REL)	BNE (REL)	BEQ (REL)	BVC (REL)	BVS (REL)	BPL (REL)	BMI (REL)	BGE (REL)	BLT (REL)	BGT (REL)	BLE (REL)
3	TSX (INH)	INS (INH)	PUL (A)	PUL (B)	DES (INH)	TXS (INH)	PSH (A)	PSH (B)		RTS (INH)		RTI (INH)			WAI (INH)	SWI (INH)
4	NEG (A)			COM (A)	LSR (A)		ROR (A)	ASR (A)	ASL (A)	ROL (A)	DEC (A)		INC (A)	TST (A)		CLR (A)
5	NEG (B)			COM (B)	LSR (B)		ROR (B)	ASR (B)	ASL (B)	ROL (B)	DEC (B)		INC (B)	TST (B)		CLR (B)
6	NEG (IND)			COM (IND)	LSR (IND)		ROR (IND)	ASR (IND)	ASL (IND)	ROL (IND)	DEC (IND)		INC (IND)	TST (IND)	JMP (IND)	CLR (IND)
7	NEG (EXT)			COM (EXT)	LSR (EXT)		ROR (EXT)	ASR (EXT)	ASL (EXT)	ROL (EXT)	DEC (EXT)		INC (EXT)	TST (EXT)	JMP (EXT)	CLR (EXT)
8	SUB (A) (IMM)	CMP (A) (IMM)	SBC (A) (IMM)	*	AND (A) (IMM)	BIT (A) (IMM)	LDA (A) (IMM)	*	EOR (A) (IMM)	ADC (A) (IMM)	ORA (A) (IMM)	ADD (A) (IMM)	CPX (IMM)	BSR (REL)	LDS (IMM)	*
9	SUB (A) (DIR)	CMP (A) (DIR)	SBC (A) (DIR)	*	AND (A) (DIR)	BIT (A) (DIR)	LDA (A) (DIR)	STA (A) (DIR)	EOR (A) (DIR)	ADC (A) (DIR)	ORA (A) (DIR)	ADD (A) (DIR)	CPX (A) (DIR)		LDS (DIR)	STS (DIR)
A	SUB (A) (IND)	CMP (A) (IND)	SBC (A) (IND)	*	AND (A) (IND)	BIT (A) (IND)	LDA (A) (IND)	STA (A) (IND)	EOR (A) (IND)	ADC (A) (IND)	ORA (A) (IND)	ADD (A) (IND)	CPX (A) (IND)	JSR (IND)	LDS (IND)	STS (IND)
B	SUB (A) (EXT)	CMP (A) (EXT)	SBC (A) (EXT)	*	AND (A) (EXT)	BIT (A) (EXT)	LDA (A) (EXT)	STA (A) (EXT)	EOR (A) (EXT)	ADC (A) (EXT)	ORA (A) (EXT)	ADD (A) (EXT)	CPX (A) (EXT)	JSR (EXT)	LDS (EXT)	STS (EXT)
C	SUB (B) (IMM)	CMP (B) (IMM)	SBC (B) (IMM)	*	AND (B) (IMM)	BIT (B) (IMM)	LDA (B) (IMM)	*	EOR (B) (IMM)	ADC (B) (IMM)	ORA (B) (IMM)	ADD (B) (IMM)	*	*	LDX (IMM)	*
D	SUB (B) (DIR)	CMP (B) (DIR)	SBC (B) (DIR)	*	AND (B) (DIR)	BIT (B) (DIR)	LDA (B) (DIR)	STA (B) (DIR)	EOR (B) (DIR)	ADC (B) (DIR)	ORA (B) (DIR)	ADD (B) (DIR)	*	*	LDX (DIR)	STX (DIR)
E	SUB (B) (IND)	CMP (B) (IND)	SBC (B) (IND)	*	AND (B) (IND)	BIT (B) (IND)	LDA (B) (IND)	STA (B) (IND)	EOR (B) (IND)	ADC (B) (IND)	ORA (B) (IND)	ADD (B) (IND)	*	*	LDX (IND)	STX (IND)
F	SUB (B) (EXT)	CMP (B) (EXT)	SBC (B) (EXT)	*	AND (B) (EXT)	BIT (B) (EXT)	LDA (B) (EXT)	STA (B) (EXT)	EOR (B) (EXT)	ADC (B) (EXT)	ORA (B) (EXT)	ADD (B) (EXT)	*	*	LDX (EXT)	STX (EXT)

DIR = Direct Addressing Mode
EXT = Extended Addressing Mode
IMM = Immediate Addressing Mode

IND = Index Addressing Mode
INH = Inherent Addressing Mode
REL = Relative Addressing Mode

A = Accumulator A
B = Accumulator B

*Unimplemented Op Code

Table 7-1.

166

7.6   REGISTER DISPLAY (KEY R)

This function permits examination of the CPU's registers and may be invoked at any time the JBUG prompt is being displayed by depressing the R key. At this point, the display will indicate a four-digit hex value, the present contents of the program counter. The remaining registers may now be examined by sequencing with the G key and will appear in the following order: index register, accumulator A, accumulator B, condition code register, stack pointer. It is the characteristic of the display routine that the value displayed for the stack pointer is seven less than the actual value.

This display is circular; that is, a G key depression, following display of the stack pointer, will cause the program counter to be displayed again. The E key may be used to escape back to the monitor at any point in the display sequence. If required, the contents of any register can be changed by using the memory change function. The monitor executes an interrupt sequence when the R key is depressed. In servicing an interrupt, the MC-6800 saves its registers on a stack in memory. (It is these memory locations that the R function "examines".) On exit from the R interrupt service routine, the CPU retrieves these values and reloads its registers; hence, if the data on the stack are changed with the M function, the new data will go into the CPU. The following locations are used to stack the registers (the dollar sign identifies hexadecimal data):

$A008	high-order byte of stack pointer.
$A009	low-order byte of stack pointer.
S+1	condition code register.
S+2	accumulator B.
S+3	accumulator A.
S+4	high-order byte of index register.
S+5	low-order byte of index register.
S+6	high-order byte of program counter.
S+7	low-order byte of program counter.

When S is the current stack pointer as saved in $A008 and $A009, note that it is necessary to exit the R display function and enter the M in order to change register values.

7.7 GO TO USER PROGRAM (KEY G)

If the prompt is being displayed, and assuming that a meaningful program has been previously entered, the CPU can be directed to go execute the program simply by entering the starting address of the program (via the hex keyboard), followed by depression of the G key (hhhhG). The resulting blanking of the displays is an indication that the CPU has left the monitor program and is executing the user's program. The CPU will continue executing the user program until either an escape (E key) is entered or the program "blows." Control, indicated by the prompt dash, can normally be obtained with the E key. It is possible that an incorrect program could have caused the variable data of the monitor to be modified. In this case, it is necessary to regain control using the reset switch.

7.8 PUNCH FROM MEMORY TO TAPE (KEY P)

The punch function allows the user to save selected blocks of memory on ordinary tape cassettes. Before initiating the punch function, the memory change function should be used to establish which portion of memory is to be recorded. Using memory change, the desired starting address may be entered into locations $A002 and $A003 (high-order byte into $A002, low-order byte into $A003). Similarly, the high- and low-order bytes of the desired ending address may be entered into $A004 and $A005, respectively. The monitor prompt dash may be obtained by escaping from memory change via the E key. The system under discussion is equipped with a microphone input terminal. With the audio recorder's microphone input connected to the corresponding point on the circuit and the prompt present, the punch function is performed as follows: The recorder is placed in the "record" mode. The P key is depressed. The prompt will disappear during the punch process and then reappear to indicate that the punch operation is completed. Typically, the prompt is off for over 30 seconds since the recording format specifies that a 30-second header of all ones be recorded ahead of the data. Further details on the recording format are provided in the sections that follow.

7.9 LOAD FROM TAPE TO MEMORY (KEY L)

The load function can be used to retrieve data that were recorded on tape, using the punch function described in the preceding paragraph. With the audio and recorder's earphone output connected to the corresponding input on the circuit and with the monitor prompt present on the display, the load function is performed as follows. To load the desired record, the tape is positioned at the approximate point from which the punch was started, and then the recorder is placed in its playback mode. Most cassette recorders have some sort of measuring tape length consumed, so it would not be difficult to identify the position of the punch on the tape once it has been originally determined. The L key is depressed. The prompt will disappear, then reappear when the load function is completed. After the prompt reappears, the memory examine function can be used to examine locations $A002 and $A003. They will contain the beginning address of the block of data that was just moved into memory. The end address is not recovered by the function; hence, the data in locations $A004 and $A005 are insignificant during the load function.

7.10 BREAKPOINT INSERTION AND REMOVAL (KEY V)

Owing to the difficulty in analyzing operation while a program is executing, it is useful during debugging to be able to set breakpoints at selected places in the program. This enables the user to run part of the program, then examine the results before proceeding. The breakpoints are set by entering the hex address of the desired breakpoint followed by a V-key depression (hhhhV). This may be repeated up to five times. The breakpoint entry function can be exited after any entry by depressing the E key. The monitor program will retain all the breakpoints until they are cleared.

If at any time an hhhhV entry is made and the hhhh (hex data) do not appear on the display, there were already five breakpoints stored and the last one was ignored. At any time the prompt is displayed, entry of a V command not preceded by hex data will cause the current breakpoints to be removed. If a breakpoint is entered and the program is subsequently executed to that point, the display will show the current value of the program counter in the four indicators on the left. (This will be the same as the breakpoint address that was inserted.) The two right-hand displays will contain the data stored at that location—that is, the operating code. At this point, the G key can be used to sequence through the other CPU registers exactly as in the register display function. If it is desirable to proceed on from the breakpoint, simply push the E key (to receive the prompt) and then the G key is depressed. Here, the CPU will reload its registers from the stack and continue with the user's program until another breakpoint is encountered or the E key is used again.

7.11 TRACE ONE INSTRUCTION (KEY N)

The trace function permits stepping through a program one instruction at a time. The trace function can be invoked any time the user program is at a breakpoint or has been aborted with the E key. However, tracing cannot begin from start-up because the trace routine does not know where the starting address is located. Therefore, an hhhhV command must be given at least once before trace can be used.

The trace function is entered by first setting a breakpoint at the location from which it is desired to trace, and then, depressing hhhhG, the program execution begins. The breakpoint can be set at the very beginning of the program, if desired. The procedure assumes that the program is in RAM, since breakpoints are handled by substituting an SWI for the op code. If the program to be traced is entirely in ROM, a convenient RAM location is used to insert a jump to the desired ROM address. Then a breakpoint is set at the address of the jump instruction.

Following the hhhhG command, the program will run to the breakpoint and stop, displaying the program counter, as before. If the H key is now closed, the CPU executes the next program instruction and again halts. The display will then show the address of the next instruction (program counter) and the operating code located there. The G key can be used to sequence the other registers onto the display as for a breakpoint, if desired. The N key can now be used to trace as many instructions as desired. It is a characteristic of the trace function that all breakpoints in effect at the time trace is invoked will be removed and must be reinstalled following exit from trace.

The trace function cannot be used directly to trace through user IRQ interrupts. The NMI is higher priority and will cause the IRQ to be ignored. Repeated attempts to execute the trace command when user IRQ interrupts are active will result in JBUG continuously returning with the same address.

Interrupt service routines may be traced by setting a breakpoint at the beginning of the service routine. The GO function may then be used to start.

7.12   OPERATING EXAMPLE

The following example program is suitable for gaining familiarity with the JBUG monitor features. If the reader has actually constructed the system, he can feed the program into it and more easily understand the operation. However, by using the schematic drawings and taking more time, the operation may be absorbed as well.

The program adds the five values in locations $10 through $14 using accumulator A and stores the final result in location $15. The intermediate total is kept in accumulator A; accumulator B is used as a counter to count down the loop. The index register contains a "pointer" (i.e., x contains the address) of the next location to be added. The program, as follows, contains an error that will be used at a later point to illustrate some of JBUG's features.

In the following listing the leftmost column contains the memory address where a byte (8 bits) of the program will be stored. The next column contains the machine-language op code and data for a particular microprocessor instruction. The next four columns contain the mnemonic representation of the program in assembler format.

				*
				* Add 5 numbers at locations 10–14
				* Put answer in location 15
0020	8E	STRT	LDS $FF	DEFINE STACK IN USER AREA
0021	00			
0022	FF			
0023	4F		CLRA	TOTAL #0
0024	C6		LDAB #4	INITIALIZE COUNTER
0025	04			
0026	CE		LDX #$10	POINT X TO LOCATION 10
0027	00			
0028	10			
0029	AB	LOOP	ADDA O,X	ADD 1 LOCATION TO TOTAL
002A	00			
002B	08		INX	POINT X TO NEXT LOCATION
002C	5A		DECB	DONE ALL 5 LOCATIONS?
002D	26		BNE LOOP	BRANCH IF NOT
002E	FA			
002F	97		STAA $15	SAVE ANSWER
0030	15			
0031	3F		SWI	GO TO JBUG

If the reader has constructed the system, he can enter it and debug it as follows:

1. *Starting up and entering the program in RAM*

    a. Turn power on. Push reset button. JBUG will respond with a "–".

    b. Type 0020 followed by the M key. This displays the current contents of location 0020.

c. Type 8E. This replaces the contents of 0020 with 8E which is the op code for the first instruction, LDS.

d. Type G. This steps to the next location (0021) and displays the contents.

e. Type 00.

f. Type G.

g. Type next byte of op code or operand (FF in this case)

h. Repeat steps f and g for remaining instructions.

i. Type E. Abort input function.

2. *Verify that the program was entered correctly*

a. Type 0020M. Location 20 will be displayed.

b. Type G. Next location will be displayed.

c. Repeat step b until done, verifying data entered in step 1.

d. Type E.

3. *Enter data in locations 10–14*

a. Same as step 1 except type 0010M to start the sequence. Any data may be entered; however, for purposes of this example, 01, 02, 03, 04, and 05 should be entered.

b. Type E.

4. *Verify data*

a. Repeat step 2 except type 0010M to begin the sequence. Verify that the memory contains the values 01, 02, 03, 04, and 05 in sequential order.

5. *Run the program*

a. Type E to ensure that no other portion is active.

b. Type 0020G. The program will run down to the SWI instruction at location 31, which will cause it to go to JBUG and show 0031 3F on the display.

6. *Check the answer*

a. Type E.

b. Type 0015M. (The answer is stored in location 15.) Note that it says 0A (decimal 10). The correct answer is 0F or decimal 15; therefore, there is a problem in the program as originally defined. The next steps should help in isolating and correcting the problem.

7. *Breakpoint and register display*

a. It may be helpful to see what the program was doing each time it went through the loop. Therefore, set a breakpoint at the beginning of the loop, location 0029. To do this, type E and then type 0029V.

b.   A breakpoint could also be set at location 002F so the results may be observed. Type E. Type 002FV.

c.   JBUG must be instructed where to begin, so type E and then 0020G. JBUG will run to the breakpoint and then display 0020-AB. At this point, the program is suspended just before location 29 and is in JBUG. On detecting this breakpoint, JBUG automatically displays the PC and is in the register display mode.

d.   Type G (go to next register). The display should read 0010. This is the value of the X register.

e.   Type G. Display = 00 (register A).

f.   Type G. Display = 04 (register B).

g.   Type G. Display = DO (condition code register).

h.   Type G. Display = 00FB (stack pointer). Even though the program set the stack pointer to FF, the action of the breakpoint used a software interrupt to store the registers on the stack, thus decrementing it by seven locations. When JBUG returns to the user's program, the stack will return to FF.

i.   Type G. Display = 0029 (PC). The register display is circular and steps d through h could be repeated.

j.   Type E. Abort the register display of the breakpoint. Type G to return to the example program and resume executing. Since the breakpoint at location 0029 is in a loop, it will again be the next breakpoint and the display will contain 0029 AB. At this point, the registers may be displayed again as per steps d through i. If this were done, A would contain the partial sum and B would be decremented. The X register would be 1 greater than previously.

k.   Type E.

l.   Type G (proceed). Display will type 0029 AB. Once again, the registers may be examined.

m.   Type E.

n.   Type G (proceed). Same procedure as in step l.

o.   Type E.

p.   Type G (proceed). Display will now show 002F 97. The program has now successfully completed the loop four times, and the A register contains the incorrect sum.

8. *Correcting the program*

a.   From the above, it is evident that although the program was supposed to add five numbers, the loop was executed only four times. Therefore, the LDAB#4 instruction at locations 24 and 25 should have initialized B to five. There are two approaches to correct the problem; one is temporary, the other is permanent. The temporary approach follows:

b.   Type E.

c.   Type V, clearing existing points.

d.   Type 0026V. Set a breakpoint just after register B is loaded.

e.   Type E.

f.   Type 0020G. The program will execute up until 0026 and then go to JBUG. Display = 0026 CE.

g.   Type G five times. This displays the current stack pointer (00F8). The B register contains the counter that we wish to modify and is located at location SP+2 (FA).

h.   Type E.

i.   Type 00FAM. Display = 00FA 04.

j.   Type 05. Display will change to 00FA 05.

k.   Type E.

l.   Type G. Proceed from user breakpoint down to the SWI instruction.

m.   Type E.

n.   Type 0015M. Display = 0015 0F. The program has now calculated the correct value for the addition of the five numbers 1-5. This verifies the fix but would be inconvenient to carry out each time the program was executed. A permanent change would be as follows:

o.   Type E, then type V, clearing all breakpoints.

p.   Type 0025M. Display = 0025 04.

q.   Type 05. Display = 0025 05. This will now permanently change the LDAB#4 instruction to a LDAB#5 instruction.

r.   Type E.

s.   Type 0020G. Execute the program.

t.   Type E.

u.   Type 0015M. Display = 0015 0F, the expected answer; the program is permanently fixed.

9.   *Trace through the program*

a.   Type E. In order to execute a trace, the program must first be stopped at a breakpoint. To trace from the beginning, proceed as follows:

b.   Type V, clearing the existing breakpoints.

c.   Type 0020V, setting a breakpoint at the first instruction.

d.   Type E.

e.   Type 0020G (go to user program). JBUG will immediately get the breakpoint and type 00208E.

f.   Type N. The program will execute one instruction and display 0023 4F. At this point, the user can either display the registers by depressing the G key or continue to the next instruction. To continue:

g.   Type N. Go to the next instruction. Display register if register.

h.   Continue step g for as long as desired. (*Note:* Do not try to trace after executing the SWI instruction; a restart will be necessary before continuing.)

i.   Type E. Clear the trace mode.

10.   *Offset calculation, including register modification*

a.   Assume that the SWI instruction at location 31 is to be changed always to a branch (BRA) to location 20. This will cause the program to remain in an infinite loop (i.e., the program has no end and will run continuously unless interrupted by some outside stimuli). Type 0031 to open the memory location. Display = 0031 3F.

b.   The op code for a BRA is a 20, so type 20. Display = 0031 20.

c.   The second byte of the BRA instruction should be the two's-complement negative offset to location 20. Since doing this calculation in hex is tedious and error prone, a small unsophisticated (there was only a little ROM left) program that does offset calculation was provided at location E000 in the JBUG ROM.

d.   Type E.

e.   Type R, then type five G's. This will display the current stack pointer so that the registers can be located and set up.

f.   Type E.

g.   Type in hhhhM, where hhhh = SP+2. This displays the current B register.

h.   Type 00. This is the high byte of the destination address of the branch.

i.   Type G. This displays location SP+3 which contains the A-register value.

j.   Type 20. This is the low byte of the destination address.

k. Type G. Display high byte of X register.

l. Type 00. Insert high byte of the branch op-code address.

m. Type G. Display low byte of X register.

n. Type 31. Insert low byte of the branch op-code address.

o. Type E.

p. Type E000G. When the program is completed, it will return to JBUG via the SWI at location E013 and the PC will be displayed.

q. Type G twice. The A register is now displayed and contains ED, which is the correct offset.

r. Type G. The B register will contain an FF to indicate the branch was within range.

s. Type E.

t. Type 0032M.

u. Type ED, inserting the branch offset.

11. *Executing and aborting*

a. Type E.

b. Type 0020G. The program will begin executing and the JBUG prompt "–" will disappear since the program now contains an infinite loop.

c. Type E. This aborts (exits) the program and returns control to JBUG. The prompt has now returned.

d. Type R. Display the PC and any other registers of interest.

e. Type E.

f. Type G. Program will again execute.

g. Type E. Abort program and return to JBUG.

h. Repeat steps f and g as many times as you wish.

12. *Punch program to cassette*

a. Rewind the cassette. Type E.

b. Type A002M.

c. Type 00. Enter high byte of beginning address.

d. Type G.

e. Type 20. Enter low byte of beginning address.

f. Type G.

g. Type 00. Enter high byte of ending address.

h. Type G.

i.   Type 32. Enter low byte of ending address.

j.   Type E.

l .   Turn on cassette record mode.

l.   Type P. Wait for JBUG prompt to return (approximately 30 seconds).

13. *Load program from cassette*

a.   Turn off power. This will cause the program in memory to be lost. Turn power back on.

b.   Push the reset button and get the JBUG prompt.

c.   Rewind cassette.

d.   Start cassette in playback mode.

e.   Type L. Wait for the JBUG prompt. Test the program by any of the options described above.

EXERCISES

7-1.   You are assigned the task of designing a microprocessor-based cash register. Provide a block diagram for the system. The requirements for the system are the following: memory, CPU, keyboard, printer, display, cash drawers, and power supply.

7-2.   Could you employ a 680-based system in Exercise 1? If so, provide a block diagram.

7-3.   What should a basic microcomputer system consist of?

7-4.   Describe the abort function in the 6800.

7-5.   Describe the function of key G in the system.

7-6.   Should you decide to actually construct the 6800 system, what power-supply rating would you use?

Hardware Systems

8.1 INTRODUCTION

The microprocessor system discussed in Chapter 7 is equipped with a keyboard, display, and, if desired, cassette recorder. These devices are hardware systems which connect the microprocessor with the outside world. They enable the user to enter data into or receive data from the system. Other hardware systems—tape printers, teletype machines, floppy disks, and so on—are described below.

8.2 FLOPPY DISKS

Floppy disks have become an essential system for storage of data. The floppy disk (or *diskette* as it is often called) is a magnetic storage medium, permanently contained in a paper envelope. It is operated by an electromechanical drive which performs all the read/write functions necessary to record and recover data on the disk.

A block diagram of a floppy disk system is shown in Figure 8-1 and could be very well employed in the microprocessor system described in Chapter 7. Data are recorded serially on the floppy disk. However, if the user decides to employ the system shown in the figure to the M6800 microprocessor, it is necessary, because of the high serial data rates, to use auxiliary logic for the serial/parallel conversion, data recovery, and data error checking. The hardware that performs this function is usually called a *formatter*.

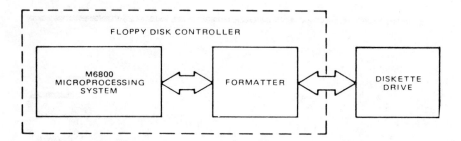

Fig. 8-1. M6800 Floppy Disk Subsystem
(Courtesy of Motorola Inc.)

This device, in conjunction with the microprocessor system, controls the diskette drive.

A functional diagram, showing all the control lines between the floppy disk system and the PIAs, is illustrated in Figure 8-2. Two PIAs are used in the system. PIA 1 is used on a data buffer; PIA 2 is used as a control, status, and interrupt interface. Peripheral register A in PIA 1 is the write clock buffer register for write operations and the read data gate for read operations. Peripheral register B in PIA 1 is the write data buffer for write operations and is used as a status signal gate for read operations. PIA 1 peripheral ports A and B are used in both inputs (read operation) and outputs (write operation). Because all data field operations must be preceded by a read ID field operation, the direction registers must be restored to all zeros in preparation for a read operation.

CA1 and CA2 of PIA 1 are used to synchronize the timing of the program to the data rate during read or write operations. Data synchronization is controlled by polling for interrupt flag 1. An active transition of the CA1 line causes interrupt flag 1 of control register A to be set to a 1. A minimum of eight cycles are required so that the CPU may recognize that the flag has been set. After the flag is recognized by the CPU, write or read data are transferred to or from the PIA. For instance, at a 1-MHz CPU clock rate, there is a minimum 8-μs delay between recognition of the service request and servicing the PIA.

The byte ready/byte request CA1 signal is one bit period in duration. It goes low at the beginning of the last serial bit time of a byte, then returns high at the beginning of the next serial byte, as shown in Figure 8-3. Because of the 8-μs program delay, the interrupt flag could be set at the beginning of the last bit period even though the data will not be ready until the end of that period. This look-ahead technique can provide additional processing time in critical timing areas of the program.

The CA2 line is the CPU's response to the disk system, indicating that the service request at CA1 has been accepted. It is used to signal overrun

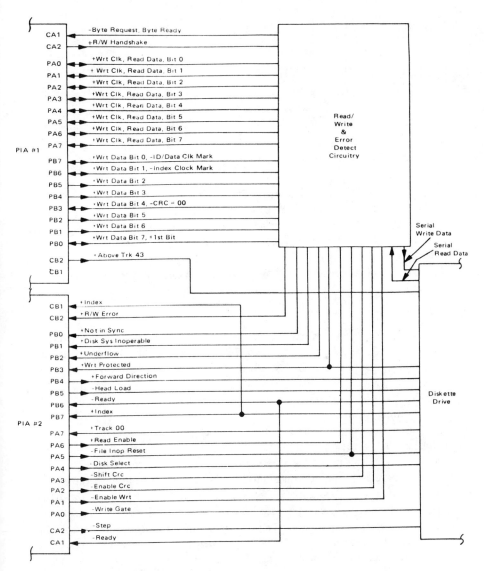

Fig. 8-2. Floppy Disk Functional Interface

errors for the read operation and underflow errors for the write operation.
The CA1/CA2 operation of PIA 1 is a handshake mode of operation in which
CA2 is set high on an active transition of CA1 and returned low by a CPU
read instruction (LDA, BIT, etc).

CB2 of PIA 1 is a control signal called "ABOVE TRK 43" that is used
only in write operations. When data are recorded on a diskette track greater

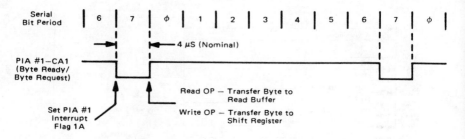

Fig. 8-3. Byte Ready/Request Interface

than 43, this line is raised high. The signal from CB2 controls the write current amplitude or inner tracks in order to reduce the effects of a phenomenon called "bit shift." The bit density of the diskette increases as the radius of the track location decreases. This means that the magnetic flux reversal of the bit being written affects the bit that had just been written. The magnetic field generated by the R/W head is approximately proportional to the amount of current in the head. The ABOVE TRK 43 signal causes less current to pass through the R/W head, thereby reducing the intensity of the magnetic field.

PIA 2 is used as a control, status, and interrupt interface. The control signals are from PA0 through PA6, PB4-PB5, and CA2. Status signals are PA7, PB0, PB1, PB2, PB3, PB6, and PB7. The interrupt signals are CA1, CB1, and CB2. The floppy disk records data on 77 circular tracks, numbered 00-76. In order to access a certain record, the R/W head must first be locked in position at the track which contains that record. The operation that performs the head movement function is called a *seek operation*. For the floppy disk, a seek operation is executed by stopping the head one track at a time. The timing between steps is controlled by an interval timer.

The restore operation is similar to the seek operation, with the exception that a restore operation always moves the R/W head to track 00. After completion of the seek operation, the only way to verify that the proper track has been accessed is to read the track address of the ID field. When track 00 is accessed, the diskette drive generates a TRACK 00 status signal from an electromechanical sensor. The restore operation is completed when the TRACK 00 signal goes active.

8.3 PRINTERS

The availability in style and quality of printers is at present extensive, ranging from slow but economical units that print out supermarket receipts to the high-quality and high speed units capable of printing 1200 132-character lines per minute.

As with any other hardware systems, printers are interfaced with the main microprocessor system through peripheral devices, such as PIAs, which control their operation. The functional diagram of a printer interface is illustrated in Figure 8-4. In this case, the printer is a cash register type. Its drum is equipped with 42 characters which may be printed in a 21-column format. Each column position has a complete character set spaced evenly around the drum. As a result of the gear ratio of the mechanism (42:1), the ratchet rotates 42 times for each complete drum rotation. Hence, each character of the set is positioned under a print hammer once during every rotation of the drum.

The basic task of the control program is to examine the text of the message to be printed and ensure that the appropriate bits in the PIA's output registers are set at the proper time. The details of timing are illustrated in Figure 8-5. In order to understand the operation, one is assisted by regarding the time for one print drum rotation as 42 equal intervals, t_0 through t_{41}. It is noted here that all similar characters in the text are printed simultaneously (i.e., all zeros are printed during t_0, all ones during t_1, etc.). For

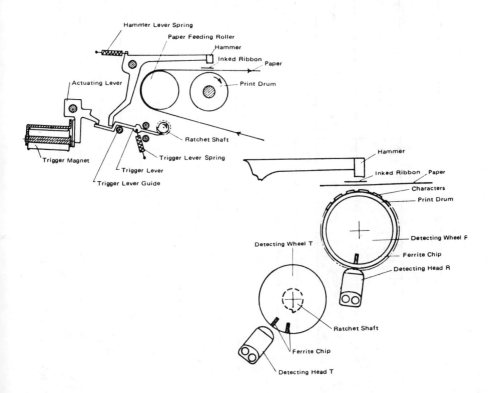

Fig. 8-4. Printer Interface

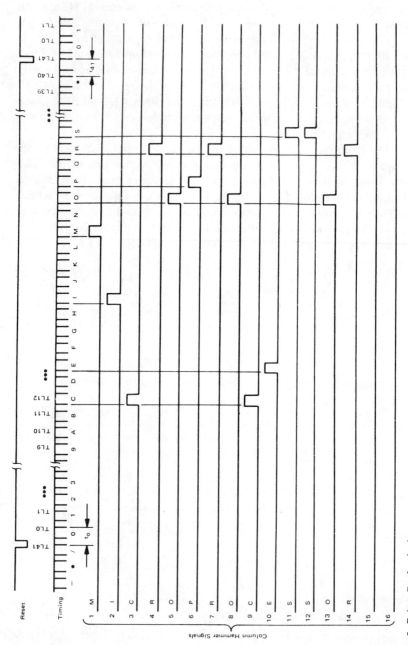

Fig. 8-5. Print Cycle timing

184

example, if the text requires the letter C in columns 3 and 9, column hammers 3 and 9 must be engaged during the time interval t_{12} during which all C's are under the hammers.

Following each TL interrupt, the CPU examines the entire message to see if there are any characters to be printed during the next time interval. The text to be printed may be either a "canned" message stored in ROM or variable information generated by the executive program and stored in RAM. Messages are stored in memory in 16-byte blocks with each memory position corresponding to a printer column position. Prior to calling the printer, the executive program loads the starting address of the message to be printed into a buffer. The printer routine then uses this address in conjunction with the CPU's indexed addressing mode to locate the desired message; this technique permits use of the same subroutine for all of the system printer requirements.

8.4 TELETYPE SYSTEMS

Teletypes are very popular hardware systems in the computer world. Their operation is very similar to that of an ordinary typewriter, with the exception that a teletyper has some additional keys, as shown in Figure 8-6. These additional keys are control keys, and their function is as follows:

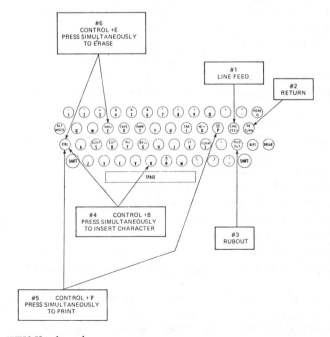

Fig. 8–6. TTY Keyboard

1. The line feed key advances the paper on which the information is printed, by one line.

2. During printing, the printing mechanism moves from left to right. The return key moves the printing mechanism to the left-hand margin.

3. Since the information is typed into the microcomputer memory, the rubout key is used to delete from memory the last typed character or control key. Additional preceding characters can be deleted by continuing to press the rubout key. This key affects the editing function of the system.

The teletype belongs to the data communications hardware system. It can be connected to the ACIA (UART) either directly or through a pair of modems. Modems enable data stored at a remote site to be transmitted over the telephone lines to a microprocessor system. Thus, the only major difference in the software required for the two systems lies in the modem control functions. A block diagram of both functions is shown in Figure 8-7. The hardware requirements to interface a teletype to the microprocessor system include the ACIA and some form of voltage-to-current interface circuit. The current interface circuits may vary to accommodate the particular teletype used within the data system.

Two of the most common methods of receiving data from a teletype are from a keyboard, such as the one described above, or a teletype paper tape reader. Furthermore, the paper tape reader can have either manual or automatic control. The automatic paper tape reader turns on and off by internally decoding words received on the serial input line. A DC1 control word turns the reader on, whereas a DC3 control word turns the reader off; DC1 and DC3 control words are teletype requirements.

A conventional interface system between the microprocessor and the teletype is shown in Figure 8-8. The manual paper tape reader requires an externally provided relay to turn the reader on and off via the ACIA. In Figure 8-8, the $\overline{\text{Request-to-Send}}$ ($\overline{\text{RTS}}$) output of the ACIA is used to control the relay; the $\overline{\text{RTS}}$ output is normally used for interfacing into a modem.

A microprocessor system can communicate over the telephone lines to a remote peripheral device by the use of a modem and an ACIA, as shown in Figure 8-9. The modem takes serial digital data and converts them to an analog signal for transmission over the telephone lines. Incoming data in analog form from the remote modem are converted to serial digital form by the on-site modem.

The ACIA provides the microprocessor system with the ability to control the handshaking requirements of the modem. The first step requires that the $\overline{\text{Data-Terminal-Ready}}$ ($\overline{\text{DTR}}$) input be low to enable the modem to complete the handshaking. Response by the remote modem to the on-site

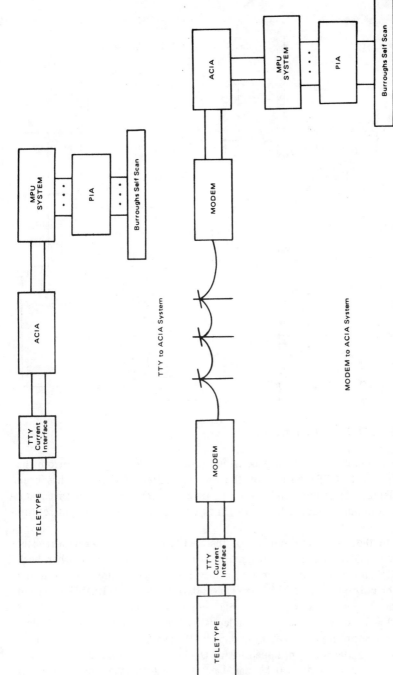

Fig. 8-7. TTY to ACIA and Modem to ACIA Interface
(Courtesy of Motorola Inc.)

187

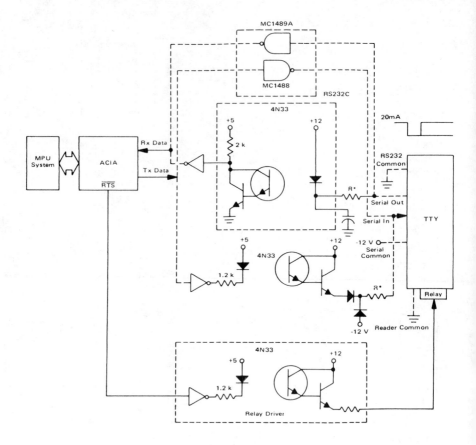

Fig. 8–8. CPU to TTY Interface

modem completes the handshaking and results in a low logic level from the Clear-to-Send ($\overline{\text{CTS}}$) output of the modem. After handshaking has been completed, the remote and on-site systems can transmit and receive data. When communications is lost between the modems, the $\overline{\text{CTS}}$ output returns high.

In the transmitter portion of the ACIA, the transmitter data register empty (TxDRE) flag and associated interrupt ($\overline{\text{IRQ}}$) are enabled when both the $\overline{\text{CTS}}$ and transmitter interrupt enable (TIE) functions are enabled. In the receiver portion of the ACIA, the receiver data register full (RxDRF) flag and associated interrupt ($\overline{\text{IRQ}}$) are enabled when both the Data Carrier Detect ($\overline{\text{DCD}}$) and receiver interrupt enable (RIE) functions are enabled; the low to high transition of the $\overline{\text{DCD}}$ input with RIE enabled generates an interrupt ($\overline{\text{IRQ}}$). In modems not equipped with a Data Carrier Detect output, the $\overline{\text{DCD}}$ and $\overline{\text{CTS}}$ inputs of the ACIA can be connected together, resulting in an interrupt ($\overline{\text{IRQ}}$) being generated when communications is lost.

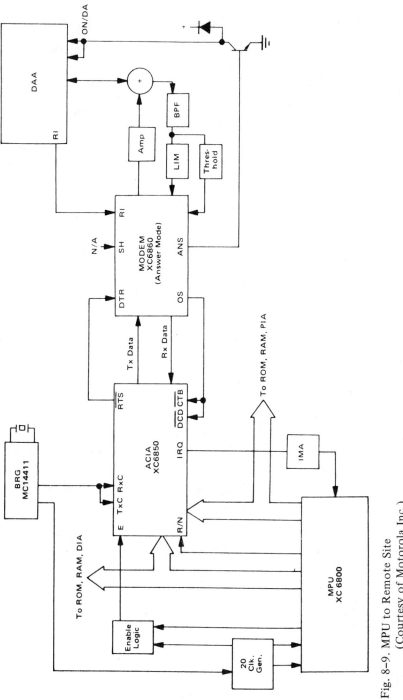

Fig. 8–9. MPU to Remote Site
(Courtesy of Motorola Inc.)

189

When used separately, the $\overline{\text{DCD}}$ and $\overline{\text{CTS}}$ inputs of the ACIA allow the use of higher-performance modems. For example, a high-performance modem will transmit on one pair of wires and receive on another pair, referred to as a *four-wire modem system*. As in the low-speed modem system, the CPU, via the ACIA, generates a $\overline{\text{DTR}}$ and, after a time delay, the $\overline{\text{CTS}}$ output of the high-performance modem goes low. The transmitter can start transferring data immediately after $\overline{\text{CTS}}$ goes low. After the on-site modem receives the carrier frequency from the remote modem, the $\overline{\text{DCD}}$ output goes low and data can be received. The transmit and receive lines of the modem are completely independent of each other. This feature, for example, allows transmission to the remote site when the other line is inoperative.

8.5 AUDIO CASSETTE SYSTEMS

The audio cassette system described in Chapter 7 is another peripheral device for manipulation of data. Most audio cassette systems employ what is known as the "Kansas City Standard" recording format, so called due to its formulation during a symposium sponsored by a microcomputer magazine in Kansas City, Missouri, in November 1975. The format is designed to eliminate errors caused by audio system speed variations. The format has the following characteristics (logical ones and zeros will be referred to alternatively as *marks* and *spaces*, respectively, in accordance with serial data transmission conventions):

1. A mark is recorded as eight cycles of a 2400-Hz signal.

2. A space is recorded as four cycles of a 1200-Hz signal.

3. A recorded character consists of a space as a start bit, 8 data bits, and two or more marks as stop bits.

4. The interval between characters consists of an unspecified amount of time at the mark frequency.

5. In the data characters, the least significant bit (LSB) is transmitted first and the most significant bit (MSB) is transmitted last.

6. The data are organized in blocks of arbitrary and optionally variable length preceded by at least 5 seconds of marks.

7. Meaningful data must not be recorded on the first 30 seconds of tape following the clear leader.

A control program in JBUG causes this format to be followed and incorporates the following additional characteristics:

1. At the beginning of the tape (BOT), the ASCII character for the letter "B" is recorded following 1024 marks (approximately 30 seconds).

2. The "B" is followed by 1 byte containing the block length (up to 256 bytes in a particular block).

3. The next 2 bytes recorded contain the starting address in memory from which the data derive.

4. Up to 256 bytes of data are then recorded and followed by 25 marks and the ASCII character for the letter "G."

The control program uses the additional features to ensure that the punch and dump functions are performed in an orderly manner.

The cassette interface circuit diagram of Figure 8-10 serves as an aid in understanding the following description of the punch and load operations. The punch (transfer of data from the microcomputer module's memory to tape) and load (transfer from tape to memory) commands are accomplished by a combination of the control program, the ACIA (or UART), and the cassette interface circuitry.

In the transmit mode (punch), the ACIA (a bus-oriented UART) accepts parallel 8-bit data from the CPU bus, adds the formatting start bit and stop bit, and then converts the data to a serial binary stream (Tx in Figure 8-10). The desired format is established by instructions from the CPU as it executes the punch command. In the receive mode (load), the ACIA accepts an incoming serial data stream (Rx Data) and a sampling clock (Rx Clk). It strips off the start/stop bits and passes each incoming byte to the CPU for transfer to memory, again under control of the CPU as the program executes. The ACIA's Request-to-Send (RTS) acts as a gating signal to switch the interface circuitry between the punch and load modes.

Timing waveforms corresponding to the appropriate signals in Figure 8-10 are provided in Figures 8-11 through 8-13 as an aid to study of the cassette interface circuitry. During a punch operation, the interface circuitry operates on the serial data to convert each logical one (mark) to an 8-cycle burst of 2400-Hz signal and each logical zero (space) to a 4-cycle burst of 1200-Hz signal, which is then recorded on tape.

The circuitry reverses this procedure during a load operation; it decodes the incoming frequency-modulated signal in order to recover the binary data and a sampling clock. In Figure 8-10, the multiplexer/demultiplexer IC, U20 (data router, for simplicity), is used to steer signals to their required points during both load and punch operations. For instance, during punch, B and C are high, while A is derived from the binary data on Tx Data. For this combination of control signals, Y is connected to Y1 (because B is high);

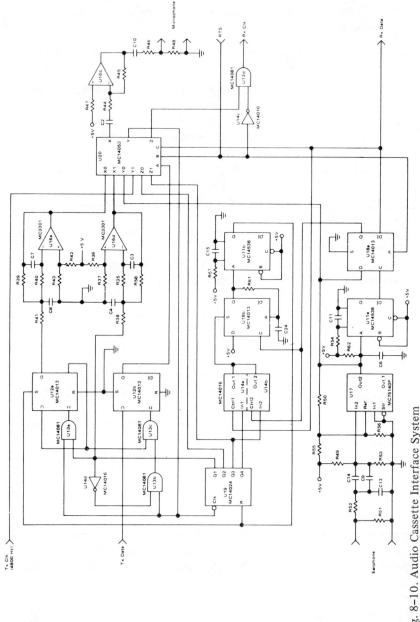

Fig. 8-10. Audio Cassette Interface System
(Courtesy of Motorola Inc.)

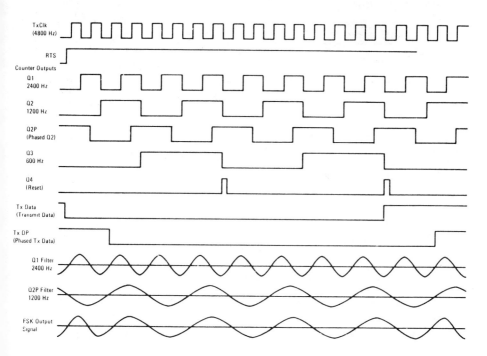

Fig. 8-11. Timing Waveforms

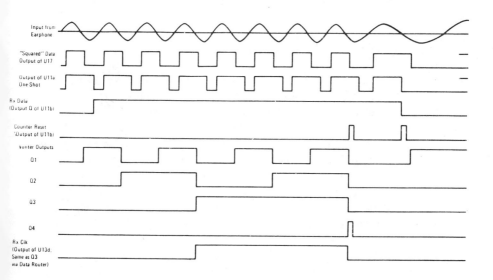

Fig. 8-12. Receive Waveforms

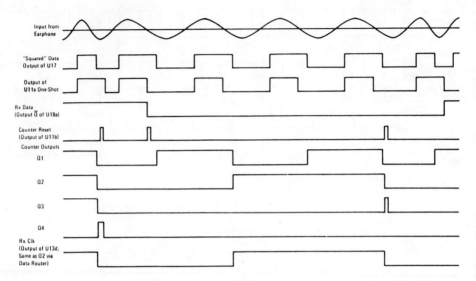

Fig. 8-13. Receive Waveforms

thus the 4800-Hz Tx Clk signal from the microcomputer module is applied to the clock input of the counter, U19. Furthermore, because C is high, Z is connected to Z1, but this signal is not used during punch. The 2400-Hz and 1200-Hz signals are obtained by selecting either the ÷2 (Q1) or the ÷4 (Q2) outputs of the counter as it is clocked at 4800 Hz. The signals at X0 and X1 are 1200- and 2400-Hz sine waves obtained via the bandpass filters of U16a and U16d. One or the other of these signals (depending on the Tx Data logic level at A) will be level-shifted, attenuated, and applied to the microphone output terminals.

It should be noted that the 1200-Hz square wave is obtained from the output of U12a rather than the Q2 output of U19. This, together with the gating of U13 and the delay associated with U12b, ensures that switching of output frequencies will occur only when the outputs of U16a and U16d are at essentially the same voltage (see Figure 8-11).

During a load operation, the incoming signal from the cassette earphone is filtered, amplified, and squared by the U17 line receiver (U17 is connected as a Schmitt trigger to reduce noise problems). This results in a signal, at digital levels, that varies between 2400 Hz and 1200 Hz according to the one–zero pattern that was recorded on the tape. This frequency-modulated signal is then converted to logical ones and zeros by the pulse-width discriminator formed by the U11a one-shot and the U18a D-type flip-flop. Incoming signals less than 1800 Hz are decoded as zeros; frequencies higher than 1800 Hz are decoded as ones. The received data will be present at the $\bar{Q}$ output of U18a.

The required Rx Clk signal, a positive transition at the midpoint of each bit time and a negative transition at the end of each bit time, is generated as follows. During load, the digital level 2400/1200-Hz signal, instead of the 4800-Hz Tx Clk signal, is steered to the counter clock input. The counter's ÷8 (Q3) and ÷16 (Q4) outputs are connected to the inputs of U14b and U14a, respectively. The control inputs of U14a and b are connected to received data and applied to the set input of U18b. The output of U18b triggers the counter reset one-shot U11b. Hence, either the ÷8 or ÷16 counter output is steered back (via X) as a reset, depending on whether the datum is a zero or a one, respectively. The counter is also reset by every mark-to-space transition via the U11b one-shot. The counter's ÷4 and ÷8 outputs are connected to Z0 and Z1, respectively. These connections combined with the reset signals result in a positive transition at the Z output of the data router after either four cycles of 2400 Hz or two cycles of 1200 Hz. Thus, the Rx Clk (Z gated by $\overline{RTS}$) has a positive transition in the middle of each bit time and a negative transition at the end of each bit time.

EXERCISES

8-1.   What is a diskette and how is it used?

8-2.   Name the device(s) used to interface a teletype with a microcomputer.

8-3.   What is the advantage of the Kansas City Standard recording system?

8-4.   What are a mark and a space? What is their cycle equivalent?

8-5.   How are 2400-Hz and 1200-Hz signals obtained in the text discussion?

8-6.   Describe a divide-by-8 counter.

8-7.   What is the difference between a UART and an ACIA?

8-8.   What is the function of a rubout key in a teletype machine?

8-9.   What is the function of a modem?

8-10. Provide a block diagram of a modem interface to a teletype.

9

Applications of Microprocessor Systems

9.1 INTRODUCTION

The text has shown thus far that a microprocessor system consists of LSI (large-scale integration) devices that perform the functions of central processing and control. The new feat use of a microprocessor is that it is *programmable*. In fact, a microprocessor may be compared to an op amp. By rewiring the basic building block of the op amp in Figure 9-1, a "programmed" circuit is created for a different transfer function. In the same way, a microprocessor is effectively rewired to perform a new function as each instruction is read from the program (Figure 9-2). As in any other design, the first step is to understand the problem that is to be solved. The aim of this chapter is to provide practical examples of microprocessor applications as they may be employed in industry and everyday life.

9.2 A SIMPLE APPLICATION

Let us consider a water tower for a small community or plant.

The Situation

The water tower must maintain the water level within certain limits to ensure adequate pressure and peak local availability.

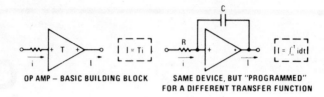

OP AMP – BASIC BUILDING BLOCK   SAME DEVICE, BUT "PROGRAMMED"
FOR A DIFFERENT TRANSFER FUNCTION

Fig. 9–1.

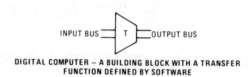

DIGITAL COMPUTER – A BUILDING BLOCK WITH A TRANSFER
FUNCTION DEFINED BY SOFTWARE

Fig. 9–2.

The Application

Obviously, the water cannot just be turned on and off, because user demand may vary. Furthermore, some sort of temperature control must be installed if the water tower is subject to freezing conditions.

Analyzing the Nature of the Application

Figure 9-3 illustrates the approach to the solution. Maximum and minimum levels, as well as a means of measuring them, have to be established. Means of controlling the water level and measuring temperature must be determined.

The design considerations are as follows:

1. Measure level or function of pressure.

2. Measure temperature.

3. Turn pumps on and off to control level.

4. Use programmable controller.

    a. Compensate for barometric pressure.

    b. Program limits for different tank capacities.

    c. Plan for adding more useful functions at no cost.

A flowchart of the solution appears in Figure 9–4. This will be the programmer's guide for writing the control program.

The solution to the problem appears in Figure 9-5. A microprocessor-

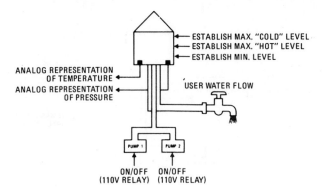

Fig. 9–3. Analyzing the situation

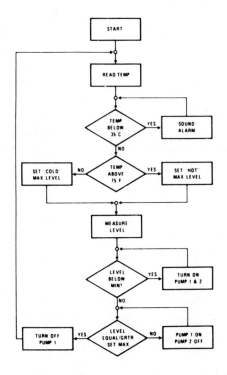

Fig. 9–4. Flowcharting the solution

based controller reads pressure and temperature and controls the pumps and alarm in accordance with the steps listed in the flowchart.

The microprocessor controller would probably consist of a simple-chip microprocessor or memory to hold the control program and data read from

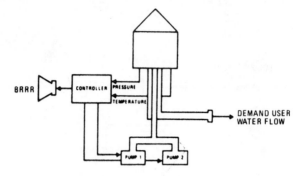

Fig. 9-5. Overview of the solution

the measurement devices, and some I/O device chips to communicate with the pressure and temperature transducers and with the pump controls, as shown in Figure 9-6.

The basic system in the figure may be expanded by adding a heater and several flow meters prevent freezing in the tank and to detect the condition of the pumps. Pump needs can also be anticipated by monitoring user flow.

Thus it is seen that once the problem has been placed in the proper perspective, the application of a microprocessor-based system becomes rather clear. However, there are some problems associated with the use of microprocessors. Prior to the design of a system, the following points should be thoroughly investigated:

1. Hidden costs.

2. Long delivery.

3. Availability of family chips.

4. Performance.

5. Computer overkill.

6. System checkout.

7. Personnel.

8. Software development.

Furthermore, a microprocessor does not stand alone. Support components, equipment, and services are needed. The designer should be aware of these costs in advance. These costs, which may be "hidden," include:

1. Peripheral and memory chips.

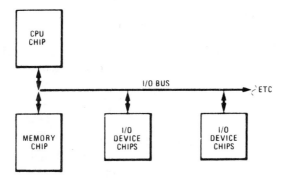

Fig. 9-6. Electronic solution of the situation

2. A PROM programmer.

3. An ultraviolet light.

4. Software programs.

5. Time-share costs.

6. Development systems (accessories).

7. Teletype.

8. Peripherals.

9. Employee training (software).

9.3 ANALYSIS OF PROBLEMS

Family chips (those designed to work with the microprocessor) often determine whether or not a processor will work in an application. These chips include ROMs, PROMs, RAMs, timing elements, line drivers, and interface adapters. These are usually available *after* the microprocessor itself is available. If they are not immediately available, it should be determined when they will be, and how difficult it would be to replace them with readily available components.

Performance should include a number of questions which must be resolved. It may be best to build in more potential performance than is needed in the first production systems.

Overkill means using more microprocessor power than is needed to do the job. Since CPU performance is directly related to CPU cost, extra performance increases hardware cost. However, the extra performance could be small relative to total development costs.

9.4 APPLICATION AREAS

Depending on the word length required, the various application areas for 4-bit, 8-bit, and 16-bit microprocessors, as well as their key characteristics, are as follows:

4-Bit
Arithmetic or Simple Control Functions

Typical applications	BCD display, control, or calculation. Electronic cash registers. Business and accounting systems. Credit-card verification. Intelligent instruments. Appliances. Game machines.
Key characteristics	Controller or arithmetic processor. Simplified I/O. BCD arithmetic instructions. Address-formation capabilities. Small-parts count for minimum systems.

8-Bit
Controller

Typical applications	Intelligent terminals and instruments. Data concentrators or front ends. On-board computer (automobile). Process, numeric, and machine control. Text-editing typewriters. Traffic control. Education, computer science courses, or computer design projects. Medical electronics. Measurement systems.
Key characteristics	Flexible I/O. Hardware to reduce software overhead and simplify I/O. Multiple addressing modes. Interrupt feature. Speed.

1G-Bit
General Purpose

Typical applications	Data-acquisition systems—A/D, D/A processing. Process monitoring and alarm. Supervisory control—gas, power, water distribution. Navigational systems. Automatic test systems. Word-processing systems. Peripheral control.
Key characteristics	Flexible I/O. Hardware to reduce software overhead and simplify I/O. Multiple addressing modes. Interrupt feature. Speed.

9.5 MORE COMPLICATED APPLICATIONS

Let us examine a security system, such as one used in a government service or a bank or in many security-entry applications—to open a door or to gain coded access to files, safes, and so forth. Operation of the system is summarized as follows:

1. Eight-bit employee-access code is input one bit at a time via the data set and data enter switches.

2. Entered code is compared to a prestored reference in memory.

3. If code is valid, accept indicator lights and lock opens; if code is invalid, reject indicator lights and system is reset to zero.

The system is shown in Figure 9-7. It must indicate to the employee when to enter data; this is done via flag 0 (F0) and its associated enter data indicator. When the indicator is on, the system is ready to accept data, and when the indicator is off, the system is reading the status of the data set switch. Flags 1 and 2, respectively, are used to specify code-accept and code-reject conditions. LEDs are used for the enter-data, code-accept, and code-reject indicators; since the devices are inherently current limiting, no surge resistor is required in the base of the transistor, and no series resistor is required in the collector circuit.

One other function is required for system operation—some way of determining when 8 bits (the complete access code) are entered. Referring to

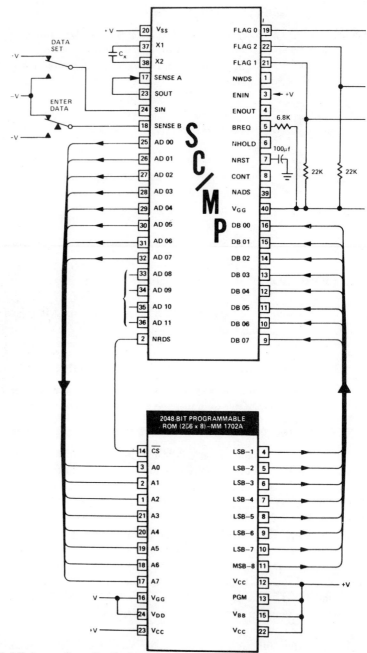

Fig. 9-7. Minimum Security System
(Courtesy of National Semiconductors)

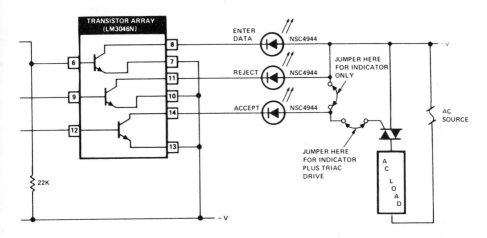

TRANSISTOR ARRAY (LM3046N)

ENTER DATA — NSC4944
REJECT — NSC4944
ACCEPT — NSC4944

JUMPER HERE FOR INDICATOR ONLY

JUMPER HERE FOR INDICATOR PLUS TRIAC DRIVE

AC SOURCE

A C L O A D

22K

+V
−V

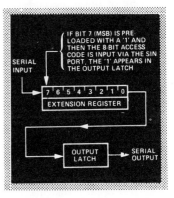

IF BIT 7 (MSB) IS PRE-LOADED WITH A '1' AND THEN THE 8-BIT ACCESS CODE IS INPUT VIA THE SIN PORT, THE '1' APPEARS IN THE OUTPUT LATCH

SERIAL INPUT

7 6 5 4 3 2 1 0
EXTENSION REGISTER

OUTPUT LATCH — SERIAL OUTPUT

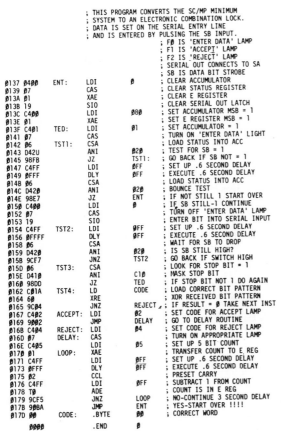

```
          ; THIS PROGRAM CONVERTS THE SC/MP MINIMUM
          ; SYSTEM TO AN ELECTRONIC COMBINATION LOCK.
          ; DATA IS SET ON THE SERIAL ENTRY LINE
          ; AND IS ENTERED BY PULSING THE SB INPUT.
                         ; FØ IS 'ENTER DATA' LAMP
                         ; F1 IS 'ACCEPT' LAMP
                         ; F2 IS 'REJECT' LAMP
                         ; SERIAL OUT CONNECTS TO SA
                         ; SB IS DATA BIT STROBE
Ø137 Ø4ØØ  ENT:    LDI    Ø      ; CLEAR ACCUMULATOR
Ø139 Ø7            CAS           ; CLEAR STATUS REGISTER
Ø13A Ø1            XAE           ; CLEAR E REGISTER
Ø13B 19            SIO           ; CLEAR SERIAL OUT LATCH
Ø13C C4ØØ          LDI    Ø8Ø    ; SET ACCUMULATOR MSB = 1
Ø13E Ø1            XAE           ; SET E REGISTER MSB = 1
Ø13F C4Ø1  TED:    LDI    Ø1     ; SET ACCUMULATOR = 1
Ø141 Ø7            CAS           ; TURN ON 'ENTER DATA' LIGHT
Ø142 Ø6    TST1:   CSA           ; LOAD STATUS INTO ACC
Ø143 D42U          ANI    Ø2Ø    ; TEST FOR SB = 1
Ø145 98FB          JZ     TST1:  ; GO BACK IF SB NOT = 1
Ø147 C4FF          LDI    ØFF    ; SET UP .6 SECOND DELAY
Ø149 ØFFF          DLY    ØFF    ; EXECUTE .6 SECOND DELAY
Ø14B Ø6            CSA           ; LOAD STATUS INTO ACC
Ø14C D42Ø          ANI    Ø2Ø    ; BOUNCE TEST
Ø14E 98E7          JZ     ENT    ; IF NOT STILL 1 START OVER
Ø15Ø C4ØØ          LDI    Ø      ; IF SB STILL-1 CONTINUE
Ø152 Ø7            CAS           ; TURN OFF 'ENTER DATA' LAMP
Ø153 19            SIO           ; ENTER BIT INTO SERIAL INPUT
Ø154 C4FF  TST2:   LDI    ØFF    ; SET UP .6 SECOND DELAY
Ø156 ØFFFF         DLY    ØFF    ; EXECUTE .6 SECOND DELAY
Ø158 Ø6            CSA           ; WAIT FOR SB TO DROP
Ø159 D42Ø          ANI    Ø2Ø    ; IS SB STILL HIGH?
Ø15B 9CF7          JNZ    TST2   ; GO BACK IF SWITCH HIGH
Ø15D Ø6    TST3:   CSA           ; LOOK FOR STOP BIT = 1
Ø15E D41Ø          ANI    C1Ø    ; MASK STOP BIT
Ø16Ø 98DD          JZ     TED    ; IF STOP BIT NOT 1 DO AGAIN
Ø162 CØ1A  TST4:   LD     CODE   ; LOAD CORRECT BIT PATTERN
Ø164 6Ø            XRE           ; XOR RECEIVED BIT PATTERN
Ø165 9CØ4          JNZ    REJECT ; IF RESULT = Ø TAKE NEXT INST
Ø167 C4Ø2  ACCEPT: LDI    Ø2     ; SET CODE FOR ACCEPT LAMP
Ø169 9ØØ2          JMP    DELAY  ; GO TO DELAY ROUTINE
Ø16B C4Ø4  REJECT: LDI    Ø4     ; SET CODE FOR REJECT LAMP
Ø16D Ø7    DELAY:  CAS           ; TURN ON APPROPRIATE LAMP
Ø16E C4Ø5          LDI    Ø5     ; SET UP 5 BIT COUNT
Ø17Ø Ø1    LOOP:   XAE           ; TRANSFER COUNT TO E REG
Ø171 C4FF          LDI    ØFF    ; SET UP .6 SECOND DELAY
Ø173 ØFFF          DLY    ØFF    ; EXECUTE .6 SECOND DELAY
Ø175 Ø2            CCL           ; PRESET CARRY
Ø176 C4FF          LDI    ØFF    ; SUBTRACT 1 FROM COUNT
Ø178 7Ø            ADE           ; COUNT IS IN E REG
Ø179 9CF5          JNZ    LOOP   ; NO-CONTINUE 3 SECOND DELAY
Ø17B 9ØBA          JMP    ENT    ; YES-START OVER !!!!
Ø17D ØØ    CODE:   .BYTE  ØØ     ; CORRECT WORD
     ØØØØ          .END   Ø
```

205

the extension register and output latch shown as a screened inset in Figure 9-7, it is seen that if the most significant bit (bit 7) is preloaded with a one and then the 8-bit access code is inputted, the preloaded value of one is shifted into the output latch. If the latch is preloaded with a zero (which is done by the 50-ft wave) and is connected to sense A, the system can determine when the code is complete (8 bits are entered) simply by checking sense A after the entry of each bit. When sense A equals 1, the input code is accepted, compared with a prestored reference, and if the two codes are in agreement, the lock is opened. If the two codes do not agree, the reject indicator lights.

Reviewing the operation, the user looks to see if the enter data indicator is on—if so, the least significant bit of the authorization code is selected with the data set switch and entered with the enter data pushbutton. While this bit is being read, the enter data indicator goes off and then returns to on; at this time, the set-data/enter-data sequence is repeated for the second bit of the access code. At the end of the eighth entry, a 1 appears at the serial output port (sense A). The sense A line is tested at the completion of each entry, and, when the output latch is equal to 1, the code is complete and is checked against a prestored reference for validity. The program is set up in such a way that entry is timed for 20 seconds; if the next bit is not entered within this time period, the system resets to all zeros. This prevents partial entries from disabling the system.

In the system described above, coded access is provided for a "single" lock, drawer, or door. The same basic system can be expanded to serve several access points; such a system is shown in Figure 9-8. The added component is a CMOS 1-of-10 line decoder with a high current pullup capability at the output. As shown, three inputs to the decoder are supplied by flags 0, 1, and 2; the fourth input is supplied by the inverted output of the SOUT line. Code-entry and code-reject features are similar to those of the basic system. As long as the serial output (SOUT) line is a logic zero, and every flag is a logic zero, the data entry line (pin 9) is selected. When flag 0 is high, and other inputs are the same as before, the rest (ready for data) line is selected.

9.6   A/D AND D/A CONVERSION WITH MICROPROCESSORS

General concepts of how a microprocessor-based system may be used as a general-purpose A/D converter are shown in Figure 9-9. The analog source may be any device capable of producing a current or a low-voltage output over a predetermined range. Outer program control and system timing parameters as well as the analog source is sampled by the A/D converter, and the resulting output is a digital word with 8-bit resolution. The digital word

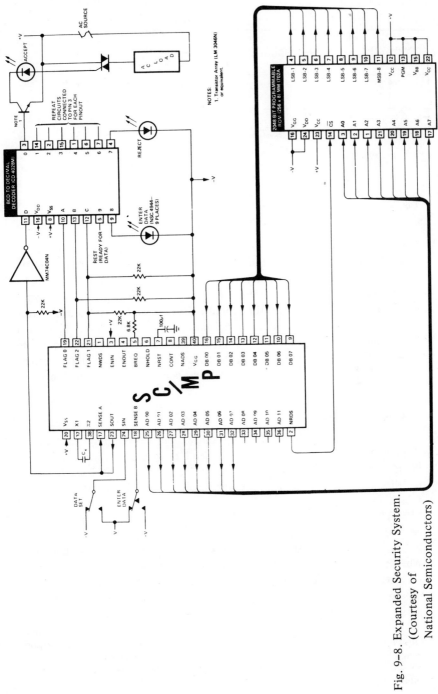

Fig. 9–8. Expanded Security System.
(Courtesy of
National Semiconductors)

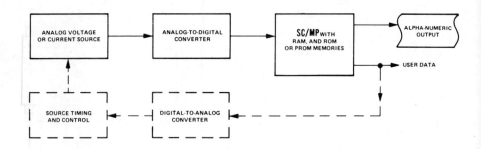

Fig. 9–9. Principles of A/D and D/A Conversion

is stored in RAM, where, under program direction, it can serve a number of functions. For example, the converted data can be compared to a previously stored reference value; thus, in a quality-control configuration, for example, a pass or a reject decision may be made. As another example, the difference between the input data and the stored reference can be treated as an error signal, and, when reconverted to its analog equivalent (shown in dashed blocks and lines), it can be used in applications that require coordinate control. The output data also can be listed alphanumerically for statistical studies in applications where time is plotted against some other variable.

System Operation*

Other than supply voltages, the single-input converter system requires a start pulse, clock pulses, an output-enable gate, and, of course, an analog input. Provided that a valid start-converter pulse is present (logic 1 at pin 6), the conversion starts on the trailing edge (high-to-low transition) of the first clock pulse and continues for 40 cycles.

When the conversion is completed, an 8-bit digital word is loaded into an output latch, and an end-of-conversion (EOC) logic level is generated. The binary output (DB0–DB7) is tristate, to permit use of common bus lines. When a valid address is received, an output-enable signal is generated; at this time, the digital output enters the accumulator of the microprocessor and, subsequently, is stored in a designated memory location. Valid data are held

---

*The microprocessor-controlled A/D converter shown in Figure 9–9 is well suited for applications such as simple machine control, single-parameter testing, data acquisition, and other single-input functions. Requiring few components, minimum memory, and a simple program, the single-input A/D converter is easy and inexpensive to implement.

in the output latch from the end of one conversion to the end of the next; thus, data transfers to memory can be implemented asynchronously.

Timing for one conversion cycle is shown in Figure 9-10. The conversion begins on the trailing edge of the clock pulse; thus, the start converter gate must be at least as wide as, and preferably somewhat wider than one clock cycle. Referring to Figure 9-10, it is seen that the width of the start gate (STRT CONV) is determined by the write strobe (NWDS) of the microprocessor. If the A/D clock is slower than NWDS, a pulse-stretching circuit similar to that of Figure 9-11 is required.

When the conversion cycle starts, the analog input is admitted at pin 12 of the converter chip and the end-of-conversion (EOC) gate is set low. During the next 40 clock cycles, the input is sampled continuously and, via a process of successive approximation, the analog signal is converted into an 8-bit digital word. At the end of the 40th clock cycle, the conversion is complete and two things happen—the EOC gate is set high and the digital word is loaded into an output latch on the converter chip.

When the output is enabled (output enable set high), the latched data (DB0-DB7) are available at pins 13, 14, 16, 17, and 1 through 4, respectively. In a similar manner to the STRT CONV gate, the output enable gate is generated via an arbitrary address—in this case, 0400_{16}. The output enable gate is synchronized by the address strobe (NADS) from the microprocessor, and the gate remains active high until the bus request line (BREQ) is released (goes low) by the microprocessor. The output control functions are under software control and, as shown in Figure 9-10, are implemented by a flip-flop.

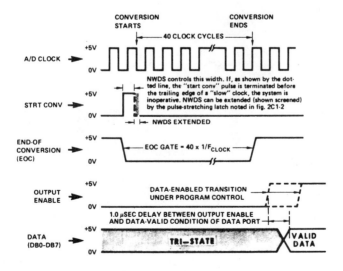

Fig. 9-10. Timing Waveforms for one conversion

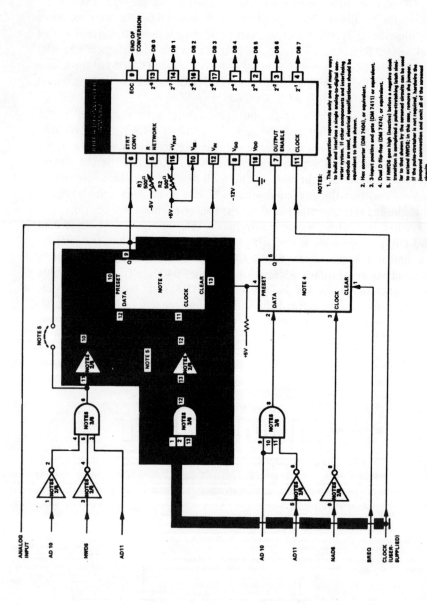

Fig. 9-11. Single-converter A/D System   (Courtesy of National Semiconductors)

210

With supply voltages as shown, the A/D converter in Figure 9-11 is designed to operate over an input range of 10 V (±5 V). Two adjustments (R1 and R2) are provided to optimize conversion accuracy. The potentiometer R1 is the zero adjustment, and, for a 10-V scale, it is set for a transition from "11111111" to "11111110" to occur at 19.53 mV (i.e., one half of the least-significant-bit value). If the voltage difference between pins 5 and 15 is more than 10 V, then the half-bit zero-adjustment value is obtained by dividing 528 (the number of half-bit values) into the difference voltage. For instance, if the voltage between pins 5 and 15 is 10.24 V, R1 is adjusted for 20 mV at the transition point—"11111111" to "11111110." Potentiometer R2 is the full-scale adjustment, and, for a 10-V scale, it is set for the transitions from "00000001" to "00000000" to occur at 58.6 mV (i.e., one and one-half times the least-significant-bit value). Again, if the difference voltage is 10.24 V, R2 is adjusted for 60 mV at the transition point—"00000001" to "00000000."

The flowchart and program listing in Figure 9-12 shows how the single-input A/D converter system can be software-controlled to provide the functions described under system operation. Referring to Figure 9-11 and 9-12, the software-hardware interface can be summarized as follows.

At the start of the program, P2 is loaded with the starting address, X'0800 (lines 6-9), the store instruction is executed, and the 12-line address port of the microprocessor is latched at X'0800 for the remainder of the input/output cycle. Accordingly, AD10 goes low, AD11 goes high, and at write strobe (NWDS) time the conversion starts. Since there are seven instructions executed prior to the load instruction, the NOPs are not required unless the converter clock rate is slowed down. If the clock rate is considerably less than 1.0 MHz, more delay may be required.

Once the A/D conversion is completed (after 40 clock cycles), the digital data are accepted by the microprocessor and are stored in a specified memory location. As indicated by lines 15-20 of the program, P2 is loaded with the address for "data acceptance"—in this case, X'0400—and P3 is loaded with the "memory-destination" address (X'0200). When the LD instruction (line 21) is executed, the 8-bit digital output of the converter is read into the accumulator, and when the next instruction (STORE, line 22) is executed, the data are stored in memory location X'0200. Observe that, when the X'0400 address is valid, the output data are gated into the accumulator via the address strobe (NADS) rather than the read strobe (NRDS); the NADS signal provides adequate time for the transfer of data, whereas the NRDS signal may not.

9.7 AN AUTOMATED TELEPHONE SYSTEM

Let us now look at a telephone system which might be used in a hotel or, with some alterations, in other applications.

Most private-branch telephone exchanges are not expected to produce

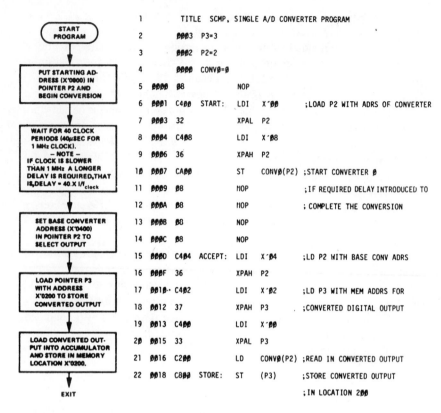

Fig. 9-12. Flowchart of Single-Converter System

automatic wake-up calls, but the modern ones in hotels and motels can do just that. The secret to this—and other features needed by the lodging trade in its telephone systems—is microprocessor control, which permits adapting a PBX to a variety of business applications.

Let us assume a system that would provide needed features for hotels with no more than, say, 112 extensions. An 8-bit CMOS microprocessor is selected as the central control section. It provides low power dissipation, a suitable I/O structure, and a CMOS or TTL interface.

The device can handle both driven and polled interrupts. By pulling down an input line, extensions gain the immediate attention of the microprocessor, or the processor can periodically scan all lines to determine if service is needed. Cycle time would not be critical, since the system need only scan 112 lines every 500 ms.

The block diagram of the system is shown in Figure 9-13. The microprocessor controls a time-division-multiplexed switch, and formats and transmits data to the peripheral devices. A cassette may be used to load the

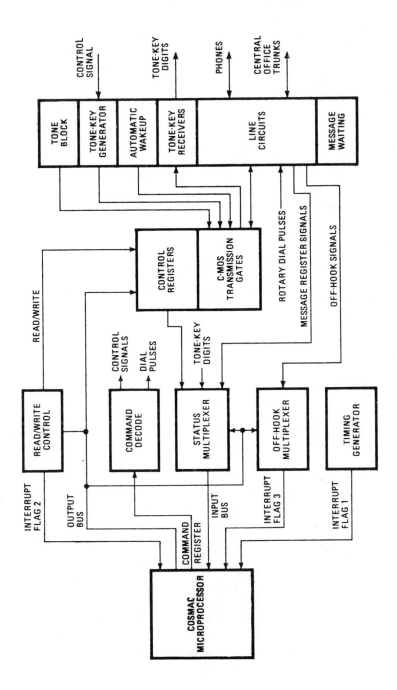

Fig. 9–13. Automated telephone system

213

program into memory, a feature that would provide further flexibility to the capabilities of the system.

The system should interface with an integral display console that provides the video terminal, keyboard, and printer most hotel operators want for storing registration information and processing guests' telephone charges. The exchange (TDM) switch interfaces with the room extensions, outside lines, central office trunks, and a multibutton operator telephone that serves as inexpensive attendant console.

The microprocessor controls most of the specialized lodging functions through the TDM switch. It writes data into the control shift registers to make phone connections and reads back data from the registers via the status multiplexer. The registers act as an extension of the microprocessor memory, because their memory is under processor read/write control.

Addressing the "off-hook" multiplexer permits the microprocessor to monitor all off-hook signals. By scanning these signals, the processor counts the dial pulses and determines which connections should be made.

The status multiplexer scans the message-register signals to keep a running total of all local phone calls from each room. It also reads the digits provided by tone-key receivers. While the system shown in Figure 9–13 is equally adaptable to rotary-dial installations, the discussion here assumes that the installation is of the newer, tone-key type.

The microprocessor controls the main functions of the switch via the command-decode block. For example, it generates dial pulses and routes them to a central-office trunk line by sending the commands to the command-decode block. The dial pulses go through the line circuits providing the proper interface to the trunk lines. The ability of the microprocessor to provide dial signals for outside numbers is necessary for the abbreviated dialing features, in which frequently called numbers may be reached by keying in a pair of digits.

The control shift registers for each extension interface with MOS switches that actually are CMOS transmission gates. The gates conduct whenever a logic 1 appears on the output of the controlling shift register, making the input to the transmission gate go positive.

The recirculating shift registers are being clocked at the same rate as the time-slot counter, which determines which one of the 20 time slots—that is, bit positions—for each shift register is controlling the conduction or non-conduction of the switch. At the point shown in Figure 9–14, no phone connections have been made. The microprocessor can read or write to a specific time slot in a shift register by providing a read/write command and the number of the slot to the decode block. The command is executed when the counter turns up the same time-slot number as the one provided. The command affects all shift registers during the designated time slot.

When any phone is taken off the hook, the microprocessor writes a

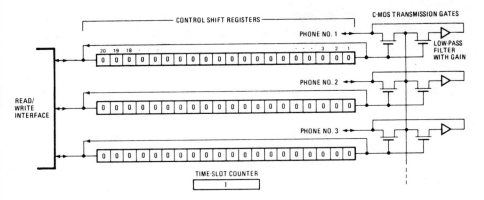

Fig. 9-14. Making connections

1 in the time slot of the shift register controlling that phone and of the shift register controlling the dial tone. It also sets a bit in time slot 1 of the register that controls the gating of the signal to the receiver. As the bit circulates around each of these three registers, a sample of the dial-tone signal is taken each time it reaches the last stage of the register. This sample passes through the low-pass filter, and the phone receives a dial tone.

As the caller begins to key in the numbers, the microprocessor removes the 1 stored in time slot 1 of the dial-tone register so that the phone no longer receives a dial tone. As numbers are keyed in, the signal generated from the phone is sampled and reconstructed in the low-pass filter. The microprocessor then reads the digits to determine the telephone number being called.

If, in Figure 9-14, phone 1 is calling phone 3, the microprocessor writes a 1 in time slot 1 of the register controlling phone 1 and writes a 1 in the register controlling the ring-back tone. It sets a bit in time slot 2 of the control register for phone 3 and in the ring-back-tone control register. It sets a bit in time slot 2 of the control register for phone 3 and in the ring-tone control register, which causes phone 3 to ring.

When phone 3 is picked up, the processor writes a 1 in time slot 1 of the control registers for the two phones and removes the bits in the ring-back-tone control register and the ring-tone control registers. This results in a connection between the phones, and the conversation can begin.

With an eye toward the long-term design goal of large-scale integration, it is essential to control as much of the switching as possible, thereby minimizing the number of small-scale integration logic circuits needed. However, excessive time spent servicing the switch would starve the peripheral devices.

Since it is difficult to determine in the early design state how many peripheral operating features will be required, it is difficult to determine how much margin for their operation must be left. However, too much margin causes the costs to soar. Ultimately, the answer lies in design experience rather than in hard and fast rules.

EXERCISES

9-1 What is the function of A/D converters?

9-2 Name some typical application areas for microprocessors other than those described in the text. Briefly explain each application.

9-3 Design a basic traffic-light system.

10

Character Generators

10.1 INTRODUCTION

Character generators should have been discussed in Chapter 4. However, it was decided to go into more detail on this important subject.

A huge new market for person/machine interfaces is being created by the increasing availability of low-cost data processing through computer time sharing, LSI calculators, minicomputers, and digital business and control systems. Equal pressure has been given on the design of CRT terminals, displays, and teleprinters that are at least as compact and inexpensive as the new data processors. Thus, manufacture of ROMs and shift registers with adequate storage capability has created an appreciable dent in terminal and printer costs. Entire alphanumeric character fonts (see the glossary, Section 10-7) and CRT refresh channels are now available as single-chip arrays.

10.2 BASIC CHARACTER GENERATION

Generating the standard 64 ASCII-selected characters in a 5 X 7 font requires a storage capacity of at least 5 X 7 X 64. Each logical 1 bit stored in the ROM produces a black dot on a printout or a bright spot on a CRT screen, and each 0 bit produces a blank space. Thus, one typical ROM is ample for a standard 5 X 7 or 7 X 5 font. The added capacity can implement special needs, such as dropping comma tails below the other character and symbols.

A basic digital character generator and CRT refresh memory is shown in Figure 10-1. In a refresh memory, register outputs are fed back to the inputs. On each recirculation, the data readdresses the ROM, regenerating (refreshing) the display. The recirculation times must correspond to the CRT scanning time to keep the display legible. MOS register delay times are relatively insensitive to temperature variations because they are established by system clock rates rather than by physical parameters. Furthermore, special requirements of data entry and output for display formating and editing can be implemented much more easily with registers than with physical delay lines. Data bit positions in the recirculation loops are maintained in alignment, and can be monitored and modulated precisely by the control logic (one recirculation loop is needed for each data bit—six loops, for example, in an ASCII-addressed system). Data entry and output for display or transmission thus becomes a straightforward exercise in logic design.

10.3 CRT RASTER SCAN DISPLAYS

The basic refresh made in Figure 10-1 limits the number of characters that can be displayed. A better way of generating and refreshing raster scan displays, particularly those with many rows or lines of characters, is outlined in Figure 10-2. Figure 10-3 illustrates the timing and logical implementation for a multiple-row system. As previously, coded data from a communications link or the console keyboard passes through the registers and addresses the generator. In these examples, the 6-bit ASCII input and the 3-bit control logic input generate raster scan character formats that allow a conventional TV monitor to be used as a display. Communications codes other than ASCII can be used.

If the ROM contains a 5 X 7 font, each 5-bit character line output will form five horizontal bright spots on the CRT. That is, each ROM output generates one seventh of each character in a row of displayed characters. The

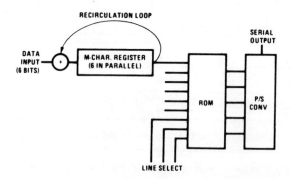

Fig. 10-1. Basic Digital Character Generator and CRT Refresh Memory

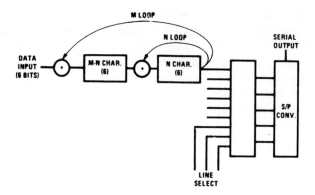

Fig. 10-2. Technique for large page displays

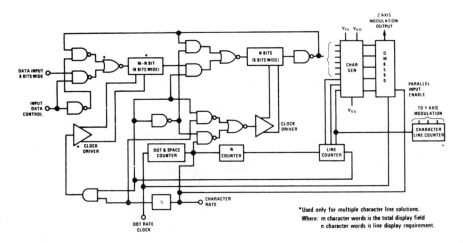

Fig. 10-3. Multiple Row Roster Scan Display System
(Courtesy of National Semiconductors)

output is serialized by the TTL register and used to intensity modulate the CRT beam as it sweeps across the screen.

The refresh memory registers are divided into M-N and N sections to facilitate page displays. M is the total number of characters displayed in several rows (lines of the page) and N is the number of characters in each row. To form such a display with single-loop registers, as in Figure 10-1, would take seven recirculations of all M data words during each refresh cycle of the CRT. The technique in Figures 10-2 and 10-3 only requires high-speed recirculation of N bits at a time.

Let us assume that, on the first sweep of the CRT beam, the ROM is being addressed by the six register outputs representing characters N1,

N2, N3, and so on. The first horizontal 5-dot line of each character in the display row are displayed in sequence. Then the line address inputs to the ROM from the control logic change to their second state at the time that N1 has completed its recirculation to the N register's outputs. Thus, on the second CRT sweep, the second series of 5-dot lines are displayed horizontally for all N characters. At the end of seven recirculations, the complete row of N characters is on the display.

Now, the contents of the N register are not returned to the input of the N register. Instead, they are fed back to the input of the M-N register, and this register is clocked to load the N register with the second group of N characters. The M-N register is then held still while the N register recirculates seven times to generate the second row of characters on the display. After all M characters are on the display, the first group of N characters is reloaded into the N register and the entire process is repeated to refresh the display.

Human factors—chiefly the response time of the eye—dictate that the display be refreshed at least 30 to 35 times per second for good legibility. Most designers prefer to refresh at a power-line frequency of 60 Hz because it is generally the most convenient frequency.

In addition to generating the line address inputs (i.e., the number of recirculations of the N register), the control logic keeps track of the number of dots and spaces in the output bit stream. The spaces between characters in a display row are inserted as zero bits when the ROM outputs are serialized by the TTL register. The counters also control the loading and recirculations of the MOS registers in the refresh memory subsystem.

For a 5 $\times$ 7 font, the new single-chip character generators are simply programmed to generate all 5 bits in each dot line from a 9-bit address. Standard programming provides the 64-character ASCII set, but special characters can be substituted by changing the stored dot patterns. The reprogramming process consists of altering an etching mask that controls gate insulation thickness in the MOS field-effect transistors of the storage array. If the oxide is left thick, the transistor will not switch when selected by the decoding logic, generating a 0 output from that location.

10.4   CONTROL LOGIC

Starting with the dot/character or dot and space counter in Figure 10-3, the counter moduli are set to accomplish the following functions:

—The dot-and-space counter determines the number of horizontal spacing bits between characters in the character row on the display. Its output is loaded into the parallel inputs of the serial-in/parallel-out shift register. For a 5 $\times$ 7 font, for example, a modulus of six inserts

1 spacing bit (logical zero bit) between each 5-dot group in the serialized stream. During live recirculation periods, this counter also drives the N counter at the character shift rate of the N register.

—The N counter causes the line select counter to change state at the end of every recirculation of the row data in the N register. It generates a pulse at intervals of 6N dot clock periods (assuming 1 spacing bit).

—The line select counter generates seven sets of the three address bits that sequence dot-line selection from the ROM.

—A character line counter is needed in some raster-scan displays to keep track of which page line has just been generated. This time is signified by the C or D output of the line select counter.

Outputs of the first three counters actuate the register clock drivers, keeping the line select bits in synch with the data code. If the line select counter is a 4-bit binary device, eight states are available on the ABC outputs (000 through 111). The D output can be used to provide a ninth state and the reset function. Only seven states are needed for line select, so the eighth and ninth states provide the interval needed for loading the N register from the M-N register.

10.5 PRINTING APPLICATIONS

The application of character generators in a printing application is normally quite different from that of the display system. Most printers require that a total character font be available before the print is executed. An example of a practical method of accomplishing this is illustrated in Figure 10-4. The method sequences the character generator element through

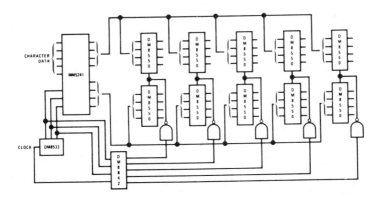

Fig. 10–4. Printer Application

the font sequence. Each of the character columns or rows is addressed. The character generator output data at each of these address intervals is transferred into bipolar memory. This memory not only satisfies the memory storage but also the general power buffer which is required between the MOS character generator and the electromechanical or thermoelectric printer. In the printer application, there may be a requirement to buffer the input data with data storage because of the relative differences in data and printer rates, but generally there is no need to retain the printed character intelligence.

The data transfer from the character generator to the bipolar memory in Figure 1-4 is accomplished by sequencing the column address lines and enabling the appropriate memory simultaneously.

10.6 LARGER SYSTEMS

Most low-cost terminal designs have been based on the 5 × 7 font because of the high cost of diode matrices and wideband video circuits. However, it is by no means the most legible font. A 5 × 7 font is acceptable for applications in which the display changes slowly, but human engineering studies indicate that severe eyestrain results when an operator reads rapidly changing data.

The greatest portion of the discussion has dealt with a 5 × 7 font. A full 64-character display can be coded into a single MOS package. However, with the introduction of LS1, a trend toward larger, more stylized font has taken place. The 8 × 10 font is much better, and 12 × 16 is almost optimum for legibility.

System designers, considering these fonts for low-cost displays, run into CRT cost problems. The least expensive displays are television-type CRTs with limited video bandwidth. Bandwidth also limits the number of characters that can be displayed simultaneously. Not counting the times required for beam retrace and functions other than character generation which reduce the time available in a refresh cycle for dot handling, the necessary bandwidth is roughly:

BW = (dots and spacing bits per character) × (characters per display row or page) × (refresh rate)

TV-type CRTs have a maximum bandwidth of about 4 MHz, of which only 2.5 MHz is generally useful. If one uses a 5 × 7 font with 1 spacing bit (6 × 7 total) at a 60-Hz refresh rate, each displayed character requires 2.52 kHz of bandwidth, so the limit is about 1000 characters. In contrast, the new ROMs take as little as 700 ns to generate a dot line, or about 5 μs/character. That is fast enough to generate 200,000 characters/second, or a display of more than 3000 characters at the 60-Hz refresh rate. The actual dot rate in the serial bit stream to the CRT can approach 10 MHz. And if larger fonts are generated in some multiplexed addressing mode, the required bandwidth can be much higher.

Fortunately, these problems are not insurmountable and there are alternatives to using oscilloscope-quality CRTs or storage tubes, which are suitable for high-performance applications but are too expensive for low-cost terminals.

10.7 GLOSSARY OF TERMS

Column. In a dot-character matrix for vertical scanning, a column is a vertical series of dots: On a page display, a column contains several vertical by aligned characters.

Dot Character. A character formed by a pattern of bright dots on a CRT screen or dark spots on hard copy, rather than by continuous strokes. The dot pattern corresponds to bit-storage patterns in a digital memory.

Font. A set of printing or display characters of a particular style and size. A typical dot-character font is 5 × 7, referring to the number of dot locations per character.

Line. In this discussion, line refers to the number of dots displayed in a single scan when a raster-scan character is generated. In a 5 × 7 dot character, there are seven lines of 5 dots each.

Page. A display consisting of several rows of characters, corresponding to lines on a printed page.

Row. A horizontally aligned group of characters on a display.

Part Two

Popular Microprocessors

11
The 4004 (MCS-4)

11.1 INTRODUCTION

Thus far the text has described the basic architecture of a microprocessor and its associated circuits. The purpose of this portion of the text is to familiarize the reader with microprocessor systems which have been on the market for quite some time and thus have gained popularity. Chapter 7 described such a system, the M6800, and other systems are discussed below.

11.2 MCS-4

This type of microcomputer is a pioneer in the industry, first introduced by Intel Corp. in 1971. It is a microprocessor system, consisting of the 4004 CPU, the 4001 ROM, 4002 RAM, and 4003 shift register.

The 4004 CPU is a 4-bit device, meaning that it operates on 4-bit words. It contains 16 index registers, each with a capacity of 4 bits. It is designed to operate with up to 4096 words of program instruction.

The address registers of the 4004 are arranged in a stack of four, one being used as the program counter, with the remaining three used for saving the return-to-addresses employed during subroutines. It is also equipped with 16 4-bit index registers, communicating with the remaining system via a data bus four lines wide. The latter poses a problem during the address phase of the instruction cycle, because data must be sent over the data bus in three 4-bit nibbles.

The accumulator of the 4004 has a capacity of 4 bits, and overflow provision (storage into a carry flip-flop).

The 4004 is packaged in a 16-pin DIP (dual-in-line). The pin configuration is given in Figure 11-1 along with a brief functional description of each pin:

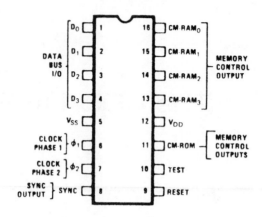

Fig. 11-1. Pin configuration of the 4004 CPU
(Courtesy of Intel Corporation)

PIN NO.	DESIGNATION	FUNCTION
1-4	$D_0 - D_3$	Bidirectional data bus. All address and data communication between the processor and RAM/ROM chips is handled via these four lines.
5	V_{SS}	Most positive supply (usually +5 V).
6-7	$\emptyset_1 - \emptyset_2$	Nonoverlapping clock signals which determine processor timing.
8	SYNC	Sync output. Synchronization signal generated by the processor and sent to ROM and RAM chips. Indicates beginning of instruction cycle.
9	RESET	Reset input. A "1" level applied to this pin clears all flag and status flip-flops and forces the program counter to 0. To completely clear all the address and index registers, RESET must be applied for 64 clock cycles (8 machine cycles).

PIN NO.	DESIGNATION	FUNCTION
10	TEST	Test input. The logical state of this input can be examined with the JCN instruction.
11	CM-ROM	This pin enables a ROM bank which can contain up to 4K words of program.
12	V_{DD}	Main supply voltage to the processor. Value must be V_{SS} – 15 V ± 5 percent (usually, –10 V).
13–16	CM-RAM$_0$ – CM-RAM$_3$	CM-RAM outputs, acting as bank select signals for the RAM chips in the system. Up to 16 RAMS can be controlled by the 4004.

11.3 MCS-4 INSTRUCTION SET

NOP (No Operation). Mnemonic for "no operation," used for delays in the system operation and as the first instruction in a program to allow any potential race conditions to die out when the system is first energized. The 4004 processor has 16 4-bit index registers that may be addressed by a 4-bit code, $R_3 R_2 R_1 R_0$. For some problems, 4 bits of capacity in the index register is inadequate. In this case, provision is made for addressing register pairs with pairs of 8 bits.

When register pairs are employed, an address code $R_3 R_2 R_1$ is used which is simply a reorganization of the old codes. Thus, it can be stated that the 4004 has 16 4-bit index registers or eight 8-bit registers. In Figure 11-2, the sixteen 4-bit index registers and the corresponding pair numbers are identified. Pair 6 and register 7 cannot be used at the same time, because, as shown, pair 6 is made up of registers 6 and 7.

FIM (Fetch Immediate from ROM). One way to load data into the microcomputer is to include them in the instruction itself. FIM is a two-word instruction that operates by loading the second word into a specified register pair as data. The previous contents of the register pair are lost.

FIN (Fetch Indirect). Mnemonic for "fetch indirect" from ROM. It is a one-word instruction but requires two instructions to execute. This is accomplished by inhibiting the program counter during the memory phase

MACHINE INSTRUCTIONS (Logic 1 = Low Voltage = Negative Voltage; Logic 0 = High Voltage = Ground)

MNEMONIC	OPR $D_3 D_2 D_1 D_0$	OPA $D_3 D_2 D_1 D_0$	DESCRIPTION OF OPERATION
NOP	0 0 0 0	0 0 0 0	No operation.
*JCN	0 0 0 1 $A_2 A_2 A_2 A_2$	$C_1 C_2 C_3 C_4$ $A_1 A_1 A_1 A_1$	Jump to ROM address $A_2 A_2 A_2 A_2$, $A_1 A_1 A_1 A_1$ (within the same ROM that contains this JCN instruction) if condition $C_1 C_2 C_3 C_4$[1] is true, otherwise skip (go to the next instruction in sequence).
*FIM	0 0 1 0 $D_2 D_2 D_2 D_2$	R R R 0 $D_1 D_1 D_1 D_1$	Fetch immediate (direct) from ROM Data D_2, D_1 to index register pair location RRR.[2]
SRC	0 0 1 0	R R R 1	Send register control. Send the address (contents of index register pair RRR) to ROM and RAM at X_2 and X_3 time in the Instruction Cycle.
FIN	0 0 1 1	R R R 0	Fetch indirect from ROM. Send contents of index register pair location 0 out as an address. Data fetched is placed into register pair RRR.
JIN	0 0 1 1	R R R 1	Jump indirect. Send contents of register pair RRR out as an address at A_1 and A_2 time in the Instruction Cycle.
*JUN	0 1 0 0 $A_2 A_2 A_2 A_2$	$A_3 A_3 A_3 A_3$ $A_1 A_1 A_1 A_1$	Jump unconditional to ROM address A_3, A_2, A_1.
*JMS	0 1 0 1 $A_2 A_2 A_2 A_2$	$A_3 A_3 A_3 A_3$ $A_1 A_1 A_1 A_1$	Jump to subroutine ROM address A_3, A_2, A_1, save old address. (Up 1 level in stack.)
INC	0 1 1 0	R R R R	Increment contents of register RRRR. [3]
*ISZ	0 1 1 1 $A_2 A_2 A_2 A_2$	R R R R $A_1 A_1 A_1 A_1$	Increment contents of register RRRR. Go to ROM address A_2, A_1 (within the same ROM that contains this ISZ instruction) if result $\neq 0$, otherwise skip (go to the next instruction in sequence).
ADD	1 0 0 0	R R R R	Add contents of register RRRR to accumulator with carry.
SUB	1 0 0 1	R R R R	Subtract contents of register RRRR to accumulator with borrow.
LD	1 0 1 0	R R R R	Load contents of register RRRR to accumulator.
XCH	1 0 1 1	R R R R	Exchange contents of index register RRRR and accumulator.
BBL	1 1 0 0	D D D D	Branch back (down 1 level in stack) and load data DDDD to accumulator.
LDM	1 1 0 1	D D D D	Load data DDDD to accumulator.

NEW 4040 INSTRUCTIONS

MNEMONIC	OPR $D_3 D_2 D_1 D_0$	OPA $D_3 D_2 D_1 D_0$	DESCRIPTION OF OPERATION
HLT	0 0 0 0	0 0 0 1	Halt — inhibit program counter and data buffers.
BBS	0 0 0 0	0 0 1 0	Branch Back from Interrupt and restore the previous SRC. The Program Counter and send register control are restored to their pre-interrupt value.
LCR	0 0 0 0	0 0 1 1	The contents of the COMMAND REGISTER are transferred to the ACCUMULATOR.
OR4	0 0 0 0	0 1 0 0	The 4 bit contents of register #4 are logically "OR-ed" with the ACCUM.
OR5	0 0 0 0	0 1 0 1	The 4 bit contents of index register #5 are logically "OR-ed" with the ACCUMULATOR.
AN6	0 0 0 0	0 1 1 0	The 4 bit contents of index register #6 are logically "AND-ed" with the ACCUMULATOR
AN7	0 0 0 0	0 1 1 1	The 4 bit contents of index register #7 are logically "AND-ed" with the ACCUMULATOR.
DB0	0 0 0 0	1 0 0 0	DESIGNATE ROM BANK 0. CM-ROM_0 becomes enabled.
DB1	0 0 0 0	1 0 0 1	DESIGNATE ROM BANK 1. CM-ROM_1 becomes enabled.
SB0	0 0 0 0	1 0 1 0	SELECT INDEX REGISTER BANK 0. The index registers 0 - 7.
SB1	0 0 0 0	1 0 1 1	SELECT INDEX REGISTER BANK 1. The index registers 0* - 7*.
EIN	0 0 0 0	1 1 0 0	ENABLE INTERRUPT.
DIN	0 0 0 0	1 1 0 1	DISABLE INTERRUPT.
RPM	0 0 0 0	1 1 1 0	READ PROGRAM MEMORY.

Fig. 11-2.

of the second cycle. During the address and memory phases of the first cycle, the FIN instruction is fetched from program storage. During the execution phase, the CPU is set up for the second cycle.

During phases A_1 and A_2 of the second instruction cycle, the contents of index register pair 0 are sent out on the bus as an address. Of course, 12 bits are required to specify an address, but an index register can only hold 8 bits. The 4004 compensates for this by sending out the 4 high-order bits of the program counter during A_3. This manipulation permits addressing of a memory location with the 8-bit contents of an index register. However, by using the 4 high-order bits of the program counter, a restriction is automatically imposed, that is, only locations that are on the same page as the FIN are addressed.

During M_1 and M_2, the contents of the addressed location are sent over the bus to the CPU. At that point, they are loaded into the index register pair specified in the FIN. There is, however, an exception to this process. If the FIN is located in the last address on the page, the 4 high-order bits sent out during A_3 are not those of the program counter. Instead, the 4 high-order bits of the program counter are incremented by one and sent out during A_3. Thus, the data retrieved by the FIM will *not* be from the same page as the FIM, but from the next page. This is dangerous programming practice and should be avoided.

Once the desired data are entered in one of the index registers, it is easy to operate on them. Many of these operations will be performed in the accumulator. The simplest way to load the accumulator is with a load accumulator instruction (LD). This instruction causes the contents of the particular index register to be loaded into the accumulator, and the actual transfer takes place during the execution phases.

LDM (Load Data to Accumulator). This instruction is a simpler way of loading the accumulator and is the mnemonic for "load immediate." In both the LD and LDM, the previous contents of the accumulator are lost, but the carry flip-flop is unaffected.

XCH (Exchange Index Register and Accumulator). This instruction loads the 4-bit content of the designated index register into the accumulator. The prior content of the accumulator is loaded into the designated register, and, again, the carry flip-flop is unaffected.

ADD (Add Index Register to Accumulator with Carry). This instruction adds the 4-bit content of the designated index register to the content of the accumulator with carry. The result is stored in the accumulator. The carry flip-flop is set to 1 if a sum greater than 15_{10} was generated to indicate a carry out; otherwise, the flip-flop is set to 0. The 4-bit content of the index register is unaffected. Example:

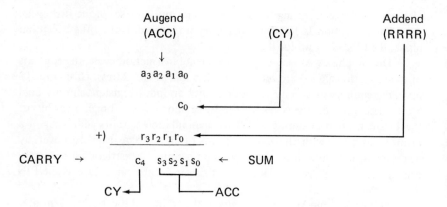

SUB (Subtract Index Register from Accumulator). This instruction complements (one's complement) the 4-bit content of the designated index register to the content of the accumulator with borrow, and the result is stored in the accumulator. If a borrow is generated, the carry bit is set to 0; otherwise, it is set to 1. The 4-bit content of the index register is unaffected. Example:

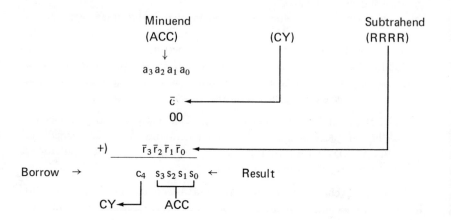

INC (Increment Index Register). The 4-bit content of the designated index register is incremented by 1. The index register is set to zero in case of overflow. The carry flip-flop is unaffected.

BBL (Branch Back and Load Data to Accumulator). The program counter is pushed down one level. Program control transfers to the next instruction following the last jump to subroutine (JMS) instruction. The 4 bits of data DDDD stored in the OPA portion of the instruction are loaded to the accumulator. BBL is used to return from subroutine to the main program.

JIN (Jump Indirect). The 8-bit content of the designated index register pair is loaded into the low-order eight positions of the program counter. Program control is transferred to the instruction at that address on the same page (same ROM) where the JIN instruction is located. The 8-bit content at the index register is unaffected. Exception: When JIN is located at the address (P_H) 1111 1111, program control is transferred to the next page in sequence, and not the same page where the JIN instruction is loaded. That is, the next address is (P_H+1) (RRR0) (RRR1) and not (P_H) (RRR0) (RRR1).

SRC (Send Register Control). The 8-bit content of the designated index register pair is sent to the RAM address register at X_2 and X_3. A subsequent read, write, or I/O operation of the RAM will utilize this address. Specifically, the first 2 bits of the address designate a RAM chip; the second 2 bits designate 1 out of 4 registers within the chip; the last 4 bits designate 1 out of 16 4-bit main memory characters within the register. This command is used also to designate a ROM for a subsequent ROM I/O port operation. The first 4 bits designate the ROM chip number to be selected. The address in ROM or RAM is not cleared until the next SRC instruction is executed. The 8-bit content of the index register is unaffected.

HLT. The processor sets the halt and stop flip-flops. Program counter incrementer and data input buffers are inhibited. The processor executes NOP continuously; continuation can occur by means of a stop or interrupt control.

In this mode, the program counter +1 is gated out at A_1, A_2, and A_3 times on the data bus. M_1, M_2 times will contain the addressed ROM instruction on the data bus. X_1, the 4-bit accumulator contents, X_2 and X_3 will contain an 8-bit SRC register.

BBS. This instruction is a combination of branch back and SRC. The effective address counter is decremented and program control is returned to the location saved by the forced JMS which occurred at the beginning of the interrupt routine. In addition, the content of the SRC register is sent out at X_2 and X_3 of the instruction cycle, thus restoring the I/O port selection. This instruction will also turn off the INTA line, reenabling the CPU for interrupt.

The previously selected index register bank also will be restored during this instruction.

LCR. The 4 bits of the command register are transferred to the accumulator. This allows saving the command register values before processing the interrupt.

OR4. The 4-bit contents of index register 4 are logically OR-ed with the accumulator. The result is placed in the accumulator and the carry flip-flop is unaffected. Examples:

$$
\begin{array}{rl}
\text{(ACC)} & 0\ 1\ 0\ 1 \\
\text{(RRRR}_4) & 1\ 0\ 0\ 1 \\
\hline
\text{ACC} & 1\ 1\ 0\ 1
\end{array}
$$

$$
\begin{array}{rl}
\text{(ACC)} & 0\ 0\ 0\ 0 \\
\text{(RRRR}_4) & 1\ 0\ 0\ 0 \\
\hline
\text{ACC} & 1\ 0\ 0\ 0
\end{array}
$$

OR5. The 4-bit contents of index register 5 are logically OR-ed with the accumulator. The carry flip-flop is unaffected.

AN6. The 4-bit contents of index register 6 are logically AND-ed with the accumulator. The result is placed in the accumulator and the carry is unaffected. Examples:

$$
\begin{array}{rl}
\text{(ACC)} & 0\ 1\ 1\ 0 \\
\text{(RRRR}_6) & 0\ 1\ 0\ 0 \\
\hline
\text{ACC} & 0\ 1\ 0\ 0
\end{array}
$$

$$
\begin{array}{rl}
\text{(ACC)} & 1\ 1\ 1\ 1 \\
\text{(RRRR}_6) & 0\ 0\ 0\ 1 \\
\hline
\text{ACC} & 0\ 0\ 0\ 1
\end{array}
$$

AN7. The 4-bit contents of index register 7 are logically AND-ed with the accumulator. The carry flip-flop is unaffected.

DBI (Designate ROM Bank 1). The most significant bit of the command register, CR3, is set. On the third instruction cycle following its execution, it causes CM-ROM$_1$ to be activated.

SB0 (Secret Index Register Bank 0). The index register bank select flip-flop is reset. Index registers 0-7 and 8-15 will be available for program use. This bank is to be selected with a reset.

SB1 (Select Index Register Bank 1). The index register bank select flip-flop is set. Index registers 0*-7* and 8-15 will be available for program use.

RPM (Read Program Memory). This instruction can be used only with the 4289 standard memory and I/O interface chip. The contents of the previously selected nibble of R/W program memory are transferred to the CPU and loaded to the accumulator.

EIN. Enable interrupt. The internal interrupt detection logic is enabled.

DIN. Disable interrupt. The internal interrupt detection logic is disabled.

JUN (Jump Unconditional). Program control is unconditionally transferred to the instruction locator at the address $A_3 A_3 A_3 A_3$, $A_2 A_2 A_2$-A_2, $A_1 A_1 A_1 A_1$.

JMS (Jump to Subroutine). The address of the next instruction in sequence following JMS (return address) is saved in the pushdown stack. Program control is transferred to the instruction located at the 12-bit address. Execution of a return instruction (BBL) will cause the saved address to be pulled out of the stack. Therefore, program control is transferred to the next sequential instruction after the last JMS.

The pushdown stack has four registers. One of them is used as the program counter, and, therefore, nesting of JMS can occur up to three levels.

JCN (Jump Conditional). If the designated condition code is true, program counter control is transferred to the instruction located at the 8-bit address $A_2 A_2 A_2 A_2$, $A_1 A_1 A_1 A_1$ on the same page (ROM) where JCN is located. If the condition is not true, the next instruction in sequence after JCN is executed. The condition bits are assigned as follows:

$C_1 = 0$	Do not invert jump condition.
$C_1 = 1$	Invert jump condition.
$C_2 = 1$	Jump if accumulator content is zero.
$C_3 = 1$	Jump if carry/link content is 1.
$C_4 = 1$	Jump if test signal (pin 10 on 4004) is zero.

ISZ (Increment Index Register Skip if Zero). The content of the designated index register is incremented by 1. The accumulator and carry flip-flop are unaffected. If the result is zero, the next instruction after ISZ is executed. If the result is different from 0, program control is transferred to the instruction located at the 8-bit address $A_2 A_2 A_2 A_2$, $A_1 A_1 A_1 A_1$ on the same page (ROM) where the ISZ is located. Exception: If ISZ is located on words 254 and 255 of a ROM page, when ISZ is executed and the result is not zero, program control is transferred to the 8-bit address located on the next page in sequence and not on the same page where ISZ is located.

RDM (Read Ram Character). The content of the previously selected RAM main memory character is transferred to the accumulator. The carry flip-flop is unaffected. The 4-bit datum in memory is unaffected.

RD0 (Read RAM Status Character 0). The 4 bits of status character 0 for the previously selected RAM register are transferred to the accumulator. The carry flip-flop and the status character are unaffected.

RD1, RD2, RD3 (Read RAM Status Character 1, 2, 3). Same as RD0 but for different status character.

RDR (Read ROM Port). The data present at the input lines of the previously selected ROM chip is transferred to the accumulator. The carry flip-flop is unaffected. If the I/O option has both inputs and outputs within the same four I/O lines, the user can choose to have either zero or one transferred to the accumulator for those I/O pins coded as outputs, when an RDR instruction is executed.

WR0, WR1, WR2, WR3 (Write Accumulator in RAM Status Character 0, 1, 2, 3). The content of the accumulator is written into the RAM status character 0, 1, 2, 3 of the previously selected RAM register. The accumulator and the carry flip-flop are unaffected.

WRR (Write ROM Port). The content of the accumulator is transferred to the ROM output port of the previously selected ROM chip. The data are available on the output pins until a new WRR is executed on the same chip. The ACC content and carry flip-flop are unaffected. The least significant bit of the accumulator appears on I/O_0. No operation is performed on I/O lines coded as inputs.

WMP (Write Memory Port). The content of the accumulator is transferred to the RAM output port of the previously selected RAM chip. The data are available on the output pins until a new WMP is executed on the same RAM chip. The content of the ACC and the carry flip-flop are unaffected.

ADM (Add from Memory with Carry). The content of the previously selected RAM main memory character is added to the accumulator with carry. The RAM character is unaffected.

SBM (Subtract from Memory with Borrow). The content of the previously selected RAM character is subtracted from the accumulator with borrow. The RAM character is unaffected.

CLB (Clear Both). Set accumulator and carry flip-flop to 0.

CLC (Clear Carry). Set carry flip-flop to 0.

CMC (Complement Carry). The carry flip-flop content is complemented.

STC (Set Carry). Set carry flip-flop to 1.

CMA (Complement Accumulator). The content of the accumulator is complemented. The carry flip-flop is unaffected.

IAC (Increment Accumulator). The content of the accumulator is incremented by 1. No overflow sets the carry flip-flop to 0; overflow sets the carry flip-flop to 1.

DAC (Decrement Accumulator). The content of the accumulator is decremented by 1. A borrow sets the carry flip-flop to 0. No borrow sets the flip-flop to 1.

RAL (Rotate Left), RAR (Rotate Right). The content of the accumulator and carry flip-flop are rotated left or right.

TCC (Transmit Carry and Clear). The accumulator is cleared. The least significant position of the accumulator is set to the value of the carry flip-flop. The flip-flop is set to 0.

DAA (Decimal Adjust Accumulator). The accumulator is incremented by 6 if the carry flip-flop is 1 or if the accumulator content is greater than 9. The carry flip-flop is set to 1 if the result generates a carry; otherwise, it is unaffected.

TCS (Transfer Carry Subtract). The accumulator is set to 9 if the carry flip-flop is 0. The accumulator is set to 10 if the carry flip-flop is 1. The carry flip-flop is set to 0.

KBP (Keyboard Process). A code conversion is performed on the accumulator content, from 1 out of n to binary code. If the accumulator content has more than 1 bit, the accumulator will be set to 15 (to indicate error).

The carry flip-flop is unaffected. The conversion table is as follows:

(ACC) BEFORE KBP	(ACC) AFTER KBP
0 0 0 0	0 0 0 0
0 0 0 1	0 0 0 1
0 0 1 0	0 0 1 0
0 1 0 0	0 0 1 1
1 0 0 0	0 1 0 0
0 0 1 1	1 1 1 1
0 1 0 1	1 1 1 1
0 1 1 0	1 1 1 1
0 1 1 1	1 1 1 1
1 0 0 1	1 1 1 1
1 0 1 0	1 1 1 1
1 0 1 1	1 1 1 1

(ACC BEFORE KBP	(ACC) AFTER KBP
1 1 0 0	1 1 1 1
1 1 0 1	1 1 1 1
1 1 1 0	1 1 1 1
1 1 1 1	1 1 1 1

DCL (Designate Command Line). The content of the three last significant accumulator bits is transferred to the command control register within the CPU. This instruction provides RAM bank selection when multiple RAM banks are used. (If no DCL instruction is sent out, RAM bank zero is automatically selected after application of at least one RESET.) DCL remains latched until it is changed.

11.4 PROGRAMMING THE MCS-4

Suppose that a series of 10 clock pulses must be generated, perhaps to drive the clock line of a 4003 port expander. Let us assume that RAM 3 is to be used. The high-order 2 bits of data sent out at X_2 time during an SRC instruction selects the RAM chip. Hence 1100 (binary equivalent for 12) is required at X_2 to select RAM 3.

Since the port on RAM 3 must be selected, the following is required:

FIM 0, OCOH; 192

SRC 0

This pair of instructions sets up the desired port for use. To generate the clock pulses, we must alternately write a 1 and a 0 into the appropriate port bit. Let us assume that we will use only the high-order bit of the port on RAM 3 and that it is initially set at zero (so that the program does not have to be reset). Furthermore, let us assume that we do not care about the other 3 bits of the port.

First let us set the accumulator to 0.

LDM 0; set accumulator to 0.

We may then complement the high-order bit of the accumulator by the following sequence:

RAL	Rotate left (accumulator and carry).
CMC	Complement carry.
RAR	Rotate right (accumulator and carry).

This achieves the operation by shifting the bit into the carry flip-flop, complementing it, and shifting it back.

An alternative way to complement the high-order bit is to add 8 (binary 1000) to the accumulator. We may set the contents of one register, say register 15, to 8 by the following sequence:

LDM	8	Load DDDD (1000) to the accumulator.
XCH	15	Exchange contents of index register 15 and accumulator.
LDM	0	Load (0000) to accumulator.

The first instruction loads the binary number 1000 into the accumulator and the second places the contents of the accumulator into register 15. Since the prior contents of register 15 also are placed in the accumulator, an LDM instruction is then executed to clear the accumulator.

Now the operation ADD 15 will add the binary value 1000 to the accumulator, because register 15 contains the value 8.

Note the difference in how the LDM and the XCH and ADD instructions utilize the second half of the instruction. The LDM loads the accumulator with the value carried by the instruction (i.e., in binary code LDM 8 appears as 1101 1000 and loads the accumulator with 1000). However, the ADDX and XCH select a register, and the contents of the register are used as data. That is, ADD 8 would add the contents of register 8 to the accumulator, not the value 8.

To generate the sequence of 10 clock pulses, one could repeat the following 4 instructions 10 times:

ADD 15	Add the contents of register 15 (1000 previously stored in the register) to the accumulator.
WMP	Write the contents of the accumulator into the previously selected RAM output port.
ADD 15	
WMP	

However, this would take some 40 instructions. The indexing operation available with the ISZ instruction allows a program loop to be repeated 10 times.

The ISZ instruction increments a selected register. If the register initially contained any value other than the value 15 (binary 1111), the instruction performs a jump to an address specified by the instruction. This address must be on the same page (within the same ROM) as the instruction immediately following the ISZ.

If, however, the register originally contained 15, the CPU will proceed to execute the next instruction in sequence. By loading a register, say register 14, with the value 6, on the tenth execution of an ISZ, the processor will proceed to the next instruction in sequence rather than jump.

Execution of the ISZ does not affect the accumulator, so the accumulator does not have to be saved prior to its execution.

The program sequence which performs the desired action is then as follows:

INSTRUCTION NO.	ADDRESS NAME	MNEMONIC	OPA	DESCRIPTION
(1)		LDM	8	Load 1000 to accumulator.
(2)		XCH	15	Exchange contents of index register 15 and accumulator.
(3)		LDM	6	Load 0110 to accumulator.
(4)		XCH	14	Exchange contents of index register 14 and accumulator.
(5)		FIM 12	0 0	Fetch immediate from ROM, data (1100 0000) to index register pair location 0.
(6)		SRC	0	Send address (contents of index register pair 0) to RAM.
(7)		LDM	0	Set accumulator to 0.
(8)		ADD	15	Add contents of register 15 to accumulator.
(9)		WMP		Write contents of accumulator into RAM output ports.
(10)		ADD	15	Add contents of register 15 to accumulator.

INSTRUCTION NO.	ADDRESS NAME	MNEMONIC	OPA	DESCRIPTION
(11)		WMP		Write contents of accumulator into RAM output ports.
(12)	LOOP	ISZ	14,LOOP	Increment contents of register 14. Go to ROM address A_2, A_1 (called Loop) if result $\neq$ 0; otherwise, skip.

Explanation of Program

1. Instructions 1 and 2: loads the number 8 (1000) into index register 15 (1111).

2. Instructions 3 and 4: loads the number 6 (0110) into index register 14 (1110).

3. Instruction 5: fetches the address of the desired RAM and stores it in an index register pair.

4. Instruction 6: Sends the stored address to the RAM bank and selects the desired RAM.

5. Instruction 7: Initializes the accumulator to 0000.

6. Instructions 8, 9, 10, 11: Generates one clock pulse as follows: Complement of highest-order bit of accumulator and send back to RAM output port (instructions 8 and 9)

Highest-order bit of accumulator is complemented again and sent back to the RAM output port (instructions 10 and 11)

7. Instruction 12: The contents of register 14 are incremented by 1 (0001). The number 7 (0111) is now stored in register 14. Since this result is not equal to zero, program control jumps to the address specified in the second word of this instruction. In this case, the address stored in the second word is the address of instruction 8. The program then executes the next four instructions

in sequence, and generates a second clock pulse. This sequence is repeated a total of 10 times, thus generating 10 clock pulses. The tenth time, when the contents of register 14 are incremented, it goes to the value 0000 and the program skips to the next instruction in sequence and gets out of the loop.

EXERCISES

11-1.   Is the 4004 a 4-bit or an 8-bit device?

11-2.   What is a fetch indirect?

11-3.   Give an example of "add index to accumulator with carry."

11-4.   Repeat Exercise 3 for "subtract."

11-5.   How are the 4 bits of the command register transferred to the accumulator? Provide an example.

11-6.   Describe "jump to subroutine."

11-7.   Show a sequence program for testing the status of a single switch connected to the 4004 on the test input (pin 10).

11-8.   Show a sequence program for testing the status of a switch connected to the port of ROM 2.

11-9.   What is meant by a "4-bit machine"?

12

The 8080

12.1 INTRODUCTION

The 8080 CPU has been one of the pioneer devices in the field of microprocessors, and, although first designed and produced by Intel, it is also second-sourced by other semiconductor manufacturers.

The 8080 is an 8-bit microprocessor housed in a standard 40-pin dual-in-line package. The chip is fabricated using N-channel silicon-gate MOS technology. It has a 16-bit address bus that is capable of addressing up to 65K bytes of memory and up to 256 input and 256 output devices. Data are routed to and from the 8080 on a separate bidirectional 8-bit bus. These data are also tristate, making direct memory addressing (DMA) and multi-processing applications possible. This CPU directly provides signals to control the interface to memory and I/O ports. All buses, including control, are TTL-compatible.

A basic microcomputer program, utilizing the 8080, is shown in Figure 12-1. An asynchronous interrupt capability is included in the CPU to allow external signals to change the instruction sequence. The interrupting device may vector the program to a particular service routine location (or some other direct function) by specifying an interrupt instruction to be executed.

Some of the features of the 8080 are the following:

—74 instructions—variable length.

—general-purpose registers—six plus accumulator.

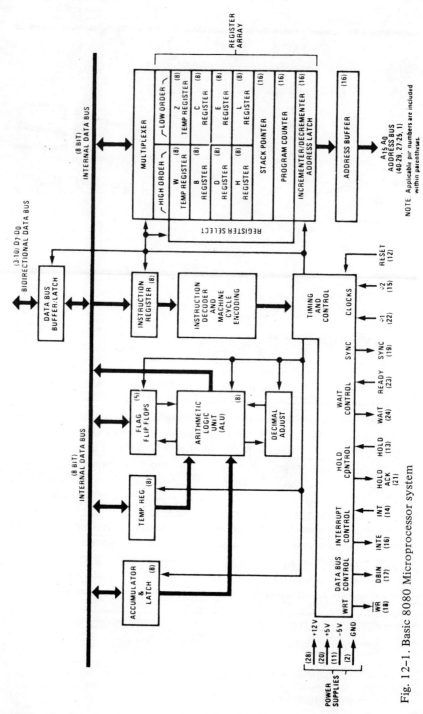

Fig. 12-1. Basic 8080 Microprocessor system

244

—Direct addressing up to 65K bytes.

—Variable-length stack accessed by 16-bit stack pointer.

—Addresses 256 input and 256 output ports.

—Provisions for vectored interrupts.

—Tristate bus for DMA and multiprocessing capability.

—Tristate TTL drive capabilities for address and data buses.

—Decimal arithmetic capability.

—Direct.

—Register.

—Register indirect.

—Immediate.

Figure 12-2 is a pin layout of the 8080 which is fairly standard among the various manufacturers. The function pin definition is described next.

12.2 INPUT SIGNALS

Ready. When high (logic 1), indicates that valid memory or input data are available to the CPU on the 8080 data bus. The ready signal is used to synchronize the CPU with slower memory or input/output devices.

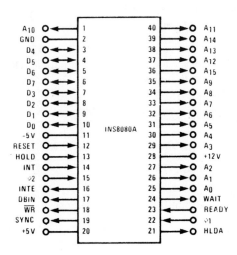

Fig. 12-2. Pin configuration of the 8080
(Courtesy of National Semiconductors)

If the 8080 does not receive a high ready input after sending out an address to memory or an input/output device, the 8080 enters a wait mode for as long as the ready input remains low (logic 0). The CPU may also be single stepped by use of the ready signal.

Hold. When high, requests that the CPU enter the hold mode. When the CPU is in this state, its address and data buses both will be in the high-impedance state. The hold mode allows an external device to gain control of the 8080 address and data buses immediately following the completion of the current machine cycle by the CPU. The CPU acknowledges the hold mode via the hold acknowledge (HLDA) output line. The hold request is recognized under the following conditions:

—The CPU is in the halt mode.

—The ready signal is active and the CPU is in the t_2 ($\emptyset 2$ pulse width) or t_W (output data) microcycle.

Interrupt (INT) Request. When high, the CPU recognizes an interrupt request on this line after completing the current instruction or while in the halt mode. An interrupt request is not honored if the CPU is in the hold mode (HLDA = logic 1) or the interrupt enable flip-flop is reset (INTE = logic 0).

Reset. When activated (high) for a minimum of three clock periods, the content of the program counter is cleared and the interrupt enable and hold acknowledge flip-flops are reset. Following a reset, program execution starts at memory location 0. It should be noted that the status flags, accumulator, stack pointer, and registers are not cleared during the reset sequence.

$\emptyset 1$ and $\emptyset 2$ Clocks. Two non-TTL-compatible clock phases which provide nonoverlapping timing are references for internal storage elements and logic circuit of the CPU.

The electrical characteristics of the 8080 are the following:

V_{DD} supply: +12 V.
V_{CC} supply: +5 V.
V_{BB} supply: -5 V.
Ground: V_{SS} (0 V) reference.

Output Signals

Synchronizing (SYNC) Signal. When activated (high), the beginning of a new machine cycle is indicated and the status word is outputted on the data bus.

Address (A_{15}-A_0) Bus. This bus comprises 16 tristate output lines. The bus provides the address to memory (up to 65K bytes) or denotes the input/output device number for up to 256 input and 256 output peripherals.

Wait. When high, acknowledges that the CPU is in the wait mode.

Write ($\overline{WR}$). When low, the data on the data bus are stable for write memory or output operation.

Hold Acknowledge (HLDA). Goes high in response to a logic 1 on the hold line and indicates that the data and address bus will go to the high-impedance state. The HLDA begins at one of the following times:

—The t_3 microcycle of a read memory input operation.

—The clock period following the t_3 microcycle of a write memory output operation.

In both cases, the HLDA signal starts after the rising edge of the $\emptyset 1$ clock, and high impedance occurs after the rising edge of the $\emptyset 2$ clock. Figure 12-3 illustrates the timing diagram of the 8080.

Interrupt Enable (INTE). Indicates the content of the internal interrupt enable flip-flop. The enable and disable interrupt (EI and DI) instructions cause the interrupt enable flip-flop to be set and reset, respectively. When the flip-flop is reset (INTE = logic 0), it inhibits interrupts from being accepted by the CPU. In addition, the interrupt enable flip-flop is automatically reset (thereby disabling further interrupts) at the t_1 microcycle of the instruction fetch cycle, when an interrupt is accepted; it is also reset by the reset signal.

Data Bus In (DBIN). When high, indicates to external circuits that the data bus is in the input mode. The DBIN signal should be used to gate data from memory or an I/O device onto the data bus.

12.3 INPUT/OUTPUT SIGNALS

Data (D_7-D_0) Bus. This bus comprises eight tristate input/output lines. The bus provides bidirectional communication among the CPU, memory, and input/output devices for instructions and data transfers. A status word (which describes the current machine cycle) is also outputted on the data bus during the first microcycle of each machine cycle (SYNC = logic 1). A status word chart for the 8080 is provided in Figure 12-4.

12.4 8080 STATUS

Instructions for the 8080 require from one to five machine cycles for complete execution. The 8080 sends out 8 bits of status information on the

Note: Timing measurements are made at the following reference voltages. CLOCK '1' = 8.0V, '0' = 1.0V; INPUTS '1' = 3.3V, '0' = 0.8V; OUTPUTS '1' = 2.0V, '0' = 0.8V.

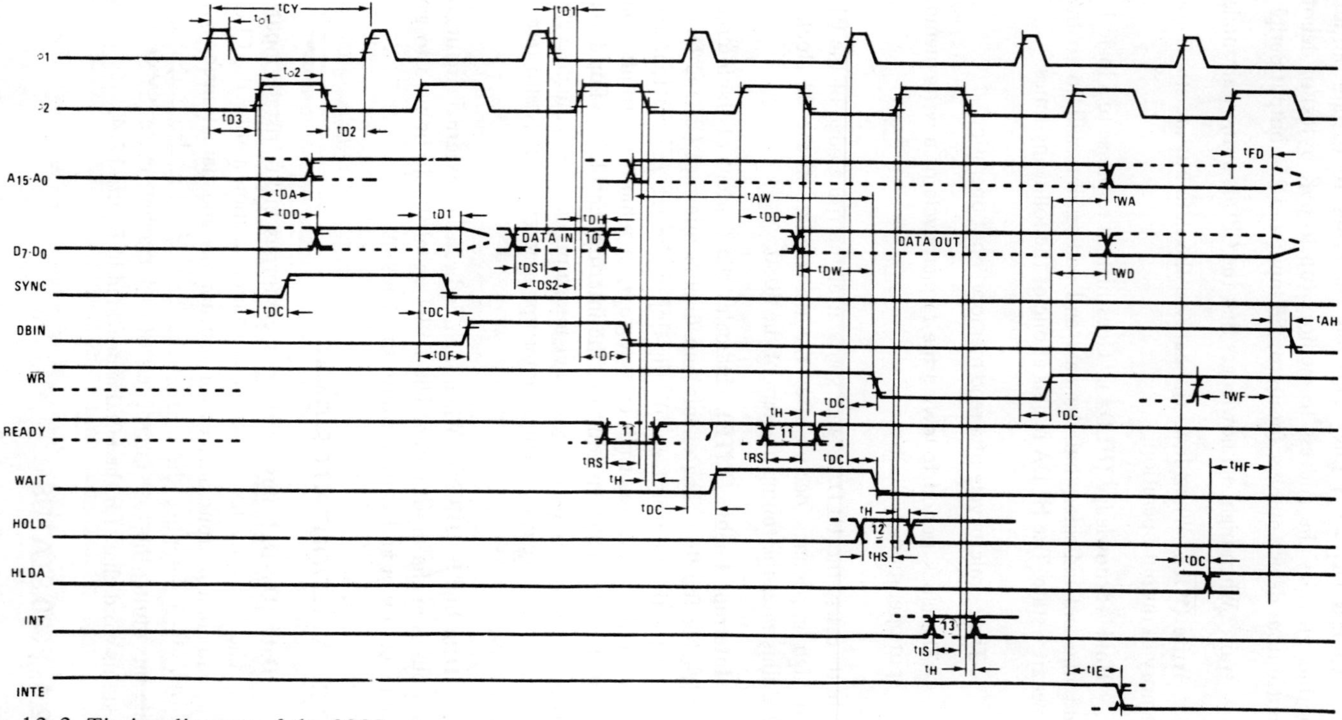

Fig. 12–3. Timing diagram of the 8080

Machine Cycle	Type	Data Bus Bit							
		D_7	D_6	D_5	D_4	D_3	D_2	D_1	D_0
Instruction Fetch	1	1	0	1	0	0	0	1	0
Memory Read	2	1	0	0	0	0	0	1	0
Memory Write	3	0	0	0	0	0	0	0	0
Stack Read	4	1	0	0	0	0	1	1	0
Stack Write	5	0	0	0	0	0	1	0	0
Input Read	6	0	1	0	0	0	0	1	0
Output Write	7	0	0	0	1	0	0	0	0
Interrupt Acknowledge	8	0	0	1	0	0	0	1	1
Halt Acknowledge	9	1	0	0	0	1	0	1	0
Interrupt Acknowledge While Halt	10	0	0	1	0	1	0	1	1

Fig. 12–4. Status Word Chart of the 8080

data bus at the beginning of each machine cycle (during SYNC time). The table in Figure 12-5 defines the status information.

12.5 TIMING WAVEFORMS

The timing waveforms of the device are shown in Figure 12-3. Timing measurements are made at the following reference voltages:

Clock: "1": 8.0 V, "0": 1.0 V.

Inputs: "1": 3.3 V, "0": 0.8 V.

Outputs: "1": 2.0 V, "0": 0.8 V.

The following notes would be helpful in observing the timing diagrams of the device:

1. Data input should be enabled with DBIN status. No bus conflict can then occur and data hold time is assured.

2. Data in must be stable during the period marked with a circled "10" in the diagram during DBIN.T_3. Both the data setup time during Ø1 and DBIN (t_{DS1}) and t_{DS2} must be satisfied. In the case of the 8080, t_{DS1} is 30 ns, and t_{DS2} is 150 ns.

3. The ready signal must be stable for the period marked with a circled "11" on the diagram. This state must be externally synchronized.

4. The hold signal must be stable for the period marked with a circled "12" during T_2 or T_W when entering the hold mode, and during T_3, T_4, T_5, and T_{WH} when in the hold mode. No external synchronization is required.

Symbols	Data Bus Bit	Definition	Symbols	Data Bus Bit	Definition
INTA*	D_0	Acknowledge signal for INTERRUPT request. Signal should be used to gate a restart instruction onto the data bus when DBIN is active.	OUT	D_4	Indicates that the address bus contains the address of an output device and the data bus will contain the output data when WR is active.
$\overline{WO}$	D_1	Indicates that the operation in the current machine cycle will be a WRITE memory or OUTPUT function (WO = 0). Otherwise, a READ memory or INPUT operation will be executed.	M_1	D_5	Provides a signal to indicate that the CPU is in the fetch cycle for the first byte of an instuction.
			INP*	D_6	Indicates that the address bus contains the address of an input device and the input data should be placed on the data bus when DBIN is active.
STACK	D_2	Indicates that the address bus holds the pushdown stack address from the Stack Pointer.	MEMR*	D_7	Designates that the data bus will be used for memory read data.
HLTA	D_3	Acknowledge signal for HALT Instruction.			

*These three status bits can be used to control the flow of data onto the INS8080A data bus.

Fig. 12–5. Status definition

5. The interrupt signal must be stable during the period marked with a circled "13" of the last clock cycle of any instruction in order to be recognized on the following instruction. External synchronization is not required.

6. The timing diagram of Figure 12-3 shows timing relationships only; it does not represent any specific machine cycle.

The complete ac electrical characteristics of a typical 8080 device are given in Figure 12-6.

Instruction Set

The last portion of this chapter provides the instruction set for the 8080. There are five condition flags associated with the execution of instructions on the 8080. They are zero, sign, parity, carry, and auxiliary carry, and each flag is represented by a 1-bit register in the CPU. A flag is "set" by forcing the bit to 1, "reset" by forcing the bit to 0. The bit positions of the flags are indicated in the PUSH and POP PSW instructions, defined in the instruction set.

Unless indicated otherwise, when an instruction affects a flag, it affects it in the following manner:

ZERO (Z). If the result of an instruction has the value 0, this flag is set; otherwise, it is reset.

SIGN (S). If the most significant bit of the result of the operation has the value 1, this flag is set; otherwise, it is reset.

PARITY (P). If the modulo 2 sum of the bits of the result of the operation is 0 (i.e., if the result has even parity), this flag is set; otherwise, it is reset (i.e., if the result has odd parity).

Symbol	Parameter	Min.	Max.	Unit	Test Condition
$t_{CY}{}^{3}$	Clock Period	0.48	2.0	μs	
t_r, t_f	Clock Rise and Fall Time	0	50	ns	
$t_{\phi 1}$	ϕ_1 Pulse Width	60		ns	
$t_{\phi 2}$	ϕ_2 Pulse Width	220		ns	
t_{D1}	Delay ϕ_1 to ϕ_2	0		ns	
t_{D2}	Delay ϕ_2 to ϕ_1	70		ns	
t_{D3}	Delay ϕ_1 to ϕ_2 Leading Edges	80		ns	
$t_{DA}{}^{2}$	Address Output Delay from ϕ_2		200	ns	$C_L = 100\,pF$
$t_{DD}{}^{2}$	Data Output Delay from ϕ_2		220	ns	
$t_{DC}{}^{2}$	Signal Output Delay from ϕ_1 or ϕ_2 (SYNC, $\overline{WR}$, WAIT, HLDA)		120	ns	
$t_{DF}{}^{2}$	DBIN Delay from ϕ_2	25	140	ns	$C_L = 50\,pF$
$t_{DI}{}^{1}$	Delay for Input Bus to Enter Input Mode		t_{DF}	ns	
t_{DS1}	Data Setup Time During ϕ_1 and DBIN	30		ns	

Fig. 12–6. A.C. Characteristics of the 8080

CARRY (CY). If the instruction resulted in a carry (from addition) or a borrow (from subtraction or a comparison) out of the high-order bit, this flag is set; otherwise, it is reset.

AUXILIARY CARRY (AC). If the instruction caused a carry out of bit 3 into bit 4 of the resulting value, the auxiliary carry is set; otherwise, it is reset. This flag is affected by single-precision additions, subtractions, increments, decrements, comparisons, and logical operations; however, AC is used primarily with additions and increments preceding a decimal adjust accumulator (DAA) instruction. The latter definition is also given in the instruction set.

12.6 SYMBOLS AND ABBREVIATIONS

The following symbols and abbreviations are used in the subsequent description of the 8080 instruction set:

SYMBOL	MEANING
A	Register A (accumulator)
B	Register B
C	Register C
D	Register D
E	Register E
H	Register H
L	Register L

SYMBOL	MEANING
DDD, SSS	The bit pattern designating one of the registers A, B, C, D, E, H, L (DDD = destination, SSS = source).

DDD OR SSS	REGISTER NAME
111	A
000	B
001	C
010	D
011	E
100	H
101	L

SYMBOL	MEANING
byte 2	The second byte of the instruction.
byte 3	The third byte of the instruction.
port	8-bit address of an I/O device.
r, r1, r2	One of the registers A, B, C, D, E, H, L
PC	16-bit program counter register (PCH PCL are used to refer to the high-order and low-order 8 bits, respectively).
SP	16-bit stack pointer register (SPH and SPL are used to refer to the high-order and low-order 8 bits, respectively).
( )	The contents of the memory location or registers enclosed in the parentheses.
←	"Is replaced by."
$\wedge$	Logical AND.
$\veebar$	Exclusive OR.
$\vee$	Inclusive OR.
+	Addition.
–	Two's-complement subtraction.
*	Multiplication.
↔	"Exchange."
‾	The one's complement [for example, $(\bar{A})$] .
n	The restart number 0 through 7.

SYMBOL	MEANING
NNN	The binary representation 000 through 111 for restart numbers 0 through 7, respectively.
•	"Not affected."
0	"Reset."
1	"Set."
x	Unknown.
	Flags affected according to standard rules.

EXERCISES

12-1. Compare the 8080 with the 6800 and discuss possible advantages and disadvantages of each system.

12-2. Define the following: ready; wait; data bus.

12-3. What would be the status of the device that would provide the following:

(a) A signal to indicate that the 8080 is in the fetch cycle for the first byte of an instruction.

(b) The address bus holds the push down stack address from the stack pointer.

(c) The operation in the current machine cycle will be a write memory.

12-4. State the symbol for the following instructions:

(a) Subtract immediate.

(b) Store accumulator indirect.

(c) Rotate right.

(d) Exclusive-OR register.

12-5. If clock "1" reads 10.0 V and clock "0" 2.5 V, does this fall within the typical timing measurements of the device?

12-6. How many peripherals could an 8080 handle?

12-7. Design a basic 8080-based system with possible ROM and/or RAM to control a small traffic signal operation.

12-8. Define the status of the sign flag if the most significant bit of the result operation is "0."

12-9. Repeat Exercise 8 for (P) and (AC).

Index